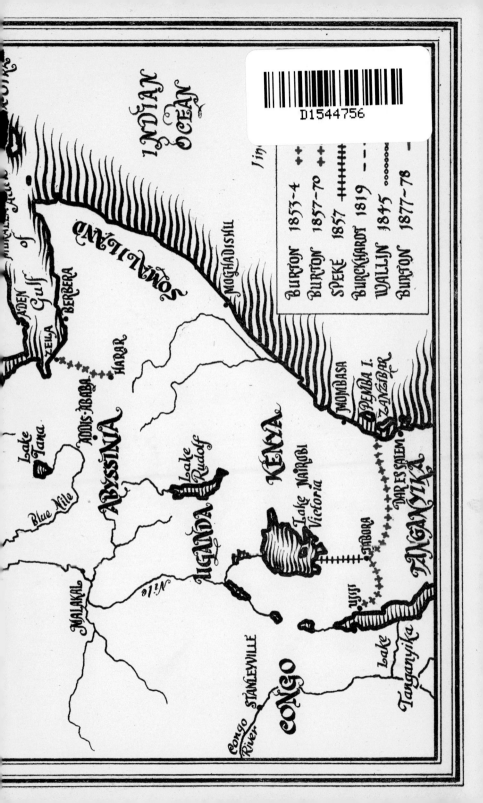

INDIAN OCEAN

SOMALILAND

Gulf of Aden

BERBERA
ZEILA
HARAR
ADDIS-ABABA
Lake Tana
ABYSSINIA
Blue Nile
MALAKAL
Nile

MOGADISHU

MOMBASA
PEMBA I.
ZANZIBAR
DAR ES SALEM
TABORA
KENYA
Lake Nairobi
Lake Victoria
Lake Rudolf
UGANDA
TANGANYIKA
Lake Tanganyika

CONGO
STANLEYVILLE
Congo River

BURTON	1853-4	++
BURTON	1857-70	++
SPEKE	1857	+++++
BURCKHARDT	1819	---
WALLIN	1845	ooooo
BURTON	1877-78	—

D1544756

THE ARABIAN KNIGHT

By the same author

GYPSY GENTLEMAN
(A Study of George Borrow)

SIR RICHARD BURTON

THE ARABIAN KNIGHT

A Study of Sir Richard Burton

By SETON DEARDEN

ARTHUR BARKER LTD. LONDON

First Edition 1936
Revised Edition 1953

80888
920
B974d

MADE AND PRINTED IN GREAT BRITAIN BY
MORRISON AND GIBB LIMITED, LONDON AND EDINBURGH

To
My Wife

Acknowledgment

THE author would wish to record once again his thanks to those who helped during the original writing of this book. The late Sir Stephen Gaselee, Foreign Office Librarian, Mr. N. M. Penzer, F.R.G.S., Mr. E. A. Reeves, Secretary of the Royal Geographical Society, and Major Cheesman, and the late Sir Percy Cox, the Arabian experts. Likewise the librarians of the Camberwell Central and Kensington Public Libraries, Mr. Burt and Mr. Jones, who threw open their Burton collections to the author, and spared no pains to assist him in every way.

For this new edition the author is particularly grateful for encouragement from his friend Mr. Christopher Tower, Arabist, collector of orientalia, and companion on many a desert journey.

Introduction

In the first edition of this book, which appeared fifteen years ago, I apologized for lack of qualifications to assess fully the life and works of a man who, among other things, was the foremost Orientalist of his day. But for an accident of circumstance, that introduction and that qualification might well have stood for this second edition of the book. The hazards of war, however, brought me myself out to the Orient to live among many of the scenes and vicissitudes which formed the background to long periods of Burton's life. Ten years of the Moslem East now lie behind me as I once more take down this book from the shelf. It might reasonably be supposed that I would wish to correct or elaborate my original interpretations of Burton's character and achievements. In fact, on re-reading the book, there is very little to be changed. Perhaps the only adjustment I would make would be that of emphasis ; a greater appreciation of the achievements in travel and erudition of this remarkable man ; a lesser sympathy for his behaviour as an official or as a psychologist.

Burton was at heart an Elizabethan. At any rate he has many of those qualities which we assign to the great figures of the sixteenth century—a restless, adventurous spirit, oddly linked with a passion for study and the acquisition of facts. A forceful yet careless directness of thought and speech, a fine contempt for established authority, and finally a sensual virility shot through with strange streaks of femininity. As an Orientalist, no European of his time, or indeed of any time except perhaps Lane, had a better practical knowledge of the structure of Moslem life and habit. For the student of Islam, Burton's footnotes are often more valuable than his narrative. It would not be untrue to say that his copious footnotes to the original translation of the *Thousand Nights and a Night*, are frequently of more interest than his somewhat clumsy prose rendering of the original.

As a student and recorder of human habit, as a tireless collector of facts, Burton is unsurpassable. He is less gifted in his comprehension of human nature and particularly oriental psychology, that subtle, sliding spirit of the Semite so deftly evoked by Doughty or by Palgrave. Burton can describe eastern scenes and ventures with realistic effect, carrying along his reader in a fine sweep of narrative. Who can for example forget the voyage of the pilgrim " hell ship " down the Red Sea, of the pitiless journey on camel-back to Mecca, or the scenes at the sacrificial " customs " of King Gelele of Dahomey ? It is when he comes to the delineation of character that he is less fortunate. Perhaps his best attempt at depicting an Oriental is his " boy Mohammed " in the " Pilgrimage " ; and how far short does this not fall of, let us say, " El Nejumy " in Doughty or " Abdullah of Riadh " in Palgrave ?

This failure to understand character, this indifference to the feelings and opinions in others, are the chief defects in Burton's character and writings. In travel, in marriage, in his official career these are the traits which mar his progress. " *Au moyen orient,*" a wise old Turk in Syria once warned the author of this book, " *avant de faire un pas il y'a toujours trente-trois considerations.*" This is a motto which every young man going East should hang upon his office wall. Alas, it is these " *trente-trois considerations* " which always defeated Burton. Perhaps with more sensitivity and less indifference, more sympathy and less boldness, more insight and less learning we might have had fewer and better books. But should we have had that matchless courage and endurance that sent him alone to deadly Harar, or that perfect contempt for danger that dared him to enter the Ka'aba of Mecca in the midst of a fanatic mob ?

And yet, though he did not understand Arabs, surely he impressed them ? Arab memories are short, and to-day you may roam the Fertile Crescent and find no memories of Doughty, and few of Lawrence. You may still trace, here and there, recollections of Gertrude Bell, faint now as " the desolate mansions of Khaula." Yet there are still to be found legends of Burton ; though he preceded them all.

Wandering through Damascus in the summer of 1943 to try to trace that house in Salahiyyeh so well described by Lady Burton in her *Inner Life of Syria,* and where Burton began his final translation of the *Nights,* I came on several memories of the great Orientalist. An old dragoman of the British Consulate ; that same who once kept Doughty's pictures of Medain Salih ; had a story of the famous iron walking-stick. In the Ommayad

Library they showed me the corner where Burton used to work.
After searching for weeks it was almost by accident that I
stumbled on the house itself, still much as he had lived in it.
" Yes," said the owner, " this was once the house of a great
Englishman."

In the East the student of travel comes to associate
certain scenes with certain travellers. By chance a passage
remembered from a traveller's book as you stand to gaze at
some street, some mountain or some desert well, that he
visited long before you, fuses the scene with his personality,
forming a background sharp and static as a Florentine painting ;
so that ever after when you think of him it is against this
timeless and haphazard landscape. Thus Burckhardt I see
limned against the dark Ruwalla tents in their *dira* near Bir
Bassiri where a hundred years before me he sat to make his
notes on " Beduins and Wahabis." Gertrude Bell, thin, tired
and thirsty will stand for me eternally by the dirty water-hole
at Ain el Beida, just as she once came riding in from the south,
and where thirty-five years later I myself lay for three days in
suffocating heat and boredom. And it was as I entered the old
house of Said el Yusef in Damascus that my host putting his
hand on my arm as we stood in the huge shadowy *liwan* said,
" here is where Doughty came to ask of my father leave to go
with the caravan to Medain Salih." And instantly, imperish-
ably, I saw the tired, gentle, red-bearded face of Khalil framed
against a background of old marble, trailing vines and soaring
frescoes.

And so with Burton. It is here, in this old Damascus house,
near to the trams that now grind their way up the Muhajarine
that I shall always see him. It is evening, and over the hills
there blows that soft wind the Damascenes call the *unnibiye*,
redolent of vines. On the roof-top overlooking the city, which
lies like the wing of a white bird spread across the green oasis,
there are seated four persons, as strange an assembly as might
be found anywhere in the world. There is the hero of the
" Pilgrimage " to " Al Madinah and Meccah," now at the peak
of his career, elaborating in his harsh, but pure Arabic some
detail from his day's labours at the *Thousand Nights and a
Night* ; there is the Emir Abdul Kader el Jezairli, the Algerian
prince—perhaps last in the line of antique Arab chivalry—
who had fought for freedom in the Mogreb, suffered exile in
France, and retired to Damascus to increase an already great

reputation for piety and generosity by protecting Christians in the Moslem massacres of 1860 ; and finally there is Jane Digby, Lady Ellenborough, the English aristocrat who renounced a European life to marry a Syrian tribal chieftain and became a Moslem ; old now and wise in her years, yet still retaining somehow the graces of the Regency drawing-room. Ah what wonderful talk rising from the roof-top under the stars ! Even Isabel coming from time to time to join them is entranced. These are his happiest days, far from deserts and jungles, hardships and cruel disappointments. The future is dark ahead, but he does not know it. Here let me in memory leave him.

Amman
Hashemite Kingdom of Jordan
1951

Chapter One

TOWARDS the end of the year 1849 a sick and helpless man was carried on board the British brig *Eliza* in the harbour at Bombay and made as comfortable as possible below. He was half-blind with rheumatic ophthalmia, intermittently delirious, and so wasted by fever and nervous prostration as to resemble a mere yellowish skeleton. Friends came to shake the emaciated hand and make their adieus for what they believed to be a much longer voyage than the sea journey, and propped up in his bunk the human travesty endeavoured to scrawl a few lines of farewell to his mother in England. Then the old wooden vessel raised anchor, dipped her flag to the fort, and tacked ponderously out into the Arabian Sea for the long homeward voyage round the Cape.

As she began to lift to the swell of the open sea, her failing passenger turned his head to the porthole and strained his feeble eyes at the low Indian hills fast sinking below the eastern horizon. Over the Gateway of India the setting sun threw a warm radiance, dressing the squalor and ugliness of the city in a momentary beauty, lighting the sombre precipices of the shore, and the soft contours of the Hills of Silence, where the Parsi dead lie staring sightlessly at the sky, with shafts of purple and gold. At this last salute of nature, there must have crept into the eyes of the sick man an expression of mingled bitterness and despair. The fire of life, burning so low in him, quickened into a brief flare of anger. Well may he, crowding back the weak tears of rage, have raised a trembling fist and cursed the monstrous injustice which he felt was sending him home to die. Behind those hills, now fading astern, lay buried seven years of unsparing labour. Seven years of youth and health, of deferred hopes, of struggle and painful achievement. No man, among the thousands working there, had done more than he ; no man deserved more of his career. And what had been the result ? The insidious whisper of government interest —that corrupt interest that lay at the rotten core of British Indian Administration—had ruined him and set his whole world tumbling about his ears. Graft had broken him, as it had broken many a good man with a hasty and injudicious tongue. Had he only a glib tongue, could he only have crooked the knee a little more to those at their desks in Bombay ; instead of creeping home as a failure to die, he might even then be fulfilling the dearest wish of his heart and following the guns that were rolling northwards to avenge Anderson in the Punjab.

He lay thus for awhile with his eyes on the sky now darkening over India. Brooding, he let his mind run down the crowded past. The lines of the mouth hardened and that sullen glare of the opaque eyes which spoke of the independent spirit within showed for a moment in the yellow, haggard face as he contemplated once more the events of his last few months of misery. Then the fires died, the face seemed to shrink again into sickness. A few stars sprang out ; the air freshened, and then night closed down on the water, and with it the fever swept round him again like a blanket of fire.

§

Only seven years earlier, almost to this very month, the young, heavily moustached Ensign Burton had stepped ashore on the Apollo Bunder, fresh from England, and with high hopes in his heart. What ignorance, dreams, and unbounded optimism had been his then ! The career for which he had longed since childhood was, after a long struggle, his at last. The chance of foreign service had set his foot on the first rung of the ladder of quick promotion. India lay before him like an oyster of which his youth was to be the prise. And an assured future surely lay before a soldier with such evident capacity for hard work, a talent for the acquisition of language, and the essential graces of horsemanship and mastery of the sword.

It was the Afghan revolt of 1842, with the massacre of Burnes and his officers at Kabul, that had given him his opportunity. Fretting miserably at Oxford, and destined by a narrow-minded father for the church, he had seized the opportunity, while England was still ringing with alarm at the tragedy, to get himself sent down ; and to persuade his vacillating and bewildered parent to purchase him a commission in the East India Company's Service. Carried on the wave of popular indignation, he had succeeded. Under pressure from the women folk of the family, Colonel Burton had conceded the point that made his son a soldier of Leadenhall Street instead of a soldier of Christ, and on 18th June of that year he had sailed from Greenwich with the combined blessings of the family on his head.

It was a time of great public excitement. A British force of some 13,000 men had been annihilated in the frozen Jagdalak Pass by Afghan hordes. In every young imagination there burned the tragic picture of that solitary survivor, Dr. Brydon, staggering wounded through the gates of Jellalabad with his urgent message that Akbar Khan's men were pouring down the passes in their thousands. News trickled home but slowly. Every young ensign leaving England on Indian service shook with anger at this audacious tweaking of the lion's tail; every young dreamer saw himself, baton in knapsack, leading the avenging armies from the south. Richard Burton, the son of a soldier, and with a soldier's blood in him, caught the fever with the rest and longed to fight.

A week in the unbelievable filth of the British Hotel in Bombay had soon rubbed the gloss off some of these ideals. The dreams of meeting, sword in hand, the murderers of Macnaughten and Burnes had vanished in the first puff of sultry heat from the shore with the pilot's news that the revolt was long over and dead. And soon the jejune hope of batons in knapsacks, stars, and crosses crumbled at the bitter knowledge that the Company's officers, though they held Her Majesty's commission, were regarded by the regular army as mere hired auxiliaries, were treated as social inferiors, and debarred from rising above a certain rank. And was it with this scarecrow Sepoy army that Britain held her own ? was Burton's thought as he looked at the badly officered, lank, and slouching creatures on parade.

This was the India of a decade before the Mutiny ; an India exploited, drained, and corrupted by the stranglehold of a trading company. Bombay and London waxed fat on the possessions they guarded with an army that was a disgrace to the country and interest it represented. At Baroda, where the young ensign was sent to join his regiment, he found himself in a bungalow with a door lintel still scarred and slashed from the sabre cuts that had been directed by thieves at his predecessor's head. Officers were stabbed in their tents, or strangled by dacoits on the common highway without causing the slightest ripple to disturb the placidty of East India House. Such was the anarchy among the troops that most officers of the garrison army were forced to hire a native bodyguard to protect life and property. Thus did Leadenhall Street preserve its own.

It was disillusionment; but to a sanguine nature this is often the spur to mental activity and solid effort. Contemplating regimental life at Baroda, with a commander who sat placidly among his sprawling native family, and officers who, with some few execptions, spent their time either playing billiards, chasing native women, or sticking pigs, Burton came to the conclusion that the officer on station in India was faced by only two alternatives of leisure—sport or languages. Sport was well enough for the physical enthusiast, and Burton was always that, but his intense mental energy required something as well on which to employ itself. The scientific and inquiring streak in him was stimulated by the enormous amount of material ready to hand. Ethnology, and its sister sciences of anthropology and philology drew him most, and he plunged into the study of languages with an unflagging energy and tireless research.

For language and for the study of peoples he seemed from the first to have an uncanny faculty. A sensitive ear, an observant eye, and a scientifically retentive memory which were combined with a passion for accuracy of detail, soon showed that here was a young officer with a future in foreign service. Nothing came amiss to his insatiate curiosity. Even his native mistress, the perquisite of every officer in those days, became to him more than the mere hygienic and economic convenience she was accustomed to be taken for. Of her he made what Marshal Lyautey once described as *un dictionnaire en peau de fesse*, the disappearance of which has much thinned the ranks of the cadre of European Oriental linguists. In her arms he spelt out slowly the intricate argot of the *bazaars*. One may well believe it was from her lips he heard the first whispers of those *Thousand-and-One Nights*, which later were to be his own best claim to immortality. Nor was his talent for language entirely innate; from birth he had wandered with his parents about the continent of Europe, lisping French at three years of age, Italian at six, Spanish and Bearnais at ten, and German at fifteen. His language sense was developed to a high degree, and coupled with a love of the minutiæ of dialect and a faculty for intense concentration over long periods, enabled him to forge ahead where others crept but slowly.

With the assistance of Gayangos, the Spanish Orientalist, he had started Arabic to amuse himself at Oxford. Continuing with a brief course in London under the ægis of an old eccentric linguist, Duncan Forbes, he had managed during the passage to India to keep at nodding distance with the language by frequenting the society of the native servants. He now plunged into a ten-hour-a-day course in Arabic and Hindustani under the ceaseless tuition of two native teachers. The long, grilling days passed by his companions in rest, or light recreation under soothing punkahs, were spent by him in a perspiring wrestle with broken plurals and the mysteries of the Vedic cerebral l. In the amazing space of six months he was gazetted as " passed interpreter in Hindustani," another four months added the dialect of Gujarati; and at the end of the year when he was transferred to the province of Sind he had added fluent Persian to his list, and made a fair inroad into Punjabi.

This was a man of worth to the Company, and they were not slow to recognize it. The moment was ripe. That " very advantageous, useful, humane piece of rascality," [1] the annexation of Sind, in which Great Britain, following a policy of justifying the means by the end, violated a treaty, forced an issue that could have but one result, and at Meeanee walked into a province with some illegality and sat down in it, throwing open a vast and virgin territory to the surveyor and the student. The country was uncharted, and the subtle Sindi and fierce Belochi and Brahui tribes and their customs were almost unknown. A bleak, barren land, sliced by a great river valley, a valuable springboard to Afghanistan, inundated periodically with Nilotic floods which left in their wake fever-ridden, stagnating pools; a strange medley of races, lawless and fearful, corrupt and oppressed, faced the newcomers. Order had to be produced from chaos, and there were few to do it. " Now," wrote Napier the conqueror, " my fearful work of settling the country begins. I have to collect revenue, administer justice, arrange the troops, survey. . . . I have to get a thorough hold of a conquered country, and establish a government, and have really hardly anyone to assist me; all is confusion . . . I am gradually finding fine fellows, but there are no great number to select from."

[1] Napier.

Burton found himself appointed as Assistant in the Survey. In this capacity his talent for observation, study, and self-obliteration found its best expression. For weeks at a time he was sent to wander alone over wide stretches of country, mixing with none but the natives, filling his notebooks with maps, geological, botanical, and ethnological information. By ceaseless study, long hours of close attention to detail, and his uncanny faculty for perfect imitation, he familiarized himself with the native tribes, their dialects and customs, so that he could pass as one of themselves. He would, it is told, crouch talking to an old native woman, watching her every lip movement, studying the play of her hands, her shoulders, and her voice, following the circuit of her thought ; he would pursue a pedlar through a *bazaar* with the persistent watchfulness of an actor watching his principal. He began to make essays in disguise, staining his face and hands with henna and slipping out at nightfall in the larger towns to pick up the stray whispers of *bazaar* talk. Napier heard of him, and took to using him in the rough Intelligence Service he had organized to gauge the temper of this newly won country.

Indian Intelligence in those days was a makeshift affair, but it was a particularly valuable method of dealing with the tortuous Oriental mind. Its history will never be written, but it played its part. To Napier and his gallant troops belongs the official glory for the victory of Meeanee, when 3000 British rolled back and put to rout an army of 20,000 Belochi tribes-men. Their achievement has been described as one of the greatest feats of British arms in India. But would it, one wonders, have been so if British Intelligence had not, with the Company's rupees, suborned the Belochi gunners before the battle to elevate the muzzles of their guns ? How many other " glorious victories " have taken their laurels from such venal roots ?

It is because it is venal, and invariably underrated by those who employ it, that the Intelligence Service is always a thankless job. It also demands a certain servility and diplomacy to those in command that a proud, independent and rather fiery young subaltern found difficult to supply. That model spirit of tact and caution which characterized Burton among the natives when in disguise was shed when he washed the henna stain from his skin. In uniform he became a different personality. By nature he was hasty, impatient, and careless of convention. Outspoken, abrupt, and often contemptuous of his immediate superiors, his quick, imperious temper and biting sarcasm built up a wall of prejudice against him and made him dangerous enemies. Between Napier and himself, however, there sprang up a mutual regard born of kindred temperament and genius. The gruff, outspoken eccentric veteran of Corunna, and the eager, intolerant young interpreter found in one another's outlook much in common. Both had a dislike of convention and society as especially manifested in the Indian army. The reaction of both to its manifestation was a certain coarseness in behaviour, an irrepressible *schadenfreude*, rudeness, or taste for schoolboy smut which shocked or delighted their companions. Both looked on their service as a weapon rather than a crutch, and despised openly those gentlemanly officers who regarded it as a term of exile. Above all both were possessed of that rare and invaluable gift—an inexhaustible fund of energy and the faculty for intensely concentrating it.

The history of Napier's command in Sind is the record of a piece of military and organizing genius. From a wild and turbulent province in which murder, corruption, and riot were rife ; in which trade was at a standstill, and every village strained its eyes in constant terror towards the menace of the surrounding hills, this ailing old man transformed it into one of the most peaceful and fruitful of the possessions. " Is the country quiet ? " someone asked a Belochi during this period. " Yes," was the reply, " if you catch a wasp in your hand it does not sting you ! " A greater compliment was never paid by a native to his conqueror.

For five years Burton worked in Sind on the more difficult and frequently unpleasant details of Intelligence work. His tasks were many and varied. For a time he would labour on the Survey in the comparative comfort of his European uniform, superintending and reporting on irrigation and agriculture. Then, dressed as a Dervish, in tatters and carrying a staff, he would slip into the hills and wander with the Belochi and Brahui tribes, about whom little was known, to listen to the currents of the minor political intrigues always surging to and fro behind the scenes. Again, with long hair falling about his shoulders and a black beard hiding all but his sombre eyes, he would limp through the towns calling his pedlar's wares of fine linen, calicoes, muslins, and cheapjack *bijouterie* from Birmingham. In such a disguise he was even permitted to display his wares in the hidden *harem*—often the very fountain-head of Oriental politics. While posturing and haggling in the argot of the *bazaars*, he would be listening and noting down the gossip of tavern, *harem*, and street-corner. At other times he would sit in sweet shops in the *bazaars* and brood for hours among the flies, somnolent but secretly alert. Or, as a native workman, he would toil with the Jats and camel-men on the work of levelling the canals, finding time at nights to write a thesis on their dialect. His information, pouring back to Bombay for study, was invaluable. Napier looked on him as one of his most useful young men. His future seemed assured.

But from some quarters he was being watched askance. The Indian army of those days, exemplified in the person of the sahib of the stiff-necked, nigger-crushing school, was anti-pathetic to eccentricity and independence in its subordinate officers. A man who rode roughshod through red tape, who lampooned his superior officers in witty and biting verse, who declared that he was so bored with his mess companions that he would henceforth eat with monkeys, proceeded moreover sarcastically to do so, and further started to compile a vocabulary of Simian terms, was scarcely likely to appeal to the conventional nabob of the 'forties. Burton's exploits, his tremendous physical strength and expert swordsmanship, combined with his hard-drinking, bawdy, essentially virile temperament made him the delight or envy of his brother officers, but a perpetual thorn in the sides of his superiors. He lacked the discretion which is much the better part of valour in military preferment. He knew it not, but he was later to pay for his tactlessness dearly.

The blow fell from a quarter where it might have been least expected.

During this difficult and exhausting period of Intelligence work, native spies brought to headquarters the information that Karachi, the apple of Napier's eye, then a mere straggling small town by the sea, was harbouring three bordels of the most degraded sort. Here, the reports ran, boys and eunuchs lay for hire, the former demanding nearly a double price for obvious reasons. As the town was scarcely a mile distant from the camp, Napier exhibited some natural perturbation at the report, especially as he may have believed Burton's theory that pederasty is geographical and climatic rather than racial, and that the British soldier might not be immune from temptation.

He decided upon an immediate investigation and, as Burton was the only British officer speaking Sindi, the latter was invited indirectly to carry out this task and make a detailed report. He had no direct or official orders, for in this matter not even the Governor himself cared to set pen to paper; and Burton made a stipulation that the report of his investigation should not be forwarded to Bombay. This was promised. Then, staining his body with henna, he put on the dress of a merchant, and, adopting the name of Mirza Abdullah, took a native companion and vanished into the back streets of Karachi, where, at some risk to his life, he obtained entry to the notorious lupanars.

If Headquarters required a glossed report, dealing in generalities and euphemisms, they had sent the wrong man. Burton's passion for detail of whatever sort combined with his personal interest in all forms of the erotic compelled him to commit to paper everything he saw. He saw sights which must have startled even his phlegmatic temperament, yet which filled him with interest. He left nothing out. His report is a model of accuracy and detail, noting even the market value of a scrotum.[1] Napier received it, read it with official interest and no doubt unofficial amusement, and filed it. Then he forgot it. Neither he nor Burton was to guess what an effect, during the rest of the latter's life, this pamphlet was to have.

When Napier was recalled from Sind shortly afterwards Burton's report lay forgotten in the office files which awaited the Governor's successor. This was a man of very different calibre from Napier, and when at length his attention was drawn to the document he was revolted. He forwarded it to Bombay where it was viewed with violent distaste. Such a subject and such a passion for pornographic detail in a supposed officer and gentleman! It was insupportable. Several officials demanded Burton's instant expulsion from the service he had so disgraced, and though this extreme was not acceded to, the young officer's name was covered with odium, and he was scarcely received into decent society.

It is difficult to understand this extreme attitude, even in those days, except by the light of Burton's previous tactlessness of behaviour. He had made himself personally disliked, and

[1] *Report on Karachi Manners and Customs*, R. F. Burton, 1855, Bombay. Also "Terminal Essay," *Arabian Nights*.

his enemies must have seized this weapon to attack his vulner-
ability. Socially he was unperturbed, he sneered at the stiff
backs turned upon him, and was simply amused by the fulmina-
tions of outraged virtue. He felt more deeply, though he did
not show it, the official reprimand and the black mark it would
put against his name.

By now the years of hard work in the Indian climate were
beginning to tell on him. A constitution, even of iron, will
not stand up indefinitely against long periods of subsistence on
sparse and filthy native food, physical labour under torrid suns,
and repeated attacks of fever. He did not spare himself;
besides his military duties and his long hours of linguistic study,
he found time to compile material for several anthropological
essays, a book of travel, a series of fiction translations, and the
opening chapters of a compendious book on the sword.[1] He
was on the verge of collapse when he was ordered to take a short
rest. It was while he was doing so at Goa, the old Portuguese
colony, that an event occurred which precipitated his debacle.

This was none other than the news, in the spring of 1848,
of the murder of the British official Anderson and a companion
by Nao Mall of Mooltan. It was followed shortly by the eagerly
awaited official information that a Mooltan campaign was imminent, and that Napier was returning from England to command
it. The thought of action again at last rang through the India
stations like a clarion and officers hurriedly wrote for their
exchanges. Burton, idling in Goa and still weak with convalescence, was roused like the rest. The long-cherished dream
of campaigning with Napier startled him from his lethargy of
weakness. He returned hastily and made his preparations,
feeling life flow back into his veins with every hour of action.
One by one his brother officers were ordered up and left him.
Hurriedly he wrote to Headquarters setting out his exceptional
qualifications and begging to accompany the force as interpreter.
He spoke Hindustani, Gujarati, Persian, Mahratti, Sindi,
Punjabi, Arabic, Telugu, Pushtu, Turkish, and Armenian,
besides having the best working knowledge in the army of
Mooltani. He was the ideal, indeed the only, man for the post.
Might he go ?

[1] His Indian period produced four books. *Sind, or the Unhappy Valley*
(1851), *Sind and the Races that inhabit the Valley of the Indus* (1851), *Goa and the
Blue Mountains* (1851), and *Falconry in the Valley of the Indus* (1852). He also
contributed to the Asiatic Society, prepared some material for *Vikram the
Vampire* (1870), and the early draft of his unfinished *History of the Sword* (1884)

But now one must assume the interest at work against him struck. A letter from Headquarters, in reply to his, curtly informed him that the post he asked for was already filled by another officer. The name was mentioned, and when he saw that name Burton knew that he was looking at the writing on the wall. He had been purposely passed over for a man with only one-tenth of his linguistic attainments, a man who spoke one language only, and that Hindustani. There were forces against him, and it was hopeless to go on. " The dwarfish demon called ' interest ' has fought against me," he wrote in anguish and fury, " and as usual has won the fight. My career in India has been a failure, and by no fault of my own." [1]

This last thrust to his failing health was the finish. He collapsed. There was one thing only to do ; go home. The medical board passed him hastily, a long furlough was granted him, and as men and guns were rumbling along the streets towards the Second Sikh War, the man who had so longed to join in it was carried helpless and bitter aboard his ship, with death in his eyes and despair in his heart.

[1] *Life of Sir Richard Burton,* by Lady Burton.

Chapter Two

BURTON, it is recorded, left Bombay virtually a dying man. Prostrated in health, dejected in spirit, he seemed to have lost all will to live. Indeed, were it not for the ceaseless care of his devoted Moslem servant, it is very probable that long before the Cape was reached he would have taken that last weighted dive into the sea. But the recuperative power of youth is boundless ; even with the incubus of a failing spirit, the body, given the slenderest encouragement will always miraculously drag itself back to health. While the change of scene and the brisk action of seaboard life lulled his mind into restfulness, the fresh breezes, salt spray, and incessant movement invigorated his blood and blew the last traces of fever from his yellow cheeks. A month of beating across the Arabian Sea saw him tottering on deck again, and by the time the *Eliza* had fought her way round the Cape seas and was tacking up the long stretch home, he was drawing out of convalescence and able to look round him.

All thoughts were now bent on his homecoming, on the beloved family he had not seen for seven years and with whom he was shortly to be reunited. Pressure of work had kept them mostly from his thoughts during his long absence, but he was now seized with an uncontrollable prodigal longing to greet a familiar face again. The moment the brig docked in English waters he hurried to London and, though he arrived in the city at the inconvenient hour of two in the morning, he at once made for the house of a maternal aunt and awakened her. From her he learned that his parents and married sister were in Pisa, and he scarcely gave himself time to transact the accumulated private business of seven years before he posted down, travelling night and day to greet them. The meeting, taking place as it did in a country filled with childhood memories, was a particularly happy one. It was the first time the whole family had been together for nearly ten years. Parents, daughter, and two sons greeted each other with a warmth that was the more fervent because each knew that it was only temporary.

Colonel Joseph Netterville Burton, his father, was one of those individuals who might easily have stepped from the pages of Thackeray. The son of an Irish cleric and one of a large family of brothers and sisters, he had early escaped from home life by enlisting in the 36th regiment, taking with him the wildest and more dangerous of his father's tenants. He saw service in Sicily, distinguishing himself by pistolling a brother officer in a duel, nursing him tenderly back to health, and then pistolling him again. Removed to Genoa, he became Town Major, and was occupying that position when the unhappy Queen Caroline, junketing across Europe with her immodest dresses, her lax morals, and paramour Bergami, paid the town a visit. She shocked the civilians, but charmed the garrison ; she radiated kindness, and her generosity, both of purse and person, was irresistible. Joseph Burton, strict moralist though he was, fell completely under her spell, and, when recalled to England at Wellington's orders to stand in the witness box and testify in the charges formulated against her by the King, flatly refused. He was gravely warned of the danger to his career rising from such insubordination, but continued to be obdurate, remembering as no doubt Colonel Newcome would have, that though he was an officer, he was a gentleman as well. The results were drastic. The Queen was condemned without him, but that did not lessen his crime. Whitehall reduced him to half-pay, thus barring the door to any promotion; and, having with the most magnificent gesture of his life extinguished himself, Joseph married a plebeian young lady with money and retired from active life to cultivate the habits of a gentleman in greater seclusion. In character he was a quixotic and vacillating moralist, with a love of etiquette combined with a wild streak of romance. Gambling for money horrified him, but he squandered thousands on financial speculation. He had a passion for amateur chemistry and while filling his household with stenches, worked feverishly at finding, among other things, a soap which he could market and so make his fortune. He was almost aboriginally superstitious, believing fervently in signs and portents, beneficent and evil stars, and other occult twaddle, never spoke of his health without touching wood, or of his age, which to his death no one knew, for fear of some dire calamity overtaking him. He suffered from asthma and general hypochondria, making the former the main excuse for the continual change of scene that his restless spirit craved.

For nearly thirty years, during which time three children had been born to him, grown up, and left him, the Colonel and his undistinguished little wife had rattled over thousands of miles of European post roads in their yellow post-chaise. Restlessness, change, and genteel excitement were the keynotes of their lives. This could not fail to have its effect on the children. Across the stream of their childhood memories flitted always a phantas-magoria of strange faces and scenes, a dangerous sense of un-reality and impermanence which must have impressed itself on their characters. In spite of their father's rigid strictness, all the more rigid because he had destined them for the Church, the boys grew up wild and uncontrolled. Dragged across Europe with tutors, governesses, maid-servants, and mountains of baggage, neglected completely for long periods, they spent the greater part of their childhood in violent escapades with street *gamins*, learned fancing from grooms, cock fighting, smoking and swallowing opium from common soldiers. It is related that at Oxford it was discovered that Richard did not know the Lord's Prayer, and had never even heard of the Thirty-nine Articles. Now and again the Colonel, at some more startling escapade than usual, would descend upon them with a riding-whip and flog them unmercifully, but for the most part they were left alone, and their tutors seem to have been helpless.

But now, as Richard breathed the soft sunlit Italian air and felt the torrid nightmare of the past year receding from his mind, he discovered a delight in wandering with his brother Edward over the scenes of their childhood and reviving the more memorable of their adventures. There was scarcely a large town that had not for them the memorable milestone of some boyish escapade. At Naples they recalled the exciting time when the cholera epidemic had swept the town and, with a horrid, irresist-ible fascination, they had followed the dead-cart with its terrible load, and watched the black, rigid corpses being tossed one by one into a plague pit from the foul depths of which shone a blue glow of corrupting human flesh. At Florence, wandering down the Chiaia, they broke into chuckles as they relived their adventure with the Florentine women, when, burning with pure and ardent love, scarce in their teens, they had clambered nightly over the roof-tops from their bedroom window, with carving-knives stuck in their girdles, to keep a tryst with an amused couple of professional prostitutes. They remembered their constant feud with their hated tutor Du Pré, putting bullets through his hat for a bet, smoking behind his back, being beaten by him, and finally physically overthrowing him.

There could have been no better way than this for a young, sick, and disillusioned man to heal and refresh himself and forget his failure in a temporary Nirvana. He had three or four manuscripts from his Indian work in his baggage, but in the backwater in which he was living, he was content for a while to do nothing but amuse himself and catch up with his arrears of health.

The following year he returned to England where for a time he moved between the Malvern and Leamington spas. But from childhood he had always hated his native country, finding the climate depressing and the people alien to his polyglot temperament. In 1851, therefore, seeking for a place to work, amuse, and recuperate himself completely, he crossed to Boulogne, then one of the fashionable watering-places, with his brother Edward, and took up residence in an hotel, where he was later joined by the rest of the family.

He found Boulogne to his liking. The climate was bracing, there were good clubs, interesting people, pretty faces, and ample opportunity for physical exercise and work. He soon had his time proportionately divided between his study, his club, the salons of his acquaintances, and Constantin's, the fencing-school. He had with him the notes and uncompleted MSS. of two books on Sind, *Sind, or the Unhappy Valley* (1851), *Sind and the Races that Inhabit the Valley of the Indus* (1851); remarkably faithful and valuable accounts of his life and work and of the character and customs of the people as observed by him during his long service in the province, and *Goa and the Blue Mountains*, an account of an expedition he made while on furlough in (1851) India. There was also a small treatise on *Falconry in the Valley of the Indus* (1852), an accurate if rather dull description of a long-dead sport still surviving among a native race. Besides numerous Government reports and contributions to the Asiatic Society, these books kept him fairly busy.

Unfortunately they fell more or less stillborn from the press. Their subjects, though they attracted some notice in scientific circles, were never likely to be popular. They were crammed with data, often ill-digested, written hastily, as all his literary work was, and composed in a style that though occasionally pungent and vivid was mostly too harsh and difficult, too full of circumlocution and self-coined words to strike the popular taste. They were, however, to stand him in good stead when, a year later, he put a proposition, still at this date maturing in his mind, before the Royal Geographical Society.

For exercise he took long walks, swinging an enormous solid-iron walking-stick,[1] which served to keep his wrists supple ; and he fenced at Constantin's. At this fencing-school he rapidly became a famous figure. He was one of the last great swordsmen, loving the art of fence with that almost rapt passion of the great masters of the eighteenth century. The exercise, combining as it does agility, physical strength, coolness of head, ardour, and watchfulness, was admirably suited to his peculiar temperament.

The *salles d'armes* of Constantin housed from time to time some of the finest swordsmen in Europe. An anecdote from a fellow officer, Colonel Shuldham, of Burton's bout with a sergeant of French Hussars will show him characteristically at his best.

The news that he was going to fight always drew a crowd, and on this occasion, as his opponent was to be a famous French swordsman, most of the Boulogne colony of English and French were there. The appearance of the two men was greeted by a buzz of admiration from the spectators. The Hussar was a powerful and magnificent specimen from the Midi ; Burton, less stocky but suppler, was a fine example of English army training. With the return of health his face had taken on that dark Arab handsomeness, with raven hair, jet-black piercing eyes, dæmonically twirling eyebrows, and fierce sullen mouth which Desanges has captured in his fine painting of this period. An enormous black sweeping moustache falling below his chin added to the general magnetism of his face and enhanced that curious bipartite look which a friend once described as " the brow of a god, the jaw of a devil."

The Hussar stood forward and donned his guard, the thick leather jacket and strong iron mask universally used for protection. Burton astounded the spectators by merely baring his neck and rolling up his sleeves, exposing mighty forearms and curiously feminine hands. Shuldham remonstrated with him, pointing out his extreme danger in fighting with no protection.

---

[1] The dragoman at the Damascus Legation, whose father had worked with Burton in 1870, told the author in 1946 that he well remembered his father's description of this famous walking-stick ; one of his strongest memories of the former consul.

Burton's terse reply was that it was of no consequence. They saluted and fell on guard. A moment of preliminary feinting was followed by a quick cut from the Frenchman, a lightning riposte from the Englishman, and then a tricky downward slash from the latter's powerful forearm which sent the Hussar's weapon flying from his hand.[1] An admiring murmur from the spectators presaged a few moments later a repetition of the feat. Seven times did the unprotected Englishman disarm the bewildered Frenchman, until at length the latter retired, complaining that Burton had nearly dislocated his wrist by the force of his blows. " To me," wrote the delighted Shuldham, " it was a marvellous display of fencing skill, and the strange, magnetic power that he seemed to possess over everybody present was equally surprising."

Nor were his conquests only those of the sword. In the intervals when he was not writing or exercising he was engaged in carrying on a series of complicated flirtations and physical entanglements with the young women of the English colony. Any pretty face would set his eye wandering, and the prettier and less intelligent the owner, the more assailable was Burton's heart. Having once had his fancy caught, he would pursue the object of it, regardless of the consequences, to the sweet or the bitter end. It is said that he pursued one young lady right into her mother's arms. " What are your intentions towards my daughter ? " demanded the latter indignantly, having no doubt heard something of the young man's reputation. Burton's reply was a sardonic grin. " Strictly dishonourable, Madam, I regret to say. Strictly dishonourable." And he bowed himself out.[2]

Some attempt to whitewash his unusually sensual nature has been made by writers who have taken their cue from his own lips that he was " no hot amorist." But this was a man who spent his life dabbling in the *erotica* of the Orient, a man whose compiled *ars amatoria* is by no means inferior in content to that of Ovid. The moral values of such a man could not possibly be the same as those of the ordinary Westerner. By the standards of the Orient Burton was not possibly a " hot amorist," by the standards of the West he was sensual in the extreme. Indeed love in its best sense he never knew. " I require two

[1] In the modern *salles d'armes*, where subtlety rules rather than force, such tactics would have had a different reception.
[2] *Life*, by Lady Burton.

qualities and two only in a woman," he would remark, " beauty
and affection." And again : " The English have the finest
women in Europe and least know how to use them." And in
the Terminal Essay to the *Arabian Nights*, he sums up the
Eastern attitude, and his own, in the translation :

> Rely not on women : trust not their hearts.
> Whose joys and whose sorrows are hung on their parts !

With such opinions and such careless behaviour in expressing
them, it was not long before he became a figure of some notoriety
in Boulogne. As usual he made a few staunch friends and a
number of enemies. Among the latter, brought by gossips
from India, was soon circulating the story of his Karachi
escapade, suitably embellished, and the other crop of legends
and half-truths which had gathered round his name were
whispered with disgust or delight in salon and café. The more
straight-laced of the British colony began to cut him, ladies of
impeccable virtue were heard to remark with emphasis that
they " would not and could not sit in the room with that fellow
Burton," one by one doors were shut in his face and acquaintances would hurry across the road to avoid meeting him. He
made no attempt to excuse himself. Indeed he rather veered
in the opposite direction, acknowledging, with sardonic gravity,
when taxed by some bolder spirit, the truth of the wildest
legend about himself. For he was now in the role that suited
him admirably, and which he was always indefatigable in
sustaining. Like Byron, a predecessor with whom he had many
other points in common, he took a keen delight in painting
himself blacker than he really was. He loved to keep up the
idea that he was a bold bad man, thoroughly damned and
beyond hope of salvation. He was at his happiest when playing
the role of ogre to a tableful of alarmed young ladies, and shook
with inner amusement as he watched their appetites wilt and
their faces pale as he solemnly and rather brilliantly told the
story of how he and a castaway boat's crew had once dined on
a plump cabin boy, or how he had bloodily murdered a man who
had penetrated his disguise. This is the type of humour that
is rarely appreciated on all sides, and his general manner and
behaviour scarcely tended to soften it. If it suited him, no one
could be more courteous and charming ; and his witty, vivid,
and downright conversation could often hold an audience
enthralled. But in other circumstances he could become

impatient and rude to an insupportable degree. If the company bored him, he thought nothing of taking up a book and pointedly reading it or of walking from the room with a cold disdainful stare. He would flirt openly with a woman who attracted him and show complete disinterest in a woman who did not. Thus, in days when society was a closed and narrow circle, he was already creating that prejudice later to affect his whole career.

During this life of mingled industry and dalliance, an episode occurred, trivial to himself at the time and yet in which destiny put on some of the habiliments of Ouida. "Fraught with destiny" would be the phrase by which this sensational lady writer would have described this episode. And, indeed, the jargon of the fiction writer is the only explanation applicable; for if ever life produced a character thoroughly consistent with the simple and romantic standards of fiction, a character who might have walked straight from the pages of a three-volume novel, it was the one now about to make its entrance in fitting circumstances.

Clad in a shaggy black coat and twirling his iron walking-stick in his fingers, Burton was one day sauntering along the Ramparts of the town when his speculative eye noticed two girls approaching him. They were tall and with good figures and, as they passed and he met their glance with his sidelong appraising stare, he saw that they were pretty, and that the taller of them had large deep blue eyes and a pile of brown-golden hair. He was attracted and turned round to stare at them, noticing curiously that the taller of the girls had stopped and was trembling with emotion. Scenting an amusing adventure he met them the following day at the same time. This time he was carrying a piece of chalk, and after following them for some time he scrawled on a wall: "May I speak to you?" and strolled away to watch developments. After some hesitation and furiously blushing, the taller girl picked up the chalk and wrote hurriedly: "No. Mother will be angry." Then, with one nervous glance at their admirer's amused face, they scuttled from sight with beating hearts. An hour later, immersed in other work or amusement, he forgot them.

It had been a casual moment to the man, charming, amusing, and instantly forgotten. To the girls it was different. The taller girl, in that one first instant of meeting his compelling gaze, had fallen in love with that idolatrous adoration which is as rare as it is senseless and beautiful. How chancy, how unprepared for was this meeting; how like the clumsy mechanism of a Victorian plot ! From that moment until she died, Burton was never to be out of this girl's thoughts. In the ill-starred tragedy that was his life, the foremost role had been reserved for her.[1]

§

The girls were Isabel and Blanche Arundell, daughters of one of the oldest and proudest Roman Catholic families in England, the Arundells of Wardour. Like many other families whose means were not up to their station, the Arundells were forced to economize by retiring periodically abroad where expenses were more consistent with their pockets and society made less demands on their pride. The family was large, besides the parents there were seven boys and girls. Of these Isabel, the love-struck, was the eldest. A handsome girl of nineteen with thick, golden-brown hair, a Grecian profile, and a swelling figure, she was just " out " from her first season in London, and had accompanied the family to Boulogne for the estimable purpose of continuing her French and music.

As with the other well-born families residing in Boulogne, the Arundells kept strictly behind their social rampart, meeting only the few neighbours, the Jerninghams, Molyneux-Seels, Dundases, and Chichesters. They lived in the rarefied atmosphere of the Haute Ville and under no circumstances mixed with general society, under which heading were included most of the English colony and two-thirds of the French one. Mrs. Arundell kept a strict eye on her delicately nurtured daughters. They were kept mostly indoors, and never allowed to walk out alone, except upon the Ramparts, where, pacing along the pleasant mile of shady trees, they could watch the stream of lower society —fast young women and dashing unscrupulous young men, soldiers and their wives and mistresses, and all the other muddy stream of the *hoi polloi*—from a discreet distance.

But no mother could thoroughly repress the high spirits which leaped behind the cool exteriors of Blanche and Isabel. They chattered incessantly of wild deeds and the heroes of

---

[1] Most of the following account of Burton's meeting and courtship comes from the pen of Isabel herself. The reader must decide for himself what to reject as a young lady's romantic fiction, and what is fact. See *Life of Lady Burton.*

Gothic romance ; out of their dark blue eyes they watched most earnestly for what they termed their Fates, who they were convinced would come striding like Lucifer to carry them off. They stole their father's cigars and smoked painstakingly in a loft ; they frequented fortune-tellers and lived in a cloud of auguries, and they thought themselves as wild as may be if they managed to exchange a little conversation with a peasant woman in the fish market.

Isabel was a romantic, idealistic, intensely religious, and determined young woman, who dwelt mostly in a dream world compounded of her own fertile imaginings and those of Mr. Disraeli. Since a small girl, when she played in the grounds of her English home at Furze Hall and had stolen down by-lanes for secret interviews with gipsies, she had always believed in a great Destiny for herself. And this was borne out by her horoscope which, cast for her in those early days by an old gipsy called Hagar Burton, had read : " You will cross the sea and be in the same town with your Destiny, and know it not. Every obstacle will rise up against you, and such a combination of circumstances that it will require all your courage, energy, and intelligence to meet them. Your life will be like one swimming against great waves. You will fix your eye on your polar star and you will go for that without looking right or left. You will bear the name of our tribe and be right proud of it. You will be as we are, but far greater than we. Your life is all wandering, change, and adventure. One soul in two bodies in life or death, never long apart. The name of our tribe shall cause you many a sorrowful, humiliating hour ; but when the rest who sought him in the heyday of his youth and strength fade from his sight, you shall remain bright and purified to him as the morning star, which hangs like a diamond drop over the sea. . . ."

Hours would she ponder over this Destiny which had been foretold her. Who would this man be ? Disraeli's *Tancred* was her faithful spiritual companion. This book she kept ever at her side ; she knew it by heart. In Tancred, the romantic peer, she found the lineaments of her own dream hero. Her thoughts dwelt always on the East, on lawless lands and colourful, romantic people. Like Lady Bertie and Bellair she was frequently " dreaming of Palestine amid her secret sadness." Oh, that delightful sadness ! With what deep sighs, what flushed cheeks would she not read over and over again that holy scene of Tancred and Eva in the eastern garden. " Why thou to me art Arabia. The Angel of Arabia and of my life and spirit! Thou art my cause and thou art most divine. . . ." As Eva was Tancred's cause and Tancred's destiny, so did she long to be the cause and destiny of some strong secret lover with a great mission in his life; someone of resolution, courage, and independence whom she would worship as a hero and cherish as a man. In her secret diary, the ultimate confidant of all her desires and dreams, she wrote about this time: "As God took a rib out of Adam and made a woman of it, so do I out of a wild chaos of thought form a man unto myself. In outward form and inmost soul, his life and deeds an ideal. He is a Hercules of manly strength . . . a soldier and a *man*; he is accustomed to command and to be obeyed. He frowns on the ordinary affairs of life, but his face always lights up warmly for me. He is one of those strong men who lead, the master-mind who governs, and he has perfect control over himself. . . . This is the creation of my fancy, and my ideal of happiness is to be such a man's wife, comrade, friend—everything to him, to sacrifice all for him, to follow his fortune through his campaigns, through his travels, to any part of the world and endure any amount of roughing. Such a man only will I wed. I love this myth of my girlhood—for myth it is—next to God; and I look to the star Hagar the gipsy said was the star of my destiny. . . ."

And Richard Burton, seen in that quick glimpse as he strolled with predatory eye along the Ramparts, was to be that Destiny. Instantly as he passed her and she met the glance of those black eyes set in the yellowish Arab face with its ruthless mouth hidden under the drooping black moustaches, she knew that this was the man. He had, she wrote later, " a fierce, proud, melancholy expression; and when he smiled, he smiled as though it hurt him. He looked at me as though he read me through and through in a moment, and started a little. I was completely magnetized." She had stopped suffocated with emotion. Next moment she had turned to her sister Blanche and whispered trembling: " That man will marry me."

Was it possible that she had found him at last? For weeks she dreamed and thought of this unknown man of the Ramparts. Daily she would hasten on to the Promenade, find a hidden vantage point, and watch for him in the circulating crowds. When she saw him she would try to steal nearer in order to hear his voice and watch his expression. If his eye fell on her she would quickly lower her head in embarrassment. Blind to all the dictates of her breeding, her blue eyes were always searching for him and hoping for a glance of recognition. To every scrap of conversation in her own home she listened eagerly in the hope of learning his name or some reference to him. She even tried to put out conversation feelers. But in vain : he belonged to a different social world from her own. Through the small seaside town their orbits circled but never seemed to cross. Isabel watched him from afar. He seemed to have forgotten her. When a female cousin of hers came to stay in Boulogne, a girl whose blood was of sufficiently plebeian hue for her to mix in Richard Burton's set, Isabel watched anguished while Richard flirted openly with the newcomer. At length they were formally introduced. Isabel, the sophisticated young aristocrat, stood trembling when she at last shook his hand. She who had come through a London season unscathed found nothing to say to the very ordinary young soldier. But she had time to steal a closer look at him and note that his eyes " looked through you, glazed over, and saw something behind."

She met him again at a dance. This time she saw that he was assaulting the affections of another young lady. He gave her a waltz. She swooned with happiness. The rest of the evening passed in a haze. When she got home she reverently removed the sash his hand had touched at her waist, and the gloves his hand had clapsed. She pressed them to her lips, and then put them carefully away. She never wore them again. As his books began to appear she bought and eagerly devoured them. Reading of his adventures among the Jats of India, his exploits at Goa, and his romantic labours among the hill tribes of Sind, she knew that his was the man God had created for her, the man at whose side she ought to be. In the long hours she spent pouring her thoughts into her secret diary, she wrote : " Where are all those grand passions of bygone days ? Is the race extinct ? Is Richard the last of them ? Richard may be a delusion of my brain. But how dull is reality ! "

Her cousin kindly prevailed upon Richard to write something for her, after the fashion of those days. The lines he absent-mindedly dashed off, Isabel tied up in ribbons and wore for months next to her heart. " What a curse is a heart ! " she wrote, in desperation. " With all to make me happy I pine and hanker for him, my other half, to fill this void. . . ." She disclosed this secret and consuming passion to no one but her God. Daily she repaired to the little chapel of Our Lady in

the College, and emptied her innermost heart before the altar.
If God willed it, and it was for Richard's happiness, she prayed
that he might become hers. " When one is young," she cried
in her happy misery, " it is hard to pine for something, and at
the same time to say, ' Thy will be done.' But is not sacrifice
the very essence of religion ? "

During the rest of her stay, her spirits soared and drooped
at every wayward puff of circumstance. When he recognized
her in the street and shot her his mirthless yet strangely
attractive smile she was lifted to the seventh heaven of happiness.
Then again she would sink appalled with the thought that he
did not love her, scarcely knew her, probably never even gave
her a thought. " Oh," she would weep in her diary, " if kind
Providence had blessed me with the man I love, what a different
being I might be ! Fate has used me hardly, with my proud,
sensitive nature to rough the world and its sharp edges, alone
and unprotected. . . ."

The Arundells had decided to leave Boulogne in May 1852.
The knowledge that she would soon have to say farewell to the
most wonderful episode of her life weighed on Isabel remorse-
lessly. In the intervals of packing and making the final arrangements she would tread the Ramparts and revisit for the last
time the places where she had first seen him. So little did he
think of her that he did not even know she was going away.
Should she seek him out and say good-bye ? Would her pride
permit it ? " When we leave this place," she wrote, " he will
go one way in life and I another ; and who knows if we may
ever meet again ? " But was it not better to be brave and
face her Destiny ? To see him again would only add to her pain
and be useless. Better by far would it be to slip out of his life as
unnoticed as she had entered ; and pray for his return. Let her
have faith in her Destiny—and his.

At two o'clock on the sunless morning of 9th May, the
Arundells' boat crept out from Boulogne harbour into the
Channel. After a night of farewell celebrations all the passengers
slept heavily below. On deck the solitary figure of Isabel,
wrapped in cloak and crinoline, stood under the stars and
watched the lights of the town fade astern. For as long as she
could see them she watched those fading lights. She was
miserable ; but she was proud. Miserable because of her loss,
proud because of her acceptance of it. " I could now rest,"
she wrote, lingering virtuously over every adjective, " after my

long and weary struggle, suffering, patient, and purified. . . .
I felt that I was as gold tried in fire."

§

While Isabel was thus being carried away into four years'
magnificent solitude, Richard, flirting casually with half a
dozen women, was occupying his serious moments with a
scheme which, projected during his Indian service when he
was making a study of practical Moslem divinity and social
life, had now, with the completion of his literary labours, revived
itself in his mind. It was nothing less than an expedition to
Arabia in disguise.

Contacts in India had aroused in him an intense interest
and sympathy with the Arabian language, literature, and
religion. In Bombay, Baroda, and Karachi he had sought
assiduously to perfect his knowledge of the Arabic tongue ;
under the tuition of a half-Badawi shaykh he had entered upon
a careful study of the Sufi or Gnostic faith, and the complicated
shibboleth and intricate formulæ of practical devotion. *Munshis*,
or qualified teachers, had accompanied him to the Indian
mosques, where, dressed as a Dervish or an Arab-Iranian pedlar,
he had often followed publicly in the prayers. He had accustomed himself to the etiquette of social life, almost as complicated
and essential as that of the religious, and as far as possible under
the circumstances he had endeavoured to fit himself for an
expedition he had one day hoped to make.

Kneeling there in those Indian mosques, joining in the
daily prayers at the call of the Muezzin, raising his hands,
sinking on his breast, bowing his head to that invisible, far-off
yet potent holy city which only the true Believer may see, he
would find himself speculating on the chances and dangers of an
expedition there. Here was a project worthy of his great talents,
an opponent worthy of his mettle. Mecca, the hidden city,
to which every Moslem in the four quarters of the globe turns
at sunset and sunrise in prayer ; Mecca, the forbidden, buried
in the heart of barren Hedjaz, a secret heart of civilization
beating in the uncharted peninsula of Arabia. Here was a goal
for the adventurous. Sitting brooding on the subject of that
hidden city, he had roughly sketched out in his mind a plan
by which a European, disguised as an Oriental, might explore
his way there. He dwelt on it long, inventing contingencies
in his mind and systematically providing for them ; every

conceivable accident of travel he discussed and decided upon. One day he had hoped to have the leisure to complete his project.

Now he felt that time had come. He was on furlough, revived in health and strength, sick of the pettiness and softness of civilization, and with a new itch for adventure in his blood.

In the autumn of 1852, after long thought and consideration, he communicated with the Royal Geographical Society, already the interested recipients of several of his Indian pamphlets, laid before them his project, and offered his services. " My desire," he wrote ambitiously, " is to remove that opprobrium to modern adventure, the huge white blot which in our maps still notes the Eastern and Central regions of Arabia " ; and his principal object was set out as " to cross the unknown Arabian Peninsula, in a direct line, from either Al Madinah to Maskat, or diagonally from Mecca to Makallah on the Indian Ocean." [1]   His secondary objects, beside making a careful study of the inner life of the Moslem people, were to inquire into the hydrography of the Hedjaz, and find out if any market for horses could be opened between Central Arabia and India.

His request, forwarded under the auspices of an influential friend, was favourably received by that admirable body of scientists and adventurers, the R.G.S. With their usual fore-sight they could appreciate the exceptional qualifications of the man who made it. They offered, on their usual conditions, to finance the expedition, and suggested that the young officer apply for additional furlough to the Directors of the East India Company. Burton accordingly wrote to Leadenhall Street, applying for an additional three years in which to prosecute researches in Arabia. But here he was unsuccessful. The Directors, looking at the matter in the light of a commercial rather than a scientific proposition, turned it down. " Nothing," they wrote pontifically in reply, " but a string of fatalities has resulted from the travels heretofore taken in that region." They granted, however, an additional twelve months to the time already remaining to him, " that he may pursue his Arabic studies in lands where the language is best learnt." More than that they would not do.

Twelve months ! It was not nearly enough ; but it would have to do. He flung himself into a rush of preparation, left Boulogne and returned to England for the first great expedition of his life.

[1] Arabia had already been crossed from east to west by Captain Sadlier in 1819.

Chapter Three

BURTON's destination, the Hedjaz, lies on the western coast of the sloping peninsula of Arabia. A narrow strip of territory, cut longitudinally by the ragged bastion of the granite Tehama hills, bounded on the east by arid Nejd, on the south by Yemen, and on the north by the great desert of Nafud, its empty, treacherous beaches fringe half the eastern coastline of the Red Sea. It is a hot, barren, stony land, a place of sand-swept wastes, waterless, harrowed by the distorted shapes of volcanic formations, its plains scored by deep torrent beds [1] which are parched, thorny gullies except for the short periods following the rains. Blessed sparsely here and there by the green of oases round which are huddled the scattered towns and villages, the wilder territory of its uplands, commanding the few caravan routes, was dominated in those days by the powerful and murderous Arab tribe, the Beni Harb.

For countless years this region had presented an almost impregnable barrier to the European traveller. Man and nature have here combined to resent and affront the intruder. Could he, obviating the difficulty of disguise, overcome the journey through the sands which swamped the legions of Aelius Gallus; could he resist thirst and disease; could he circumvent the ambushes and raids of the ever watchful tribes; could he even attain the comparative safety of the inland cities, he might yet, by a single slip, fall under the knives of his infuriated fellow travellers. For a slip might proclaim his identity, and mutilation and death would be the almost inevitable result.

It is a strange irony of circumstance that makes the Hedjaz, this unhallowed spot where even life itself struggles to exist, the well-spring of the Mohammedan religion, a holy land sanctified and blessed, a fanatically guarded goal of the faithful. But here, among these arid hills, Mohammed the Prophet was born, grew up under the inspiring flame of God's breath,

---

[1] Burton's name for them is *fiumaras*, a word which will be used in the subsequent narrative.

was threatened by his enemies, fled in the *Hegira*, and settled and breathed his last in the fair city of Medina, relinquishing his body to the Faithful, his soul to eternal paradise, and his Koran to the hands of his disciples, Ali and Abu Bakr. In green Medina, he died, but it is in arid Mecca, under the shadow of the House of God, that he was born ; and it is towards Mecca that he faces, like a good Moslem[1] as he lies in his deathless sleep, swinging between heaven and earth in the great Hujrah in Medina.

Mecca, then, is the very core of Moslem civilization, a city to be kept undefiled and jealously preserved from the outer world. The Christian directs his prayers to heaven, the Moslem towards Mecca. Five times a day, before sunrise, just after noon, before sunset, and just after sunset, and finally when the day has closed, it is the Prophet's ordinance that the good Moslem shall direct his face towards Mecca and his prayers towards the House of God, and that once in his life, " so be he able," he shall leave his native land and, glorying in the hardships of the way, undergo a solemn pilgrimage to Mecca to make his devotions before the very House of God itself, be purified of his sins at the Holy Well of Zem Zem, and so earn the title of Hajj and the coveted green turban. This is an ordinance whose fulfilment is an indispensable step to Paradise, a duty of intense labour and suffering which no good or wise Moslem must omit, it is a passport of respectability, social and commercial, a guarantee of piousness. To die in its performance is a surety, for however vile a sinner, of immediate and eternal bliss.

And so yearly at a certain date, from the seventh to the tenth of the month, Dhu'l-Hijja, a great historic phenomenon is repeated.[2] Drawn from the farthest confines of the Moslem Empire, from every race white and black, a great stream of the pious converges upon the arid shores of Arabia. Alexandria, Damascus, and Baghdad, the three main gateways for the pilgrims, pour their living tributaries into the deserts. From these meeting-points the great caravans used to lumber slowly on their thousand-mile trek across desert and steppe, or by sea

---

[1] The ordinance that the Moslem in his devotions should face towards Mecca was, of course, the Prophet's own. Previous to this command Jerusalem had been the cynosure of prayer.

[2] The Hajj may only be performed during the sacred month. A visitation made at any other time of the year is called an " Umrah," and is of far less sacred efficacy.

and land towards Mecca. A motley throng of nationalities and races, rich men and ragged beggars, collected for protection, paid a handful of villainous Turkish or Albanian irregulars to act as guards, and struggled forward to Eternal Bliss, braving intense hunger and thirst and attack by Badu, and dying in large numbers on the way from all three. Almost a third of this vast concourse was formerly believed to perish yearly by the way [1] from bullets, thirst, or disease, and for miles at a time the old caravan routes were marked with the calcined bones of men and animals. For these few months of the year the peninsula of Arabia is a babel of tongues and dialects. Arabic is the *lingua franca*, but the dialect variations on its native purity are almost infinite. Each man is a stranger to his neighbour, Turk rubs shoulder with Negro, Arab with Punjabi, Persian with Malay; but so long as the religious observances, the five acts of worship, are punctiliously observed, all other lapses from Arabian etiquette can be safely laid at the door of racial ignorance.

This, then, is the time most propitious for the interloper, and it was Burton's purpose to make use of it as a cover for his expedition. Entering the Hedjaz by this route and at this season, he obviated the difficulty of travelling alone in dangerous regions, was less likely to arouse the suspicions of the natives, and would be given an unrivalled opportunity for making a first-hand study of the manners and customs of the Moslems at the most critical moment of their lives. His plan was to proceed to Mecca in the disguise of a pilgrim, perform the complicated ceremonies of initiation while making a careful survey of the hidden city, and having attained the coveted green turban of a Hajj, an infallible passport to all parts of Arabia, continue into the heart of the peninsula on a hazardous survey of the unknown route to Makallah.

An examination of the three main pilgrim routes led him to fix his choice on that from Alexandria. This entailed a journey by canal to Cairo, a camel ride to Suez, by boat from Suez down the Red Sea to Yambu, and thence to Mecca and Medina by the trade route. After three years' abstinence from Oriental life of any sort, and with the difficulties of an excursion into a part of the Empire he had not previously visited before him,

---

[1] 1853. Matters are very different now: though the Hedjaz railway no longer runs from Damascus to Medina, wealthier Hajis often travel by air, and others by motor coach.

he felt that without a little tuition and familiarity with Arab manners and a refreshment of his knowledge of the minutiæ of religious custom, his disguise might well be pierced by the ever-watchful eyes that would surround him.[1] He determined, therefore, that whatever surplus time remained at his disposal should be spent at Alexandria in accustoming himself to his surroundings, studying the habits of the people, and perfecting the details of his imposture.

In 1845, Wallin the traveller had made the Pilgrimage in a Persian caravan from Hail. He had managed to enter Mecca, but the extreme danger of his presence (two Jews caught that year had been crucified alive by the infuriated pilgrims) prevented him from making any notes of value on his observations. Burton sent him a list of questions from Boulogne, but by the time they were received, Wallin was dead. His only predecessor who had left information of value was Burckhardt the Swiss, who in 1814–15 left Taif in the disguise of a Mameluke and entered Mecca in the company of three Arnaut soldiers picked up on the way. His account of the city is by far the most comprehensive and accurate yet made.[2] He was a shrewd, careful, and thorough observer, and subsequent travellers could do little but amplify his copious notes. His identity was known, however, to Mohammed Ali Pasha, who for political reasons allowed him to go free; and one or two of the most intimate ceremonies of the Pilgrimage had therefore to be avoided. Both Burckhardt and Wallin, then, in a sense had failed; the first to make any observations, the second to sustain his disguise. It remained to Burton to accomplish both successfully.

Every detail and contingency that forethought could provide for was gone over again and again during the last few weeks in London prior to his departure. He was circumcised—a painful operation at the age of thirty-two, but vitally necessary, as a foreskin was as dangerous as a Bible in Arabia. He made secret arrangements with a friend at Alexandria for his stay there. He tried out the effects of various dyes[3] on his skin, practised

[1] There would be little danger of detection through faults in the Arabic language. Among the many differences of dialect in the various countries where this language is spoken, any slips would pass unnoticed. A slip in religious procedure was a much more likely danger.

[2] See Burckhardt's *Travels in Arabia*, 1829.

[3] One can only surmise that Burton was a man of exceedingly pale skin. Most sunburned Europeans of dark complexion would pass easily as Arabs among Syrian, Persian, and Circassian pilgrims.

handling a spear, taught himself to shoe horses ; and repeatedly rehearsed the details of his disguise. When all was ready, he secretly packed in oriental baggage and sent it to Southampton to await arrival.

Above all things, Burton hated most the ceremony of " good-bye." The act of parting from a loved one invariably seemed to stop his heart and fill his eyes with tears. This boyish trait drove him to make of departure a thing furtive and unheralded, and impressed those who did not know him with a sense of his callousness. As the time for his departure on this long and hazardous adventure drew near, he found it difficult to hide from mother and sister the emotions which rose up in him. For not even they knew that he was going. The secret of his expedition was well kept. Only the R.G.S. and a handful of brother officers were aware of it. No doubt the fear of emotional scenes prevented him from communicating the secret to his family while he was yet with them. But he would not leave his mother in doubt a moment after he was gone. He accordingly wrote a letter to her, to be delivered the day after his departure, telling her briefly of his plans, leaving with her his will and his small stock of valuables to be divided, in case of his non-return, between her and his beloved Eliza. On the night prior to his departure he kissed his mother a filial good-night in the ordinary manner. The next morning he was gone.

A certain Captain Harry Grindlay was one of the few officers in his secret. Grindlay was a man with considerable experience of the Orient. It had been arranged that he should accompany Burton to Alexandria in the role of interpreter, Burton posing during the journey as a Persian prince. Both men knew that *bazaar* whispers reach far beyond the Mediterranean, and that for complete success Burton must leave London, not arrive at Alexandria, as an Oriental. A suspicion that a Persian had arrived who had not embarked might start gossip that could wreck the whole expedition and put Burton's life in jeopardy. It was to Grindlay's rooms in London, therefore, that the two men went in a cab, and it was from here that a few hours later a soft-robed Persian prince, accompanied by a deferential English interpreter, swept down to Southampton. From the moment that they left Grindlay's rooms in London until five months later when a sun-scorched importunate Afghan forced his way into the British Consul's office at Jeddah, Burton was scarcely to speak five sentences in his native language. Persian,

Hindustani, Urdu, and Arabic—from now on he was to live, dream, and think in them.

On 3rd April 1853, as Mirza Abdulla, of Bushire, he gracefully boarded the P. and O. liner *Bengal* and recited in Arabic the *fathah,* or prayer of farewell. Curiously enough it was on this first voyage that his imposture was seen through for the only time during the whole pilgrimage. A Greek from Bombay, struck by the punctiliousness of the devotions of the Persian prince, eyed him closer and recognized something familiar about the cast of his features. Burton's quick eyes noted the discovery by a man who had known him in India, and made a sign to him to keep silent. The Greek turned away, leaving the " Moslem " among his Arab companions. Nor did he open his mouth until the pilgrimage was accomplished and he met Burton in Bombay.

Embarking at Alexandria, after nine days' journey, Burton passed the first battery of eyes—the beggars clustered on the quay—with a disdainful stare. " Alhamdolillah ! " he exclaimed on setting foot on shore. " Moslem ! " murmured the watching crowd, and did not molest him.

He had arranged to make his stay in Alexandria at the house of a friend, the only person in Egypt in the secret of his disguise. Here, to lull any suspicion in the native servants, he was lodged in an outhouse overlooking the lovely Mahmudiyah canal, and here, among the fragrance of oleanders and roses, he laboured hard at his study of the minutiæ of the Moslem faith under the tuition of a religious sheikh.

By day, in the soft leisurely Egyptian air, he practised the ritual of devotion, the laws of ablution, the art of prostration, and the use of Koranic quotation on all necessary occasions.

In the intervals of study—he had put off his Persian dress— he gave out that he was an Indian *hakim,* or doctor, and with a small dispensary of drugs (mainly cathartics of various strengths) soon acquired a fair reputation as a healer. A mere smattering of medical knowledge was sufficient to obtain some miraculous cures among the ignorant *fellahin,* and soon the door of the outhouse by the Mahmudiyah was besieged by men, women, and children, all clamouring for the healing touch of the Indian doctor. That his disguise was so far successful, there could be no doubt. " Even respectable natives, after witnessing a performance of ' Mandal ' and the magic mirror, declared that the stranger was a holy man, gifted with supernatural powers and knowing everything. One old person sent to offer me his daughter in marriage ; he said nothing about dowry—but I thought proper to decline the honour. And a middle-aged lady proffered me the sum of one hundred piastres (£1) if I would stay in Alexandria and superintend the restoration of her blind left eye." [1]

His leisure hours were employed in visiting the lower parts of the town, the baths, coffee houses, and *bazaars*, trying to work himself into the skin of the Arab population.

A month's hard study sufficed to polish up his Arabic, rusted by a three-year sojourn in Europe, and give him confidence to take the road ; and he now ran his eye round the extensive gallery of Oriental types for a suitable character to adopt that would sustain his particular disadvantages without arousing suspicion. After careful consideration he decided upon that of Dervish or wandering Holy Man. No character lends itself more readily to the travelling spy than this, for of all Moslem types the Dervish is the only one who is allowed any wide latitude of behaviour. Self-appointed man of God, possessor of *baraka* or the divine essence, he may be anything from a saint to a lunatic or ruffian ; by virtue of his profession he is a man apart, he can laugh at ceremony, snap his fingers at manners and customs, can rest or wander, marry or remain single—none asks him why. The more of a curiosity and fanatic that he is, the more insults he throws over his shoulder, the more he is respected. He may ride with his servants on she-camels, or wander weaponless through an armed camp : he will be equally safe. In moments of great danger he can feign madness—which is akin to holiness in the Orient—and he will be left alone. His very eccenticities are his passport of safety, and for a man who knows his habits, his character is the easiest and most useful to assume. During his service in India Burton had been initiated into the Kadiriyah order of Dervishes,[2] and after a period of probation had been elevated to the position of Murshid, or Master, and he was consequently well acquainted with the tenets and practices of these Oriental Freemasons. He therefore gave out that he was a Persian Dervish and *hakim* ; and prepared to embark upon the second stage of his journey to the holy cities.

---

[1] *Pilgrimage to Al Madinah and Mecca.* All quotations in this section unless stated otherwise are from this book.

[2] A Sect who believe in free-will (Kadi) as opposed to pre-destination.

Putting on the Dervish's gown, large blue pantaloons and short Persian shirt, he went to the *bazaars* and bought a tooth stick, a bit of soap, and a wooden comb and tied them up in a rag; to this he added a goatskin waterbag, a Persian rug for prayer, a cotton stuffed chintz-covered pillow, a blanket, and a sheet, a large cotton umbrella of yellow, a dagger, a brass inkstand and penholder to carry in his belt, and last but not least, a heavy rosary for defensive as well as devotional purposes. Then kissing his host's hand, with humble ostentation, in front of the servants, and hearing a hurriedly whispered " Good luck ! " in English in his ear, he said farewell to his sorry patients —now amounting to about fifty, and set out for the steamer that was to take him to Cairo.

He had prudently taken a third-class deck passage on board this miserable boat, and he consequently found the passage trying—though it was milk and water to the awful passage he was to make later in the Red Sea. While the little steamer puffed noisily up the canal, the Dervish sat by day under a blazing sun which, piercing the thin canvas awning stretched above, struck the deck passengers almost speechless. At night, cold, raw dews soaked and chilled him to the skin. He squatted apart from the rest, as befitted his holy calling, smoking perpetually, with occasional breaks to mumble his prayers and finger the beads on the gigantic rosary. For food he munched bread and garlic, and his only drink was from a leathern bucket dropped into the muddy waters of the canal.

On the first-class decks a number of Europeans were travelling, and a brother officer, tripping over the squatting man, damned the Dervish's eyes as a dirty nigger for getting in his way. The Dervish scowled, muttered " *Ibn Kelb!* " under his breath, and took his grievance to the third class, where a Lahore merchant consoled him in secrecy with the first whispers of the mutiny brewing among the Sepoys in India, and how soon they were going to rise and drive the accursed English to the sea.[1]

The end of the journey was livened, however, by a happy and valuable acquaintanceship which was to bear promising fruit later. Burton got into conversation with a plump, pleasant-faced Arab with a thin red beard, shrewd, quizzing eyes, and a

---

[1] Burton transmitted this information to the War Office. The Mutiny itself came two years later.

general expression of benevolence, a sort of Oriental Mr. Pickwick. "Who art thou?" and "From whence comest thou?" are always the first questions in the East. He introduced himself as Haji Wali, an Alexandrian merchant, and with dry, inoffensive humour fired off a number of questions at the Dervish. "Thank Allah we carry a Doctor!" he cried in mock gratitude when Burton told him of his profession. But when pressed to explain himself, he declared with a roll of his expressive eyes that they were doctor-ridden. "You doctors," he complained shrilly, "what do you do? Wa'allahi! I am as good a physician as the best of you if only I knew the *dirham-birhams* [1] and a few breakjaw Arabic names of diseases!" Information was succeeded by general conversation, and by the time the Cairo quay was in sight the two men were fast friends.

It was the height of the pilgrim season in Cairo. Daily large throngs of newcomers filled the streets. The squares and open places were blinding with the blaze of crimson, gold, and silver from the rich equipages of the wealthy merchants and pilgrims travelling *de luxe* on the Hajj, festoons of beggars, clamouring that the fourth ordinance of Mohammed's creed be remembered, clung round the doors of every mosque, and importunate Cairenes forced their goods at stupendous prices on the bewildered and ignorant poorer pilgrims. Every shade of brown, from the shiny ebony of the great Nubians to the dark milk of the cold Persians, rubbed shoulders in the caravanserais, and through everything clad in tatters and clutching their knives and thick wooden staves strode sullen bands of Maghrabi pilgrims—desert men, penniless, and out for plunder.

As all the better-class native hotels were filled to capacity, Burton was obliged to secure two miserable rooms at a rent of ten piastres a week in a *wakalah* or caravanserai in the Greek quarter of the town. The place, consisting of a large square with gates surrounded on three sides by galleried rooms, was enormous, verminous, and filthy. In the square was piled all the merchandise and the servants, while the pilgrims slept in the dark filth of the surrounding rooms.

Here he met the cheerful Haji Wali again. The Haji was in Cairo on a lawsuit and expected, knowing eastern justice, to be there from any period up to a year. But he proved an able friend, for he took the younger pilgrim under his wing, saved him from too much robbery at the hands of the sharks who line

[1] Weights and measures.

the pilgrim routes to fleece the pilgrims, and constituted himself
as his guide. His first advice was to tell the young Indian doctor
to cease from posing as a Persian Dervish. " If you persist in
being a Persian," remarked the wise old man, " you will be
cursed in Egypt ; in Arabia you will be beaten because you
are a heretic ; you will pay the treble of what other travellers
do, and if you fall sick you may die by the roadside."

It was advice not to be ignored. Once again, therefore,
Burton changed his identity. He now became a Pathan, born
in India of Afghan parents, and sent to wander as is their
manner from early youth. To support the character required
a knowledge of Persian, Hindustani, and Arabic, all of which
he knew sufficiently to pass muster. He quietly effected the
needed transformation, and in a night Burton the Dervish
followed Burton the Persian prince into oblivion.

A motley collection of characters was gathered at the
wakalah ; and once more Burton laid out his drugs and
let it be bruited abroad that he had some skill as a *hakim*.
The Haji, only too eager to help a friend, most ripely spread
the propaganda, and patients of all classes came clamouring
for aid.

Came a wailing Arab slave dealer who cried that *Shaitan*
had cursed him with ill luck as two of his Abyssinian girls
snored. " And what man will bed with such thunder ? "
Worth fifteen pounds apiece and unsaleable, could the Doctor
help ? The doctor helped by dosing the unsaleable ones with
a strong cathartic, which for some unknown physiological
reason seemed to cure them. Loud in his praise was the slave
master, and Burton extracted payment by drawing from him
many of the secrets of his trade, markets, prices, places of supply
and demand which were subsequently retailed in another
dispatch to the British Government. The Haji, too, was
delighted with his friend's success, and it was not long before
the *wakalah* rang with his praises and brought to Burton's
door an almost overwhelming flood of custom.

At this sort of thing Burton was in his element. We have
a picture of him at work drawn by himself. " When you administer with your own hand the remedy—half a dozen huge
bread pills, dipped in a solution of aloes or cinnamon water,
flavoured with assafoetida, you are careful to say, " In the name
of Allah, the Compassionate, the Merciful." And after the
patient has been dosed, " Praise be to Allah, the Curer, the

Healer " ; you then call for pen, ink, and paper, and write some such prescription as this :

A.[1]

" In the name of Allah, the Compassionate, the Merciful, and blessings and peace be upon our Lord the Apostle, and his family, and his companions one and all ! But afterwards let him take bees-honey and cinnamon and album graecum, of each half a part, and of ginger a whole part, which let him pound and mix with the honey, and form boluses, each bolus the weight of a Miskal, and of it let him use every day a Miskal on the saliva. Verily its effects are wonderful. And let him abstain from flesh, fish, vegetables, sweetmeats, flatulent foods, acids of all descriptions, as well as the major ablution, and live in perfect quiet. So shall he be cured by the help of the King, the Healer. And the Peace."

For several weeks he endured the hospitality of the *wakalah*, through all the rigours of the fasting month of Ramadan when each man hates his neighbour, as a respected and admired Indian doctor, and he might have been tempted to lengthen the visit, were it not for an unfortunate *contretemps* which lost him his reputation for respectability and labelled him with another not so pleasant.

The cause of this fall from virtue was one Ali Agha, a Captain of the Albanian Irregulars, on leave from the Hedjaz. These Albanians were the terrors of Egypt and Arabia. Sneering, swaggering braggarts, they tyrannized all weaker brethren and were almost always at the root of a row. Utterly reckless and without fear, it was their habit to go about loaded with an armoury of pistols, daggers, and spears, and draw and use them on the slightest provocation. They were constantly duelling, their method being to face one another across a table and then fire their pistols point-blank. Ali Agha was a typical specimen of the class, a tall, broad-shouldered mountaineer with a simian brow, fierce eyes, and a close-shaven skull and face decorated by an enormous pair of waxen moustaches. Covered with scars, one leg shattered by a Turkish bullet—giving a limp which he tried to hide with a swagger, he was never clean and never sober, and was a perpetual thorn in the sides of all at the *wakalah*. Entering Haji Wali's room one evening, Burton found this fearsome creature leaning negligently against the wall. After an exchange of pleasantries in which several covert sneers were flung at the head of the inoffensive doctor, Burton turned his back on the man and produced a new pistol for the

[1] A monogram, the initial letter of Allah usually placed at the head of all writings.

Haji's inspection. Ali Agha leaned forward and grabbed it.
Burton instantly snatched it back. Then the brigand turned
as if to depart and waggishly seized the doctor with an eye to a
trial of strength. A quick scuffle ensued, and for the first time
in his life Ali Agha found himself matched against a man as
powerful as himself. The next moment a solid English cross-
buttock laid the astounded brigand on his back with a thump
that must have set his skull ringing. He was delighted. Far
from being offended, he sprang to his feet, patted Burton on
the head, swore eternal friendship, and called for another pipe.
Followed a catechism of his life's history, an examination and
description of every several scar on his tough body, a description
of his more colourful amours and finally an invitation to his
new friend to test himself in a drinking bout.

Alas for reputation ! For all Ali Agha's boasting and un-
savouriness, Burton could not but feel that he was a man after
his own heart. The challenge, a trial of manhood, was a temptation impossible to resist. Throwing caution to the winds, he
accepted the invitation, and repaired that evening to Ali Agha's
room. The brigand was awaiting him seated upright on a low
bed with four bright wax candles burning round it. On the
floor, wrapped in wet rags for coolness, were the materials
for the bout—a long, thin flask of powerful 'arak, or eastern
cognac, standing in an iron pot beside a bowl of curds and
cucumber, some cold soup and a dollop of cold stewed meat.
The bout began with the elaborate ceremony with which all
matters must be prefaced in the East. Ali Agha, after greeting
his guest politely, and inviting him to toss his dagger in a far
corner while he himself did the same, took up a small glass,
wiped its exterior with a grimy forefinger, filled it to the brim,
and tendered it to the doctor with an exaggerated bow. Receiving it with a low salaam, Burton tossed the contents down his
throat, turned it upside down to show fair play, and then
returned it with another deep bow, for the process to be reversed.
Then both men took a mouthful of curd and cucumber to cool
their palates, a dash of water, and another glass. As Ali Agha
was by no means sober when this contest started, an atmosphere
of hilarity was rapidly attained. With every glass he grew freer,
indulged in a little hospitable horseplay and dashed handfuls
of nauseous perfume from a jug into his friend's face. He next
declared that, to top the evening, the pious Haji Wali must be
brought in and made to drink with them. No sooner said than

performed, and arm in arm solemn doctor and tipsy brigand rolled into Haji Wali's room and haled him forth. Trembling with religious horror the old man was presented with a brimming glass of the fiery and forbidden spirit. He protested that throughout life he had been a good Moslem, he swore he was ill and would drink on the morrow, he quoted the Koran, he screwed his chubby face up into an attempt at anger and threatened to call the police. It was useless. "Drink!" said Burton, and "Drink!" said Ali Agha in a voice of thunder. Finding persuasion useless, and seeing nothing before him but mortal sin, the unhappy Haji started up and fled for his very life, leaving tarbush, slippers, and pipe in the hands of the enemy. With drunken care Ali Agha sprinkled the inoffensive belongings with reeking spirit, then wound up with a grandiloquent flourish by declaring that nothing now would satisfy him but a troop of dancing girls.

The *wakalah* was now wrapped in sleep and Burton began to have qualms. He declared that such persons were no longer allowed in caravanserais. "Who hath forbidden it?" inquired the brigand in tones of cold ferocity. Burton replied that it was the order of the Pasha, whereat, shouldering his pipe, Ali Agha started for the door declaring at the top of his voice that the Pasha should come himself and dance for them. Foreseeing a brawl Burton hurried after him, but not before, from the darkness of the passage outside, had come the shrieks of someone being belaboured by the enormous pipe, followed by yells of "O Egyptians! O ye accursed! O genus of Pharaoh! O race of dogs!" as a sorely bruised Arab stumbled down the stairs. Ali Agha was now thoroughly in his stride. Putting his shoulder to a nearby locked door, he burst it open and descended like an irate Jove upon a pair of ancient basketmakers and their wives, sleeping in a single bed. A fearful uproar ensued. Meeting him oath for oath the two aged crones drove him from the room. He reeled downstairs, fell on top of the sleeping doorkeeper, and, feeling for his dagger, announced with a frightful roar that he would drink the man's blood. The whole place was now awake and several people, including his own servant, flung themselves upon him. Bawling the Albanian war-cry of "O Egyptians! O race of dogs! I have b—-d all Cairo, Alexandria, and Suez!" he was dragged up to his room, while his drinking companion, the doctor, loaded with vituperation on all sides, crept hurriedly to the shelter of his own bed.

" You had better start on your Pilgrimage at once," declared the Haji the next morning, with a twinkle in his eye. He was right. For nearly a week nothing was talked of in the *wakalah* but the unspeakable wickedness of Albanians, and the hypocrisy of doctors who professed to come from India. Burton's reputation was gone, and its going revived awkward questions as to who and what he really was. It was time to be on the move, and he was not slow in taking the hint.

§

The Sheikh Nassar, a Badawi of Tur in the Sinai region, being on his way homewards, contracted to hire two dromedaries to the pilgrim for the sum of fifty piastres each. One dromedary and a running camel-man would have been sufficient but, wishing to leave wrapped in such tatters of respectability as he could muster, Burton decided that his attendant should be mounted also. " Besides ostentation, I wanted to make a forced march in order to ascertain how much a four years' life of European effeminacy had impaired my powers of endurance. . . . There are few better tests than an eighty-four mile ride in midsummer, on a bad wooden saddle, borne by a worse dromedary, across the Suez desert."

His heavy baggage was packed and sent on ahead by camel-train under the care of Sheikh Nur, his Indian boy-servant. A sprinkling of silver was put among the baggage, for marauding Badu will often leave a man's person alone if they successfully rifle his goods, and they have a habit of ripping up his stomach with his clothing if nothing is discovered in the latter. The rest of the silver was secreted about the person of Sheikh Nur, and Burton himself carried the gold. Two days after the heavy camel train had departed, Nassar the Badawi strode into the *wakalah* out of a mid-afternoon sun to announce that the dromedaries were saddled and ready, and that it was time to depart. Dressing himself, sticking pistols in his belt and hanging from his shoulder the crimson-corded pocket Koran in token of being a pilgrim, Burton dispensed the customary trifling presents to servants and friends and descended into the din of the courtyard. Here the dromedaries stood saddled and waiting surrounded by a number of Burton's friends and patients, among whom was the disconsolate Haji Wali and an ancient Sheikh, a fervent admirer of the doctor, who insisted, in spite of his years, on accompanying the traveller to the town gate.

Embracing the faithful Haji Wali heartily on cheeks, forehead, and shoulders, and receiving a servile exhortation from the ancient Sheikh, Burton mounted, and accompanied by his friends on foot (a great honour) sallied out of the caravanserai gate. As the beasts lumbered through the archway, the passers-by, seeing the Koran dangling from Burton's shoulder, with one accord raised their right arms and cried : " Allah bless thee, O Hajj, and restore thee to thy country and thy friends ! "

It is a solemn moment for all ; a moment most impressive to the Moslem mind. One more pilgrim is about to venture his life for his faith, perhaps to fall by the wayside from thirst, sickness, or bloodshed ; perhaps to live and stand in ecstasy while the waters of Zem Zem wash the sins one by one from his tired soul. In farewell Burton raises his hand, trots down the street leading to the desert gate and drops a blessing on the heads of officer and guard. In the East the pilgrim's blessing is one of particular power. " God speed ! " cry the guard respectfully as the gate swings open. " Allah keep thee ! " screams the stout Haji Wali, and shrilly pipes the ancient Sheikh, as the hot, hungry desert swings suddenly into view. A flicker of hands, a cloud of dust, and the pilgrim and his guides are cantering eastwards into the shimmering sea of sand.

The heat strikes them like a blow. Across his face each man draws his head mantle to shield his eyes from glare and spare his mouth and nostrils from the rising sand. A gentle canter is succeeded by a race, as with a ringing laugh the Sheikh Nassar tries to take the lead. It is a trial of manliness, and presently Englishman and Arabs, careless of the eighty-four mile inferno before them, are careering across the desert with shouts of encouragement. But soon the heat begins to tell ; a flaming wind parches their lips, the glare beats through upon their eyelids, sand rises and swirls about their knees ; man and beast flag and the latter drop to a gentle jog-trot. To refresh themselves the men prepare a pipe and pass it from mouth to mouth like Indian braves. Conversation succeeds, and the eternal Oriental questions of " Who art thou ? Whence comest thou ? " and " For how long dost thou stay," are bandied about until each man knows the why and wherefore of his neighbour. And so they turn to food, a favourite subject with the half-starved Badu of the desert. Each in turn cries out his favourite dish and vies with his neighbour in describing its excellencies.

But presently that too is exhausted and a hot, dry silence falls. Burton sinks into reflection and his companions draw their hoods across their faces till only their eyes can be seen, moving restlessly over the ever shifting immensity before them. " It is strange," reflects the traveller, " how the mind can be amused by scenery that presents so few objects to occupy it. But in such a country every slight modification of form or colour rivets observation : the senses are sharpened, and the perceptive faculties, prone to sleep over a confused mass of natural objects, act vigorously when excited by the capability of embracing each detail. Moreover, desert views are eminently suggestive : they appeal to the Future, not to the Past : they arouse because they are by no means memorial. To the solitary wayfarer there is an interest in the wilderness unknown to Cape Seas and Alpine glaciers, and even to the rolling prairie—the effect of continued excitement on the mind, stimulating its powers to their pitch. Above, through a sky terrible in its stainless beauty, and the splendours of a pitiless blinding glare, the Samun caresses you like a lion with flaming breath. Around lie drifted sand-heaps upon which each puff of wind leaves its trace in solid waves, flayed rocks, the very skeletons of mountains, and hard, unbroken plains, over which he who rides is spurred by the idea that the bursting of a waterskin or the pricking of a camel's hoof would be a certain death of torture—a haggard land, infested with wild beasts and wilder men—a region whose very fountains murmur the warning words, ' Drink and away ! ' What can be more exciting? What more sublime? Man's heart bounds in his breast at the thought of measuring his puny force with Nature's might, and of emerging triumphant from the trial."

Occupied with these reflections they rode steadily eastwards, while the sun declined, lengthening their shadows and drawing in its train a cooler desert wind, presently to unveil the stars. The freshening air lightens the spirits of the Badu, and one by one they raise their voices in a monotonous plaint, artless and yet in perfect accord with the desert mood, a song straight from the Arab heart, of bubbling rills, and cool shade and of dates that are ever fresh. " Wa'al ard mablul bi matar. . . . And the earth was wet with rain . . . ! "

As darkness crept up the eastern horizon with its reproachful call to sunset prayer, they turned off the road into the sandhills, and were suddenly greeted by a figure rising with an " Es salaam aleikum " from the darkness of a hollow. Hands flew to pistols, camels snarled, then Burton recognized the apparition as one Mohammed al Basyuni, a plump, proud-featured Meccan boy who had made his acquaintance in the Cairene *wakalah* by selling him an Ihram [1] and Kafan [2] at exhorbitant rates. The boy had tried to press the acquaintance, but Burton had repulsed him, fearing his astuteness and fondness for asking questions. The boy was typical of his race and city, " selfish, affectionate as spoiled children are, volatile, easily offended, and as easily pacified, with a matchless intrepidity of countenance, brazen lunged, not more than half-brave, and with an acute sense of honour, especially where his relations were concerned." At the *wakalah* Burton had been able to avoid him, but here in the desert the impertinent lad would take no rebuff. For reasons of his own, one of them a complete lack of money, he was determined to attach himself to the new Hajji, and attach himself he did with a vengeance. In half an hour he had commandeered Burton's foodstuffs by appointing himself as under-officer of the party, insulted the Badu by wrenching Burton's tobacco pouch from them, and flattered and smoothed his new benefactor in a way which indicated to the latter how difficult it was going to be to get rid of him.

After prayers the party moved on and spent the night under the walls of the Central Station, wetted by heavy dews, cooled by the desert wind, and serenaded by the lonely jackal. Rising with the dawn, they moved on, and at their first halt had their only adventure on the way. No sooner had they off-saddled than they found themselves among a band of half-starved Maghrabi pilgrims, miserable yet fierce, like bedraggled hawks, possessed of nothing but a *burnus*, a pair of sandals, a long knife, a bag of dry provisions, and a begging bowl. These tousle-headed predatory creatures make the Pilgrimage in hungry, desperate bands under a temporary leader known as a " Maula." No other tribe could live through the appalling hardships these Africans endure ; they trust entirely to alms, and where these fail or are not forthcoming, they do not hesitate at murder.[3] Among the whole clamouring band there was not

[1] Ihram, the pilgrim's special dress, carried on the Pilgrimage, and donned just before entering Mecca.

[2] Kafan, the shroud, which all pilgrims are obliged to carry in case they should die by the way.

[3] Such pilgrims may still be seen at all times of the year marooned penniless in towns or walking their way wearily on foot across the Libyan or Syrian deserts. They have a reputation for religious integrity which those who have lived with them will bear out.

a drop of water, and after the party had given them what water could be spared, they became threatening. For a moment it looked like trouble, the Badu drew their knives, the boy Mohammed cowered, and Burton swung his pistols. But the weapons kept them at bay, they retired sullenly muttering, and mounting relievedly the party continued on their way.

All that day they rode, pausing not for the sun, and only halting in late afternoon when Burton, his curiosity aroused, turned his dromedary off the road on the pretext of watering it, and rode up to inspect a bedraggled fort regarded by the Egyptians as the key to the Suez.

Returning, the party hastened on until the castellated peaks of Jabal Rahah rising in the distance, and the twinkling glimpes of blue sea, told them that Suez was near. As night fell they passed through the tumbling six-windowed gateway of the town and rode wearily to their quarters.

For the traveller it was an agonizing night. Eighty-four miles of jolting in a hard wooden saddle had made every bone ache, and he had lost inches of saddle-blistered skin. Also he was disquieted at the complete disappearance of his advance baggage, together with the feeble Sheikh Nur. The next morning, however, the ubiquitous Mohammed came completely to the rescue, both boy and baggage were recovered intact, and preparations were made for the hire of places on a pilgrim boat bound for Yambu.

Pilgrims arriving at the Alexandrian depot were formerly divided into three bodies, and distributed by passport by either Cosseir, Yambu, or the overland Hajj route round the Gulf of Akaba. Burton found some difficulty with his own passport which had not been visaed in Cairo ; but after some negotiation he managed to get into touch with the British Consulate and obtain a fresh one made out in the name of an Indian British subject.

Meanwhile the indefatigable Mohammed had reappeared with a party of friends, Medina men, returning after a begging tour through Egypt and Turkey. A twelve days' voyage and a four days' difficult journey awaited them ; and not one of the five had a farthing. They had " boxes to carry, customs to face, and stomachs to fill. Their boxes were full of valuables, arms, clothes, pipes, slippers, sweetmeats—but nothing short of starvation would have induced them to pledge the smallest article." Foreseeing that their company might prove an advantage, Burton "hearkened favourably to the honeyed request for a few crowns."

These penniless but complacent gentry were respectively : an effeminate-looking Circassian, plump, precise, and something of a scholar, named Omar Effendi ; a coal-black, emancipated negro with impudent manners and a penchant for pilfering, called Sa'ad the Demon ; a dirty old Sheikh known as the " Clarified Butter Seller " [1]; and a Turkish Arab half-caste, Salih Shakkar, mean, haughty, and ungrateful. Omar Effendi, a brooding, mincing youth with a hatred of women and an almost tigerish ferocity of purpose, had run away from his family in Medina to enrol himself as a pauper-student in the mosque of El Azhar. But he had not been free long before his broken-hearted parents sent Sa'ad the Demon, their manumitted family slave, after him, to implore him to return. Sa'ad had found him in an extreme of poverty and had not much difficulty in carrying out his master's orders. They were now returning together, living on what they might beg, or the boastful, brave, unscrupulous Sa'ad could steal. The " Clarified Butter Seller," Sheikh Hamid, was affecting poverty and filth for diplomatic purposes. " He will not pray because he is unwilling to take clean clothes out of his box. He can sing all manner of songs, slaughter a sheep with dexterity, deliver a grand call to prayer, shave, cook, and fight." As for Salih Shakkar, he borrowed gratefully at Suez, and mercilessly " cut " his benefactor at Medina.

Friendship having been generally established by coffee and the loans, the party commenced familiarities by prying into one another's baggage. They pulled out Burton's clothes, over-hauled his medicine chest, and criticized his pistols. His copper-cased watch aroused amusement, likewise his compass —Omar having seen one of the latter in Alexandria. Burton therefore imagined they would think little of his sextant. But here he made a grave mistake. The strange instrument [2] aroused instant suspicion, questioning looks were passed between them, and the boy Mohammed only waited for Burton to leave the room before declaring that the latter must be an infidel spy from India. The party went into instant conclave,

[1] *Samman.*

[2] Seventy years later Cheesman had to use subterfuge before he could produce a theodolite at Bahrein, such is the deep distrust among the Arab of all things mechanical. See *In Unknown Arabia*, page 21.

and for a few moments it was touch and go. Burton was still within hail of the British Consulate so he was not in actual physical danger ; but his plans would most surely be wrecked if his identity were revealed. It was fortunate that the scholarly Omar had noticed among the baggage a letter addressed to Haji Wali, and had been struck by Burton's able discussion of several matters on high theology. This letter just sufficed to tip the balance in Burton's favour. Omar Effendi declared that the Hajj was a man of knowledge and must be a true believer ; Sheikh Hamid, who probably cared not a damn either way, supported him, and both turned upon the astute Meccan youth and covered him with abuse. Burton passed the matter off with excuses, left the sextant behind him, and thereafter for a week, as a sign of special piousness, prayed five times daily with the ardour of a convert.

Having arranged to travel together, the party now bent all its energies towards securing places on the next pilgrim vessel about to sail. Sa'ad the Demon swaggered about the town bullying agents and haggling with owners, and finally closed with a rascally Arab for five places on the poop of his vessel the *Golden Thread*.

It must be understood that the whole of the transport system on the pilgrim route was a piece of blackmail and exploitation run by local Pashas. Unable to help themselves except by bribes, the poorer pilgrims were herded like cattle from point to point, robbed, overcharged, and delayed for as long as suited the pockets of the local officials. Vessels were often held back until they could be crammed to suffocation, and then were pushed off under the care of untrained sailors with their semi-suffocated and sometimes dying human cargoes.

Even Burton's hardened spirit quailed when he saw the *Golden Thread* swinging at her anchor. A sambuk of some fifty tons, she was built to accommodate sixty persons, her greedy owner had contracted to take a hundred ; and as Burton's party embarked with baggage, food, and water, and clambered up on to the already crowded poop, they found the long waist of the ship beneath them crammed with one mass of fierce, jostling, shouting Maghrabi, men, women, and children. Here and there among these matted locks and shaven skulls from the deserts of Tripoli and Tunis could be seen the fez of a few miserable old Turks and Caramanians.

The embarkation began in a turmoil and quickly developed into a fight in which the Maghrabis swept the hold of all but themselves, and stabbed a few Turks who resisted. An unwise Syrian who leaned down from the poop to help his belaboured countrymen had to be hastily hauled back to safety with a split head, half his beard gone, and deep gashes from Maghrabi teeth in his leg. Having driven all strangers into the farthest corners, the Maghrabi, like wounded dogs, sat down to lick their hurts.

The waist of the ship was a hell, but Burton and his party on the poop were in little better ease. Some eighteen souls, including three Syrians, a married Turk and family, the doddering Rais [1] and his lubber crew, were distributed, surrounded by baggage, water, and fuel about a space not exceeding ten feet by eight. A box-like cabin a little forward of them, some three feet high and about half the size of the poop, was stuffed like a slave ship with fifteen perspiring women and children. This cabin and the flimsy shadow cast by the big lateen sail was all the shade the whole vessel afforded, and above it on the massed heads of the pilgrims beat a fierce Arabian sun. Burton was fortunate in finding a sort of antiquated bedframe slung from the side of the vessel, the use of which he secured for a dollar and so escaped the unspeakable torment of night. The rest disposed themselves for their twelve days' purgatory as best as they could.

The boat itself, Burton was none too happy to notice, had neither compass, charts, log, sounding lines, nor even a solitary spare rope. Allah and the ancient captain were all they had to rely on against the manifold winds, currents, and rocks of the Red Sea—and though the former might be expected to extend some help to a load of despairing pilgrims, Burton was none too sure of the latter.

For an hour they swung cursing and jostling on the tide while the owner, hailed repeatedly and vociferously, and labelled with every insult under the sun, rowed out to them and from a safe distance listened to their complaints before commending them to God and returning comfortably home. Then, finding that nothing was to be done to ease the congestion, a dozen Maghrabis, headed by their leader, advanced to the poop and demanded that places be made for them up there. This request was treated with derision ; and the Maghrabis drew themselves up and prepared for battle.

At once, Sa'ad the Demon, who had shipped as a seaman in order to avoid paying a fare and had contributed not a little to the general atmosphere of fury by scattering insults in all

[1] Captain.

directions, rose and tossed among his companions a bundle of thick, greased fighting staves. " Defend yourselves," he bawled, " if you don't wish to be the meat of the Maghrabis ! " Omar, Burton, Sheikh Hamid, and Salih Shakkar arose and armed themselves, while Sa'ad, an awe-inspiring, glistening giant of ebony, approached the edge of the poop and addressed the enemy with : " Dogs and sons of dogs ! now you shall see what the children of the Arab are ! "

His words were drowned in the sudden rush of the Maghrabis. Armed with knives and with the agility of cats, they flung themselves in a solid body at the poop. The pilgrims met them shoulder to shoulder with their fighting staves and by well-timed blows and thrusts sent them spinning back into the hold. The shrieks of women and the hoarse cries of " Allahu ! Akbar ! " from the Maghrabis were punctuated by the war-cries of the travellers encouraging one another as they whirled their staves : " I am Omar of Daghistan ! " " I am Sa'ad— Sa'ad the Demon ! " " I am Abdullah,[1] son of Joseph ! " Behind them the old captain stood trembling and calling the *Fathah*.

The Maghrabis fought like tigers, swarming in clusters up the sides of the poop and rigging until the rickety vessel swayed at her anchor, and the harbour echoed with yells. For a while the odds stood in balance. But palm-sticks and short knives are no match against well-wielded quarter-staves, and, when presently Burton put his shoulder to a heavy water jar standing on the edge of the poop and sent it and its contents crashing into the seething mob below, the Maghrabis' ranks broke, and they slunk to the far end of the hold, whence they came later in true Moslem fashion to " make the peace " by kissing the heads, shoulders, and hands of their victors.

At length, when all was settled on board, the ropes were cast off, the patched sail bellied out, and Suez slid away. From the decks of the *Golden Thread* every pilgrim raised earnest hands to heaven, palms upturned to catch the blessing, while their earnest voices floated across the water in the solemn recitation of the *Fathah*.[2] The time was 3 p.m., 6th July 1853. As they crept slowly out of the harbour into the open sea, Burton

---

[1] Burton went by the name of Abdullah during the Pilgrimage. The Arabs, however, called him the Father of the Moustaches on account of the prodigious length to which these grew on his face.

[2] The *Fathah* is a prayer used by the Moslem on all occasions of doubt or commencement, i.e. beginning a journey, during a battle, starting on a piece of work.

could not help but throw a last wistful glance at the British flag floating serenely above the Consulate. It was a reminder of the security that would be no longer available to him. This, he was aware, was his first real step into the dark. What had passed was nothing ; ahead lay the real perils of the journey. He must brace himself to meet them. But the qualm was only momentary. He soon recovered his spirits and, as the bows of the *Golden Thread* began to lift lazily to the urge of the open sea, felt himself seized by " the heart-bounding which prospects of an adventure excite."

§

It is a custom of Arab travellers to make the first day's journey a short one, so that they may easily return if they discover that some needful article has been left behind. The first night was therefore spent by the *Golden Thread* under the lee of Mount Jabal Atakah and within sight of the lights of Suez. As night dropped down the dark slopes of the mountain, a cold, bright moon arose, and a heavy dew, raw and clammy, set the huddled pilgrims shivering as if with the ague. Burton endeavoured to snatch some rest in the broken cot, but as it measured a bare four feet by two and was slung precariously at the side of the vessel, every lurch as she took up on her hawser threatened to hurl him into the sea. Dozing was therefore scarcely safe, but he could gather a morsel of comfort to himself from the fact that his position was infinitely better than the misery of the poop, the suffocation in the cabin, or the indescribable torment of the hold.

The night passed slowly in this manner and early dawn found them coasting along in a light gale. The sun warmed their stiff bodies and loosened their tongues, coffee was boiled on small wood fires and pipes were lit and puffed while they lay and watched the broken shores and ragged peaks of Sinai scudding by. But discomfort returned with the growth of day. Overhead a torrid sun blazed down, while Burton's cot was alternately rocking skywards or drenched in slopping wavelets. When the gale dropped, and the full force of the sun smote down on the crowded decks, all who could huddled together in an endeavour to catch the moving shadow from the sagging sail. The long day passed only too slowly and night found them anchored off a spit of sand known as the Hammam Bluffs.[1]

[1] Jebel Hammam Faraun.

Here the poop passengers were enabled to stretch their legs on the sandy foreshore, to bathe,[1] catch fish, or sleep in the cool sand. A few of the bolder Maghrabis accompanied them, the rest, awestricken by the Rais's stories of ghosts and goblins, preferring rather the safety of the hold. As the sun sank below the Egyptian horizon the dirty old Sheikh Hamid ranged the Maghrabi in rows along the sands, and roused them to fervour by a truly magnificent call to prayer. So moved were these innocent desert men by the Arab's oratory that they crept forward after devotions to kiss his hands, knees, and shoulders in token of added respect. Presently coffee was boiling fragrantly, the Rais joined the poop party, and lying round their winking fires under the bright summer stars the usual story-telling began. At this the Rais was an adept. Knowing every bluff and beach of the seashores and the sailors' legends connected with each, he related the stories of wonder and mystery with such skill that the Maghrabi grew uneasy and fingered their knives at the shadows. Once more he related the story of Abu Zulaymah, the patron saint of those seas who sits for ever in a cave among the rocks watching over the safety of pious mariners, and sipping his coffee which is brought from Mecca by green birds ; once more he unfolded the story of Egypt's awful king who pursued the tribes of Israel into this very sea, of how this sea opened for the chosen of God and closed again in roaring waters upon the Egyptian might. A chorus of heartfelt " Allah preserve us " rose from the appalled Maghrabi as he told how on clear days the mariner may see far down in the green depths the long-haired Egyptians in their shining armour walking on the very bottom of the sea.

That night Burton and his party slept softly in the cool sand ; but many a Maghrabi lay wide-eyed until dawn.

Morning brought calamity. The *Golden Thread* was found to be fast stuck on a sandbank, from which not all the united efforts, prayers, sacrifices of burnt coffee to Abu Zulaymah, or *Fathahs* could move her. The Maghrabis strained and tugged, Burton and his party shouted, the Rais twittered ; but the obdurate ship remained. Finally each man in turn called upon his particular saint while the rest gave a heave. Sheikh Hamid called loudly upon his ancestor, the " Clarified Butter Seller," Sa'ad the Demon upon some obscure relative from the south, the Maghrabi tied themselves into muscular knots, the Rais prayed fervently. The *Golden Thread* still lay inert. Then

[1] Presumably in the well-known hot springs here.

Burton, who had been watching the tide carefully with an eye to the main chance, waited until he judged it had reached a suitable height, then called to the Maghrabi to range themselves round the boat, struck an impressive posture, and raising imploring hands to heaven, lifted up his voice and addressed a favourite Sufi mystic in ringing tones : " Ya Piran Pir ! Ya Abd al Kadir Jilani ! " And to the straining Maghrabi : " In the Name of Allah ! Heave ! " As one man the clinging, sinewy bodies heaved. The *Golden Thread* lurched, shuddered, and slid off into the sea—to the complete dumbfoundment of the Maghrabi, who surrounded the imperturbable traveller with cries of admiration and respect.

Embarking as quickly as possible, they scudded southwards through the dangerous currents and cross-seas of the notorious Pharaoh's Bay. That evening they anchored under a ridge of rocks, beyond which stretched the long plain of Tur. The Rais prevented all would-be explorers from going on shore by relating a series of diabolical yarns about the shadowy Badu who are supposed to haunt the place. In consequence everyone slept on board in what little comfort could be got.

A halt next morning at Tur itself, a miserable town populated by Greeks and Candians whose only means of livelihood is that of selling water to ships, was a welcome change. Night brought a fringe of cloud about the head of mount Jabal Tur, and warned the Rais that they were in for a gale. The next day, accordingly, was wisely spent in harbour while the gale raged outside. Burton's party made an excursion on donkeys to the so-called Hot Baths of Moses,[1] a spot a few miles inland, where they bathed in lukewarm bitter water, examined the spot where Moses struck the rock with his rod and where he left the marks of his nails deeply scored in the hard stone. They returned to their tent on shore to find the beach covered with parties of Persians who had disembarked from a large Persian vessel. These supercilious persons, as is their wont, swaggered haughtily about until their evening Call to Prayer nearly put a termination to their existence by rousing the Maghrabi to the remembrance that Persians are heretics. Trouble was averted only by a miracle and, as the long-bearded Persians hastily re-embarked, Burton had cause to remember and be grateful for the advice given him by the Haji Wali.

The next day at dawn they left Tur with the none too

[1] Jebel Hammam Sayidna Musa ; about 3 miles N.W. of Tur.

pleasant prospect of being unable to touch land again for some thirty-six hours.[1] It was a prospect before which even the most hardened quailed. That day passed slowly with the party on the poop lying with heads over the side to catch the few breaths of air, and the Maghrabi one mass of odorous bodies, arms and legs seemingly inextricably entangled lying bareheaded, sweating with their tongues extended, panting like dogs.

To take his mind off his physical discomfort, Burton scribbled meteorological remarks all day on a piece of paper. This is an excerpt of what he wrote lying cramped on the narrow poop of the *Golden Thread* as she crept through Sinai with her sweating cargo:

"*Morning :* The air is mild and balmy, as that of an Italian spring ; thick mists roll down the valleys along the sea, and a haze like mother-o'-pearl crowns the headlands. The distant rocks show Titanic walls, lofty donjons, huge projecting bastions, and moats full of deep shade. . . . Nothing can be more delicious than this hour. . . . But morning soon fades. The sun bursts up from behind the main, a fierce enemy, a foe that will force everyone to crouch before him. He dyes the sky orange, and the sea 'incarnadine.' The morning beams oppress you with a feeling of sickness ; their steady glow, reflected by the glaring waters, blinds your eyes, blisters your skin, and parches your mouth ; you now become a monomaniac ; you do nothing but count the slow hours that must ' minute by ' before you can be relieved.

"*Midday :* The wind, reverberated by the glowing hills, is like the blast of a lime-kiln. All colour melts away with the canescence from above. The sky is a dead milk-white and the mirror-like sea so reflects the tint that you can scarcely distinguish the line of the horizon. After noon the wind sleeps upon the rocking shore ; there is a deep stillness ; the only sound heard is the melancholy flapping of the sail. Men are not so much sleeping as half-senseless ; they feel as if a few more degrees of heat would be death.

"*Sunset :* The evening sinks behind the deep, cerulean sea, under a canopy of gigantic rainbow which covers half the face of heaven. Across the rainbow the sun throws its rays in the form of giant wheel spokes tinged with a beautiful pink. The eastern sky is mantled with a purple flush that picks out the forms of the hazy desert and the sharp cut hills. Night falls rapidly, when suddenly the appearance of the Zodiacal Light restores the scene to what it was. But after a quarter of an

[1] Presumably for lack of wells ashore.

hour all fades once more ; the cliffs are naked and ghastly
under the moon, whose light falling upon this wilderness of
white and pinnacles is most strange—most mysterious. . . .
The stars glitter with exceeding brilliance. At this hour the
planets look down upon you with the faces of smiling friends.
In communion with them your hours pass swiftly by, till the
heavy dews warn you to cover up your face and sleep. . . ." [1]

All that day they lay under a vertical sun while the wind
dropped and the sambuk hung like a tired bird with drooping
plumage. Under the fierce midday rays even the tough Maghrabi desert-men suffered exceedingly. Two Syrians fell ill and
the baby of a young Turkish mother was found to be dying,
the mother herself being in little better state. Nerves were
raw and tempers strung to breaking-point, yet Burton was
struck by the consideration with which the passengers showed
their sympathy. Pomegranates, dates, and vile Maghrabi
concoctions were pressed upon the gasping mother, men's
faces softened at the sight of the feeble child ; for a moment
a ray of beauty seemed to strike the tortured pilgrim ship.

Night at length brought release, and as a breeze tautened the
lateen sail and set the sambuk creaking and straining at her
cordage the passengers sat up, stretched their cramped bodies
to the cool blast and began to sing, jest, and tell the limitless
Oriental tales. In a square wooden box, lined with clay and
half-filled with sand and stones, a fire is made, pipes and coffee
appear, and the evening meal—a little rice, a few dates, or an
onion—is eaten frugally and with gusto. But everyone is
exhausted. The dry intolerable heat has drawn the strength
from every man's bones. Only the sapless yet tireless Omar
Effendi finds strength to perform the ablution and say his
sunset prayers. The rest lie drowsily talking under their thick
padded cotton coverlets, staring at the clear and blazing firmament overhead, or wrapping their heads in sleep.

On the 12th, stupefied from their thirty-six hours of cramp
and heat, they found anchorage at Dumayghah [2] where they
staggered ashore and bivouacked gratefully on the beach. The
next day they crept with idle sails into Wejh.

Wejh was filled with Persians lying in the only shade,
picking their rotten teeth with case-knives. No sooner landed
than the Maghrabi circled round them on tiptoe like fighting
dogs. A single spark would have led to trouble, but fortunately

---

[1] *Pilgrimage to Al-Madinah and Mecca*, chap. xi.   [2] Sherm Dumeigh.

that spark was not struck, and Burton's party proceeded to install themselves in the interior of the only café. Here some relaxation from the heat might have been obtained had not Sa'ad the Demon, in his usual vile temper, quarrelled with the proprietor, a squint-eyed, low-browed tough, and seized him by the throat. The proprietor did the same, and for a few moments both men circled leisurely, hoping their friends would separate them. Only when each was firmly gripped by his companions did their wrath become terrible to see. Villagers rushed in to join the fray, and in the succeeding fracas Omar Effendi discharged his pistol into a coffee canister. As if by magic the storm was lulled. Coffee was more important than honour, and soon it was circulating among friend and foe in perfect amity.

On the 14th they left Wejh after sleeping in the coffee house and all day wore ship, while a sailor stationed in the mast-head attempted to bellow directions above the ceaseless roar of the Maghrabi. Night was spent on a ledge of rock huddled together with the noxious Persian pilgrims, and some difficulty was found in mooring the *Golden Thread*, as by no stretch of imagination could her short anchor rope reach to the bottom. Fortunately the Rais of the Persian boat proved friendly and sent over a cable, and all was well.

Another day of heat and thirst found them in the cove of Marsa Mahar [1] where they rested on the cool sands and watched the Maghrabi lining the shore taunting the Persians, who dare not land, with being " the slippers of Ali and the dogs of Omar."

The 16th found them creeping slowly on with jaded spirits. That evening they should have made Yambu but for the laziness of the Rais, who was duly flogged. They anchored all night on the open coast, and Burton lay down to sleep in sight of the great Jabal Radhwah, the celebrated mountains of the Arabian shore.

At noon the next day, after beating slowly round the slip of headland separating them from their destination, the weary ship-load crept miserably into Yambu. They had been twelve days on their fearsome journey, and it was a miracle that some of them had not died.

While wading ashore at Marsa Mahar, Burton had felt a sharp stab in one of his toes, which on examination proved to be a puncture caused by treading on one of the prickly *Echinus* organisms which cover all the shallow reaches of the Mediterranean and Red Sea. A spine from one of these *Echina* can be

[1] Sherm Mahar.

very poisonous, and, combined with the effects of the hot sun, heavy dews, and continual washing in brine, Burton's wound had been rendered so swollen and painful that he could scarcely walk. It was an unfortunate accident to have occurred at the very gate of the Pilgrimage, and it was to prove one of his main difficulties during his subsequent journeys.

But at the moment all personal discomforts were forgotten as the port of Yambu drew near, with its promise of instant and permanent release from the horrors of the pilgrim ship. " After slowly beating up the narrow creek leading to Yambu harbour, we sprang into a shore boat and felt new life when bidding farewell to the vile *Golden Thread*."

§

Yambu is to Medina what Jeddah is to Mecca, at once a gateway of commerce and religion and a mouth to the thirsty throat of the desert. Burton found it an ugly, sprawling town, " built on the edge of a sunburnt plain that extends between the mountains and the sea . . . a long line of buildings, whose painful whiteness is set off by a sky like cobalt and a sea like indigo." To the sea it turned a fringe of warehouses, customs, and caravanserais built of limestone and crumbling coralline. A few cafés abounded in the town proper and a long market-place, overhung with latticed windows from the houses, and darkened from the sun glare by a covering of palm leaves, ran through the centre. A mosque or two and a few saints' tombs were scattered here and there, and behind it stretched the brown basaltic desert, rising slowly to the gloomy shimmer of the Hadhwah range.

Burton preceded his companions to a coffee house, where, nursing his painful foot, he sat waiting till the Arabs had successfully negotiated the customs, whence they came to join him. Finding a *wakalah* they reserved a room overlooking the sea and then proceeded to examine the town. Burton was now on the alert, for he was conscious of watchful eyes everywhere. During *Wuzu* and communal prayers, he had the sense of being narrowly watched ; a feeling to which he responded by performing his devotions with the assumed ease and nonchalance of an accomplished Moslem.

That afternoon a camel-carrier was sent for and the party began to treat for transport. The haggling was protracted, " for the Sheikh of the Camels and his attendant Badu were men that fought for farthings, and we were not far inferior to them." At length an agreement of three Maria Theresa dollars per beast was reached, half to be paid before and half on completion of the journey. Burton hired two animals, one for his servant and baggage, the other for the boy Mohammed and himself. Arrangements were made to start on the evening of the following day in the company of an escorted grain caravan, and a chill was thrown on the final proceedings by the Sheikh of the Camels' terse remark that the Hazimi tribe [1] was " out," and travellers were having to fight every day. " Sir," trembled Sheikh Nur, on hearing these words of ill omen, " we must wait till all this is over." The boy Mohammed, his boasting momentarily silenced, declared that he too deemed it safer to wait ; and Burton had to sting their yellow hides with a : " Why, ye were lions at Cairo ; and here at Yambu ye are hens ! "

The morning of the following day was spent in laying in a seven-day stock of provisions, and uneasily speculating on the future. Boxes were packed, pistols cleaned, primed, and loaded, and each traveller attired himself for the road. On the advice of a Medina man whom he met at the *wakalah,* Burton dressed as an Arab to avoid paying a capitation tax which was barbarously levied by every town chief on strangers, and he was warned that if he wished to avoid this unpleasant form of legal blackmail, he must never speak any other language but Arabic, even to his servant, in the vicinity of a village. Once more, therefore, he changed his identity and put on the big yellow and red head-dress, embroidered cotton shirt, crimson sash stuffed with flint pistols and curved daggers of the Arab ; over all he threw the gorgeously embroidered, gold towelled camel cloak called an *aba,* slung round his waist a sword, over his shoulder a matchlock gun, and gripping a palm-stick for camel guiding, declared himself ready for the road.

All pilgrims carry a *hamail* or suspended pocket Koran and by digging out the centre of his Burton was able to con al watch, pocket compass, pencils, and paper in the cavity In a secret pocket also he carried a small pistol with a spring dagger for final emergencies.

For conveyance he insisted on a *shugduf* or closed litter strapped on the camel's back, excusing himself from the more manly method of riding in the open by pleading the difficulties

[1] A despised branch of the Harb tribe. See Doughty, *Arabia Deserta,* vol. ii. p. 293 for details of this tribe, well described as " hounds, Turks, and traitors."

of his poisoned foot. He would thus be able to make what notes he required on the journey with some degree of secrecy.[1]

By 3 p.m. that afternoon the camels were standing ready loaded in single file, with the servants squabbling over places, and all was ready for departure except the most important items—the travellers themselves. In true Oriental fashion, the moment of departure found them scattered all over the town, Sa'ad the Demon blustering in a café, Sheikh Hamid at the dock greeting a new ship from Suez, Omar Effendi closeted with relatives in some remote house. It was six o'clock before all had filtered back and mounted, and not until after twilight and sunset prayer that they rode out in Indian file through the overhanging Medina gate, called out a greeting to the guard to show they were peaceful Arabs, and struck east across the desert.

A clear fresh moon was hanging high above the jagged jaws of the far-off Tehama hills, bathing the whole enormous plain in ghostly light. Every stick and stone stuck out as if carved in jet, and the silica in the sand glittered like a myriad needle points beneath the camels' pads. As their nostrils caught the clean, cool desert air the file of white-robed Badu began to sing, and singing watched the lights of Yambu slip away behind them, and the mountains of Radhwah loom up on their left.

The party consisted of twelve camels tied head to tail, " with but one outrider, Omar Offendi, whose rank required him to ride a dromedary with showy trappings," and though the country at that stage was perfectly safe, all kept fingering their weapons and after a mile or so ceased singing and fell into a deathly silence in which even the irrepressible Demon was quiet. At three in the morning they halted, piled their baggage together for safety, laid down their rugs and slept uneasily under the stars. Daylight brought reassurance in the shape of the grain caravan of 200 camels accompanied by an escort of seven villainous-looking Turkish irregular cavalry armed to the teeth. The two parties joined and proceeded with more security on their way.

[1] Among the more ignorant Arabs, it was formerly often as much as a man's life was worth to be seen with pencil and paper. The Arab has a great fear of charms and spells and looks upon any but holy inscriptions with considerable hostility. Even more travelled Arabs regarded a man who could write much with suspicion. Burton, in cases where secrecy was impossible, managed to overcome the difficulty by pandering to Arab pride. He would sit with his notes and ask his companions for particulars of their genealogy, always a matter of extreme pride to the Arab ; while pretending to write down their answers he would work away in security at his own notes.

For three days they continued eastward travelling between the sea and mountains across the wide lava plain. The routine of caravan travel began at three o'clock in the afternoon. After a satisfying meal of boiled rice, clarified butter, stale bread, and date paste washed down with dried sour milk dissolved in water, boxes would be loaded upon the groaning camels, the travellers would mount, and, under the tempered rays of a declining sun, the caravan would strike off in single file across the limitless expanse. At 6 p.m. the leader would call a short halt; prayers would be said in the soft sand and pipes lit and smoked over the fragrance of coffee. An hour would see them mounting once more and lumbering on at a steady two miles an hour, through brilliant moonlight which lit up the landscape with the remorseless clarity of an etching, outlining every stone, root, tree, and basalt formation. Each man would ride, his eyes alert for raiders on the ever-shifting horizon, wrapped lightly in a warm cloak and with his head cloth drawn lightly over nose and mouth against the heavy dew. Thus they would proceed across the silent waste while the moon sank, the stars paled, and the first fingers of dawn pressed up the rim of the eastern sky. At eight a halt would be called, tents firmly pitched, and, over little fires of camel dung, breakfast and coffee consumed and pipes drowsed over. Then, wearily stumbling to their tents, they would lie dozing fitfully or awake and sweltering through the long hours of the breathless, blazing day.

Between 10 and 11 p.m. on the second day they crawled into Al Hamra, a long, straggling village, the middle station on the Yambu–Medina route; that same Al Hamra where some sixty years later T. E. Lawrence was to ride in to meet Feisal, and make history. A slight brush with thieves who had fled at the discharge of a matchlock was their only adventure on the way. That night they slept in a circle formed by their unloaded baggage and each man spread his sleeping-rug upon his valuables with a cocked pistol by his hand.

Rising at dawn, Burton made an excursion round the village. He found that it was little else but a row of one-storied buildings, standing on a shelf of red soil from which it took its name, above a deep *fiumara*. A few shops, a *bazaar*, some stunted houses of unbaked clay, and a sprinkling of palm groves together with a ramshackle fort guarded by a small troop of Albanian cavalry completed the points of interest. On all sides rose stony mountains, precipitous rocks, and frozen torrents of lava.

He returned to the camp to find ominous rumours floating about. Somewhere in the mountain passes ahead of them a brigand called Sa'ad, or the Old Man of the Mountains, was raiding, assisted by an equally villainous brother, and had sworn to cut every throat that ventured through his defiles.

This ruthless pair were at that time the terrors of the Hedjaz. Aspiring to rule the Beni Harb [1] and therefore be uncrowned kings of the caravan routes, it was their policy to shake the native morale by periodically swooping down like thunder-blasts, closing the roads, shooting the troopers, and raiding every living thing in sight. Nor was a traveller's throat or two much of a consideration.

Sheikh Nur and the boy Mohammed shook like jellies on receiving this information, while the undaunted Demon, thrusting out his enormous negroid lips like an ape, swore that could he but meet him, he'd castrate the raiding villain himself. A reassuring background to this scene was provided by the Turkish irregulars who sat quaking in their saddles with faces the colour of dirty paper.

The following day, however, matters were improved by the appearance of a Meccan caravan, complete with escort. Burton's caravan hurried to join it, and about 5 p.m. the combined force moved off eastwards into the shadow of the mountains.

By evening they found themselves approaching a gorge, the territory of the notorious Sa'ad, and, after evening prayer, which Burton noticed was said by everyone with extreme fervency, they moved forward again with beating hearts.

Their forebodings were justified, for, as they approached the mouth of the gorge, a body of immobile and silent Badu was observed to be watching them from above the entrance. Un-easily the caravan jerked, jostled one another, and drew to a standstill; and, while men reined in their snarling beasts and felt nervously for their pistols, the whole body of Badu, as if at a signal, swept down upon them. Halting a few yards away, they peremptorily ordered the escort to return or they would refuse transit to the caravan. There was instant con-fusion, but the travellers had no time for parley or negotiation, for, before another word could be said, the escort, amounting to some two hundred men, wheeled their horses round and

[1] The Harb tribe, bounded on the north by the Shammar and the south by the Ateiba, has a territory stretching from the Red Sea to within 200 miles of the Persian Gulf.

galloped home, leaving the caravan to its fate. The Badu, however, having seen the Turks off their land, signalled to the caravan
to advance, which it did with extreme trepidation, and they then
vanished in a cloud of dust as quickly as they had come.

The night passed fortunately without incident, and the
following day as the chill wind of the false dawn pressed their
cheeks they lumbered into Bir Abbas, the last important stage
on the route.

Bir Abbas lay treeless, locust infested, and stifling at the
heel of a hill-girt *fiumara*, under a pitiless sky of brass. On the
very fringe of the Harb country, its few stone forts, coffee
house, *bazaar*, and miserable hovels stood like a weak gesture
of the Sultan's against his hereditary enemy the Old Man of
the Mountains. This stage is the most important meeting-
place for the Mecca and Medina caravans, who wait here until
they have gathered sufficient numbers to attempt the passes
beyond. The first day was spent by the travellers in watching
a parade of 500 Arnaut horsemen who were welcoming a party
of sheikhs from the neighbourhood. To the tap of the kettledrum the companies of ragged soldiers wheeled, formed line,
charged, and retired in some sort of order ; meanwhile filling
the hot air with bloodcurdling yells, and discharging their
pieces, shotted to make more noise, in all directions at im-
aginary enemies. The trained European soldier watched them
with interest, coming to the unorthodox conclusion : " they
have yet another point of superiority over us : they cultivate
the individuality of the soldier, whilst we strive to make him a
mere automaton. . . ."

That evening a fresh wave of unease filled the camp as the
far-off crackle of fire indicated a brush between the soldiery and
the Badu somewhere in the mountains. On retiring to rest,
each man slept once again on top of his valuables with a loaded
weapon to hand. A system of guards was inaugurated also,
but Burton, wakened several times during the night by the
distant ululation of jackals or the scratching of a pariah dog
prowling round the tent, saw that on every occasion the guard
had fallen asleep. Fortunately no marauders appeared and
morning discovered every man's belongings as intact as himself.

The succeeding day was spent in all the sweltering im-
patience of a forced halt. The sun cut pitilessly down through
thin tents, fraying the tempers and sapping the strength from
the pilgrims crouched smoking, drinking, and dozing there.

By evening, however, the decision to move on was made, and soon the stirring sound of the kettledrum calling the Arnaut escort to mount was heard through the camp. Each man saddled his camel and clambered hastily into the swaying *shugduf*, and about 11 p.m., as a rind of moon was just showing above the sinister peak where the notorious Sa'ad was reputed to dwell, the party moved off to a sandy flat where four caravans, banded together for safety, were waiting to take the road. Followed a hasty struggle for places in the line, for no man wishes to travel in that unguarded danger spot, the rear; and about midnight, with much shouting to camels, thwacking of sticks, swearing, praying, and squabbling, the enormous caravan moved slowly off.

They struck still eastwards across a moonlit *fiumara*, through a country " fantastic in its desolation—a mass of huge hills, barren plains, and desert vales. The road wound among mountains, rocks, and hills of granite, and over broken ground flanked by huge blocks and boulders piled up as if man's art had aided Nature to disfigure herself. Vast clefts seamed like scars the hideous face of the earth, not a bird or beast was to be seen or heard."

At early dawn on 24th July the caravan found itself approaching The Pilgrims' Pass, a gorge ill-famed as a favourite ambush of the Harb. As the long straggling line of men and camels crept slowly towards the dark entrance, a chill fell on them, and even the loudest boasters were silent.

Nor again were their forebodings without foundation. The head of the caravan had scarcely lumbered into the dark jaws of the ravine, when from high above the precipitous edge a few puffs of black smoke coiled lazily up in the air; they were followed instantly by the sharp echoing cracks of matchlocks, and a couple of Albanian horsemen reeled from their saddles and lay kicking in the sand.

Instantly all was confusion. Above the banging of pieces, the shouts and screams of bewildered men and the moans of flogged camels rose echoing up the dark cleft like a flight of startled birds. Peering through the powder smoke at the heights, Burton could see the Beni Harb, boys as well as men, leaping like goats from crag to crag, dragging huge matchlocks, or lying comfortably ensconced behind clumps of stone, firing at will into the struggling mass below. Their aim was directed principally at the Albanians; nor dare the wretched escort return the fire with any accuracy, for a dead Badawi would be the signal for the whole countryside to rise and massacre the pilgrims to a man. Dropping one after another from their saddles, the helpless men called loudly for help upon the party of elderly sheikhs accompanying the caravan. These dismounted imperturbably, spread a carpet in the midst of the mêlée, and held a solemn council over their pipes to decide what must be done. Their answer was unanimous : nothing : and all the panic-stricken lines of men could do was to blaze away as much powder as possible in the hope of hiding themselves behind their own smoke.

The caravans emerged at length on the other side, leaving twelve dead men and a score of camels to the tender mercies of the Harb.

Another two hours of hasty marching from that ill-omened spot saw them in safety at Bir al Hindi, the last stage on the caravan route to the Prophet's resting-place.

The spirits of all now rose like magic with the realization that their lives and (of equal importance) their belongings had come through in safety. Fear no longer rode them like a hag, and the camel-men, Badu of the same blood as the Harb, who had hitherto been treated with respect in their own territory, now came in for an abundance of taunts and abuse. The boy Mohammed, ever forward in such matters while his hide was safe, declared fiercely, looking around and fingering his weapons, that the beards of the camel men were now in his fist. " Where be these owls, those oxen of the desert, those beggars, those cut off ones, those Sons of Flight ! [1] Truly I will torture them with the torture of the oil. . . ." To this the infuriated Badu would retort by gripping their palm-sticks and hoarsely muttering : " By Allah ! and by Allah ! and by Allah ! O boy, we will flog thee like a hound when we catch thee in the desert."

Owing to the boy's taunts the camel-men disappeared and left the helpless party to stumble uncomfortably on inferior beasts, all through the succeeding night, which completely wrecked Burton's *shugduf* and forced him and Mohammed to cling tightly to the ruins like a couple of mournful birds.

With the welcome light of dawn, Burton awoke and shook off his lethargy and looked about him, to sense instantly a change in the tempo of the caravan. In the cold, pale morning light,

[1] A pun on the name Beni Harb, made by softening the initial consonant of " Harb."

each man could be seen hurrying his beast, regardless of the rough road, and in an almost uncanny silence.

" Are there robbers in sight ? " he asked the boy Mohammed, who was peering steadily out at the rough track in front of them.

" No," replied the boy simply, " they are walking with their eyes, they will presently see their homes."

Rapidly the whole caravan hurried through a long valley known as the Blessed, and approaching on its farther side a huge flight of natural steps surmounting a broad escarpment of black basalt clambered hastily to the top. Camels moaned and men gasped as they made their last ascent. On the summit, as if by word of command, each man halted, dismounted, and approaching the farther side gazed raptly at the scene below. Following their gaze, Burton could scarcely resist an exclamation of wonder.

" As we looked eastward, the sun arose out of the horizon of the low hill, blurred and dotted with small trees, the frontier of Nejd, staining the spacious plains with gold and purple. . . . Rightwards, broad streaks of lilac-coloured mists, here thick with gathered dew, there pierced and thinned by the morning rays, stretched over the date groves and the gardens of Kuba, which stood out in emerald green from the dull, tawny surface of the plain. . . . Below, distant about two miles, lay Al-Madinah. . . . All of us descended, in imitation of the pious of old, and sat down, jaded and hungry as we were, to feast our eyes on the Holy City."

It was an impressive moment. In silence the long line of dusty, tattered men stared down from their barren heights upon the glory below. Then words burst from them.

" Oh, Allah ! " muttered the Sheikh Hamid through his cracked lips, two tears trickling down the scarred channels of his cheeks, " this is the Sanctuary of Thy Apostle. Make it to us a protection from Hell Fire, and a Refuge from Eternal Punishment ! Oh, open the gates of Thy Mercy, and let us pass through them to the Land of Joy ! " And Sa'ad, the great negro, cried in throaty accents : " Oh, Allah ! Oh, Allah ! bless the last of Prophets with blessings in number as the Stars of Heaven, and waves of the Sea . . ." " Live for ever," shrilled the boy Mohammed, his poetic soul fired with momentary emotion, " Oh, most excellent of Prophets, whilst the west wind bloweth gently over the Hills of Nejd, and the lightning flasheth bright in the firmament of Al Hedjaz ! "

" Such," noted the traveller, " were the poetical exclamations that rose all around me, showing how deeply tinged with imagination becomes the language of the Arab under the influence of religious enthusiasm. In all the fair view before us, nothing was more striking, after the desolation through which we had passed, than the gardens and orchards about the town. It was impossible not to enter into the spirit of my companions, and truly I believe that for some minutes my enthusiasm rose as high as theirs. I now understood the full value of the phrase in the Moslem ritual : ' And when the pilgrim's eyes shall fall upon the trees of Al Madinah, let him raise his voice and bless the Apostle with the choicest of blessings. . . .' "

It was the 25th of July, and the caravan had taken eight days to traverse 130 miles of desert. The first stage of the Pilgrimage was now over.

§

The green groves and white buildings of Medina spring like miraculous verdure from the barren soil of a sandy plain. The city stands in a hollow at the confluence of a number of mountain torrents, dominated on three sides by the rugged Tehama, the holy hillock of Ohod, and the rolling hills of Nejd. Hidden from the traveller until the ultimate moments of his journey, it bursts suddenly upon desert weary eyes with the promise and beauty of the very gardens of Paradise. Around its cluster of bright buildings curls a pierced and towered wall with ancient gateways, and from the centre of the buildings, holding instantly the observer's attention, rises the enormous flashing green dome and minarets of the Hujrah or burial place of the Prophet.

Burton gazed long on this scene, the first bourne of his weary travels, but, as his eye fell on the holy building, he was reminded of his real purpose, and the dangers lying ahead of him. The burial place at Medina is as jealously guarded as the Ka'abah at Mecca, and a single suspicion that a disguised infidel walked among them would have turned the Arab into tigers. Now indeed would he have to watch tongue and hand with care ; a single slip might mean disaster.

After his first moments of enthusiasm roused by the sight of the Holy City and its effects on his companions, the emotion of the moment wore off, and the instincts of the traveller returned. Drawing apart from the rest, Burton made a quick topographical sketch of the scene ; then, concealing the papers in his sleeve, he remounted and followed his companions down into the plain towards the main gate of the city.

An eager multitude awaited the travellers on the way to the gate. Exclamations of wonder from the pilgrims were mingled with the sobs of joy and wails of Oriental happiness as mother greeted son, and brother, brother. Riding among them, touched by the picture of Arab family affection all round him, Burton was sharply aware as he entered the gateway of other eyes than welcoming ones in the crowd. Each pilgrim came under the scrutiny of a watchful stare of Madani officials. Adopting the nonchalant attitude of a hardened pilgrim, Burton rode easily past them and through the gate.

The Sheikh Hamid, who had arranged to be Burton's host during his stay, had preceded the party into the city in order to prepare for the reception of his guests. As the camels knelt before his house, the old man emerged to welcome his guests with the customary words of greeting, and Burton was amused to see a startling change in his appearance. In place of the grubby old tramp who had travelled from S'ez, a polished gentleman of Medina stood there. His tousled head was washed and freshly shaved, his beard had been brushed, trimmed and curled to a neat exclamation mark on his chin, and, in place of the filthy *jubbah* with which he had hoped to deceive plunderers *en route*, his shoulders were covered in a magnificent flowered *caftan* and his extremities in a pair of brilliant pantaloons of the finest silk.

Courtesies were exchanged and then the weary guests descended from their camels and took their rest in a cool room, where spread divans, ready-filled pipes, and braziers of boiling coffee ministered to their more immediate needs.

The Sheikh lived in a large house, filled always with guests, preyed upon by a cohort of impertinent children, and surrounded by mother, wife, and numberless relatives. Their wants were attended to by a pair of African slave-girls, and during the whole of his stay there, these were the only women of whom Burton had the slightest glimpse. On occasions when the house was empty, he was permitted to converse with the Sheikh's ancient mother, the lady being safely wrapped and hooded and hidden from him round a bend in the stair ; but, as is usual in strict Arab etiquette, of the mistress of the house, ever busy about his comforts, he saw not even a passing shadow.

§

Sheikh Hamid scarcely allowed his guest to recover from the rigours of travel before he began to bustle him about his religious duties. Constituting himself as cicerone to the new pilgrim, he determined to supervise the shibboleth of visitation and prayer which strict custom now required to be performed.

The first day after their arrival, they rose at dawn, washed, prayed, and broke their fast upon a piece of stale bread. Then, performing the Greater Ablution, they dressed in the spotless white clothes so beloved of the Prophet, and descended to the gate. A donkey had been hired for Burton (much to the sarcasm of passing Badu) on account of his poisoned foot, and, picking their way through the narrow streets, they approached the Prophet's Tomb.

This striking building, which instantly attracts the eye from the heights about the city, proved on closer acquaintance to be a disappointment. There was no general approach to it, no prospect from which one could admire its proportions. Small dwelling-houses and winding lanes pressed close against its walls. Nor did the interior seem much better. " I was astonished at the mean and tawdry appearance of a place so universally venerated in the Moslem world. The longer I looked at it, the more it suggested the resemblance of a museum of second-rate art, an Old Curiosity Shop, full of ornaments that are not accessories, and decorated with pauper splendour." [1]

But Burton had little time to cast an eye over its failings. Urgently pressed by the religious old Sheikh, he hurried through the Gate of Pity and took up his stand inside. Facing the outer wall, the pilgrim and his guide began the ceremonies by clapping both hands to their left hips and pacing slowly and in even time, like the chorus of a dance, along the echoing hall known as the Illustrious Fronting. As they paced, they chanted : " O Lord, cause me to enter the Entering of Truth, and cause me to issue forth the Issuing of Truth. O Allah ! open to me the doors of Thy Mercy, and grant me entrance into it, and protect me from the Stoned Devil. . . ."

At the conclusion of this prayer they entered the inner Garden of the Tomb and performed two salaams in honour of the temple, following this by the loud recitation of the 109th

[1] A description that the cynical traveller could apply equally to the Holy Sepulchre in Jerusalem.

and 112th chapters of the Koran. Kneeling until their foreheads touched the marble stones, they continued with the Prostration of Thanks—a heartfelt prayer of gratitude to Allah for permitting a sinful worshipper to stand in this holy spot.

It was now the recognized moment to give alms, and the hordes of beggars who sit about the temple, all day, watching the devotions, rushed forward with spread napkins to receive their charity.

Burton had arranged for this moment by giving the boy Mohammed a few handfuls of coppers and stationing him in the rear to act as almsgiver. During the turmoil of beggars, therefore, the former was able to cast a more observing eye round the architecture of the building than would otherwise have been safe.

As soon as this ceremony was over, they moved on reverent feet into the Hujrah or actual Tomb Chamber, a large, square structure some fifty-five feet across. Here, under the enormous dome, the glimmer of brass, gold, and silver filigree work, standing up against a grass-green background, delight the eye of the fervent Moslem. Here towers the Tomb of the Prophet himself, and the smaller resting-places of his daughter, the lady Fatima, and the disciples Omar and Abu Bakr, together with the so-called Place of the Archangel, and a number of minor praying places, all of which, as with every part of the Mosque, had to be approached in their proper sequence of prayer.

Under the steady glances of hundreds of watchful eyes, Burton began his prayers. He was acting now with his life at stake. Such a small thing as the position of his thumbs during the bow-prayer would, he believed, convict him of mortal heresy, and cause him to be dragged from the place and possibly slaughtered in fury outside.

Yet the air under the great arching dome was full of the murmured syllables of " Peace be upon thee ! "

" Peace be upon thee, O Apostle of Allah," muttered Sheikh Hamid, taking up position about six feet from the silver railing surrounding the Curtained Presence. " Peace be upon Thee, O Seal of the Prophets," whispered Burton. " Upon thee, O Opener of Grief . . . Upon thee, O thou bright Lamp . . . Upon thee, O thou bright Lamp . . ." came the sea of whispers from the cluster of worshippers and watching beggars.

" Allah, repay thee for us ! " chanted Sheikh Hamid and Burton together. " I deposit on this spot and near Thee, O Apostle of God, my everlasting Profession of Faith, from this our Day to the Day of Judgment, that there is no God but Allah, and that our Lord Mohammed is His Servant and His Apostle. Amen ! "

This solemn profession of faith at the very gate of the Prophet's Tomb is one of the most terrific moments of a Moslem's life. It is followed by something which to his dying day he never forgets, a peep through the window at the very tomb itself.

Sheikh Hamid signalled silently to Burton to approach this aperture and look in. It was a tense moment. This is the time when watching eyes are at their sharpest. Persians and other fanatic heretics have been known to toss bundles of filth in at the window in order to defile the tomb, an act which, if detected, has often led to a massacre of Persians in the city.

Peering into the semi-darkness of the aperture, Burton's eyes were able to make out little but a swaying curtain inscribed with gold letters, a large pearl rosary, and what is described by Koranic writers as a " brilliant star set in diamonds and pearls, believed by the vulgar to be the jewels of Paradise," but which to the cool eye of the Westerner " greatly resembled the round glass stoppers used for the humbler sort of decanters . . ."

There now followed a final short sequence of prayers, and then all was over, except the beggars.

Hurrying home, with mental notes still in his head, Burton wrote an account of the visit, concluding with the words : " Although every Moslem, learned and simple, firmly believes that Mohammed's remains are interred in the Hujrah at Al Madinah, I cannot help suspecting that the place is as doubtful as that of the Holy Sepulchre at Jerusalem."

His preliminary Zair, or ceremony of visitation, having been carried out, Burton concluded his religious duties by a visit to the Five Mosques of the Prophet, the Mosques of Kuba, the cemetery of Al Bakia, and the martyr Hamyah's tomb at the foot of Mount Ohod.[1] Sheikh Hamid then declared him free from further religious duty and permitted him to roam the town.

§

For four weeks Burton spent the life of an ordinary Madani citizen at Sheikh Hamid's house. Daily he rose at dawn, breakfasted sparsely, and rode forth on an excursion through

---

[1] Lack of space precludes more than a brief description of Burton's religious observances in Medina. A complete account can be found by those interested in the *Pilgrimage to Al-Madinah and Mecca*, chaps. xxvii–xxxi.

the city. At eleven o'clock he returned to dinner which was served on a large copper tray round which all sat and dipped in their hands. After dinner he would usually retire to some quiet part of the house where, lying naked on a divan, he would while away the siesta by reading, dozing, smoking, or writing up his secret notes, until sunset. Then followed the hour for receiving visits, which was succeeded by evening prayers and a substantial dinner. After dinner, the popular Madani pastime (frowned heavily upon in Mecca) of dressing in rags and striding the streets like Haroun al Raschid armed with fighting staves was often indulged in. Women or adventure of any sort was the object of these excursions, and no young Madani rake was worth his salt unless he returned with the scars of battle or wounds of love.

Burton's time passed easily enough in these occupations until on the morning of Sunday, 28th August, a far-off dust cloud roused the city to excitement. Drawing slowly nearer this disturbance slowly resolved itself into a crawling phalanx of men and camels, and gradually the great Damascus caravan, of some seven thousand pious souls, could be seen reeling across the plain, loaded with sick and dying, and weary from its several hundred-mile trek across the waterless Nafud.[1]

Led by a Pasha bearing a new curtain for the Hujrah, and guarded by a regiment of Turkish and 'rnaut cavalry, it crept slowly into the city all through the long day. That night passed in unspeakable clamour, and by next morning a new city had sprung up within the city, " a town of tents," wrote Burton, who watched it with amazement mixed with admiration. " How describe the utter confusion in the crowding, the bustling, and the vast variety and volume of sound ? Huge white Syrian dromedaries, compared with which those of Al-Hijaz appeared mere pony-camels, jingling large bells, and bearing *shugdufs* like miniature green tents, swaying and tossing upon their backs ; gorgeous litters carried between camels or mules with scarlet and brass trappings ; Badawin bestriding naked-backed dromedaries and clinging like apes to the hairy humps ; Arnaut, Kurd, and Turkish irregular cavalry, fiercer looking in their mirth than Roman peasants in their rage ; fainting Persian pilgrims forcing their stubborn camels to kneel ; country people driving their flocks of sheep and goats with infinite

---

[1] This is the yearly caravan which in 1876 Doughty followed as far as Hail. See *Arabia Deserta* for an unparalleled description of this ordeal.

clamour through lines of horses fiercely snorting and biting and kicking and rearing ; devout Hajis jostling one another running under the legs of camels, and tumbling over the tents' ropes in their hurry to reach the Harim ; cannon roaring from the citadel ; shopmen, water carriers, and fruit vendors fighting over their bargains ; boys with loud screams bullying heretics ; a well-mounted party of fine old Arab Shaykhs of the Hamidah clan, preceded by their varlets, performing the Aryah or war-dance, firing their duck-guns upwards, or blowing the powder into the calves of those before them, brandishing their swords, leaping frantically the while, with their bright-coloured rags floating in the wind, tossing their long spears high in the air, reckless where they fall ; grandees riding mules or stalking on foot, preceded by their crowd-beaters, shouting to clear the way ; here the loud shrieks of women and children, whose litters are bumping and rasping against one another ; there the low moaning of some poor wretch that is seeking a shady corner to die in ; add a thick dust which blurs the outlines like a London fog, with a flaming sun that draws sparkles of fire from the burnished weapons of the crowd, and the brass balls of tent and litter ; and—I doubt, gentle reader, that even the length, the jar, and the confusion of this description is adequate to its subject, or that any ' word painting ' of mine can convey a just idea of the scene."

Two days later " a splendid comet blazing in the western sky aroused the apprehensions of the Madani." A Hazimi fell out with a Hamidah (over some trifling business of a mare) ; during the whole afternoon of Tuesday, the 30th of August, the sound of firing among the mountains was distinctly heard in the city. Through the streets, parties of Badu, sword and matchlock in hand, hurried along to the fray.

This sudden flare-up among the local tribes put a decisive end to Burton's plans for a continued journey to Maskat, as originally intended. The Maskat route would be a battlefield for months and he had to be back at Bombay before the end of March under pain of losing his commission. Moreover, he had been obliged to leave behind almost all his instruments, and the benefit to geography from his crude survey could be but little. He was therefore regretfully obliged to give up all hopes of continuing eastwards, and turned his thoughts towards the journey to Mecca.

He had intended to prolong his stay at Medina until the last moment, and continue to Mecca by the *Tayyarah* or Flying Caravan, rather than the slower caravan from Damascus. But on the morning of 31st August, Sheikh Hamid returned hurriedly from the *bazaar* exclaiming :

" You must make ready at once, Effendi !—there will be no *Tayyarah*—all Hajjis start to-morrow—Allah make it easy for you !—have you your water-skins in order ? You are to travel down the Darb-al-Sharki, where you will not see water for three days ! "

Poor Hamid looked horror-struck as he concluded this fearful announcement ; but Burton was filled with secret delight. " Burckhardt had visited and described the Darb-al-Sultani, the road along the coast. But no European had as yet travelled down by Haroun al Raschid's and the Lady Zubaydah's celebrated route through the Nejd Desert."

But there was little time to ruminate over his good fortune. The water bottles had to be examined, and Burton found and patched some rat holes in them. Stores of wheat flour, rice, turmeric, onions, dates, unleavened bread, cheese, limes, tobacco, sugar, tea, and coffee were laid in. Sheikh Hamid himself kindly searched for good camel-men, an indispensable asset on the murderous Mecca road where there is no law to prevent desertion, robbery, or stabbing. He returned with a cool-eyed, short, tough old man, called Mahsud, and a sharp-eyed son.

The haggling was protracted but, when terms were finally settled, all was amity.

" Hamid then addressed to me flowery phrases of the old Badawi. After which, turning to the latter, he exclaimed, ' Thou wilt treat these friends well, O Mahsud the Harbi ! ' The ancient replied with dignity. ' Even as the Father of the Moustachios behaveth to us, so will we behave to him ! ' He then arose, bade me be prepared when the departure gun sounded, and stalked out of the room, followed by his son, who, under pretext of dozing, had mentally made an inventory of every article in the room, ourselves included."

No sooner had they disappeared than Sheikh Hamid shook his head and most earnestly entreated Burton never to let the round of a day slip by without dipping a hand in the same dish as the Harbi, for only so long as they remained on " terms of salt " with him would their lives and property be safe.

That evening friends dropped in to take their leave, and Burton felt a genuine regret as he shook the hand of the learned, yet fearless and companionable young Omar Effendi. The baggage was carried down and disposed along the ground in front of the house ready for instant departure, a few final prayers were said, and then the business of settling bills completed.

Sheikh Hamid had treated his guest with such hospitality that Burton could take back nothing of the £5 loaned at Suez. There followed a long discussion over pipes and coffee, much advice from the kindly old Sheikh, a parting present of pencils from Omar Effendi (from one man of learning to another) and then sleep.

" Thus, gentle reader, was spent my last night in Al Madinah.

" I had reason to congratulate myself upon having passed through the first danger. The next risk to be run was the journey between the two cities, where it would be easy for the local officials quietly to dispose of a suspected person by giving a dollar to a Badawi."

§

At 8 a.m. on Wednesday, 31st August, Burton's party left Medina by the Egyptian gate and struck north. Burton and the boy Mohammed shared a litter on one camel, the Sheikh Nur clung to a cot on another, and the remaining beasts, for Mahsud owned a string of nine, were ridden by a party of Turks and Meccans.

After an hour's slow riding they swung north-east and fell in with the Nejd Highway, climbing gradually out of the Medina basin. About noon a halt was made in a hollow place commanding the plain, and all the pilgrims dismounted to feast their eyes for the last time on fast-fading Medina, a final picture they would carry to the end of their lives. Then, remounting, they struck across a *fiumara* and reached the famous lava bed of the Darb al Sharki, described by Burton's predecessor Burckhardt from hearsay, but never before seen by European eyes. Nightfall found them descending again towards a low plain, from which a myriad twinkling watchfires denoted the main meeting-place of the caravans. Here pitched about the sumptuous green and silver tent of the Pasha of the caravan were the numberless tents of the Damascus and Baghdad contingents. Finding an open space, Burton's off-saddled, spread their own tents, and took their coffee and pipes under the open stars.

The dull boom of the Pasha's brass signal cannon roused the whole camp before daylight and in the cold dusk they struck tents, hastily loaded their animals, and thronged into a gloomy pass, where they struggled for good places in the caravan, an important decision, for caravan law is strict and, once stationed, marching order must never thereafter be broken. Again the cannon sounded, and was followed by a chorus of shouts, yells, thwackings of sticks and stumbling of feet as the animals took the strain on their loads and the whole mass moved slowly forwards through the defile.

For two hours they battled with their loaded animals through the congested pass, finally emerging on to another low plain on the farther side. The sun, now rising above the eastern hills, was throwing its first shafts across the vast concourse and Burton was able to see more clearly the whole panorama of the caravan spread out before him.

Seven thousand souls, was his computation as he ran his eye over the throng, on foot, on horseback, in litters, or bestriding the gigantic Syrian camels. It was an awe-inspiring, magnificent sight, this suffering, straining river of humanity thrust blindly on to death or glory by one common spiritual urge. It was impossible to contemplate it unmoved. " There were eight graduations of pilgrims. The lowest hobbled with heavy staves. Then came the riders of asses, of camels, and of mules. Respectable men were mounted on dromedaries, and the soldiers had horses : a led animal was saddled for every grandee, ready whenever he might wish to leave his litter. Not the least beauty of the spectacle was its wondrous variety of detail, no man was dressed like his neighbour, no camel was caparisoned, no horse was clothed in uniform. And nothing stranger than the contrasts ; a band of half-naked Takruri marching with the Pasha's equipage, and long-capped bearded Persians conversing with shaven Turks."

Yet in spite of the apparent disorder, a certain discipline ruled the caravan. The Pasha's cannon ordered its going and its stopping, its praying and its rising. The Pasha himself was the supreme judge of right or wrong. The daily routine was to sleep through the hot hours and travel through the long hours of darkness, as is so wisely ordained by the Prophet.

As the heat of day grew momentarily more intense, beasts and men began to fail and sink in numbers, and the wayside became lined with the corpses of dying and dead animals round which roamed bands of the starving, destitute Takruris. These beggar pilgrims, clad in filthy loin cloths, skull caps, and sandals, and carrying nothing except a wooden begging bowl and a knife strapped above the elbow, clambered like carrion about the dead beasts, hacking off the choicest steaks of quivering flesh for food.

At 3 p.m. the caravan halted and wearily made camp. The beasts had been waterless for ninety hours and it was imperative that someone should visit the local wells. The boy Mohammed rode off on a dromedary and came back after a four-mile journey with water, but black with fury at the conduct of the soldiers who had hastened ahead of the pilgrims, occupied the wells, and levied a charge on all comers. But anger was soon forgotten in sleep, and exhausted spirits took their rest under the canvas, while the jackals sang, the fires died, and Pasha's guard dozed over their spears.

The inexorable thunder of the gun dragged them from their beds at 1 a.m. and set them stumbling and cursing through the starlit gloom. Dawn found them entering a strange and fearful country thick with thorn trees which tore litters of cursing pilgrims to the ground, blinded donkeys, and slashed to ribbons the clothes of the riders. On either side the plain was encircled by the black jaws of basalt cliffs, and the air was filled with uncanny pillars of whirling sand, which trailed like bodiless fingers across the yellow wastes, flinging down men and camels in their path.

For four weary days they crept across this unhallowed, waterless country leaving a trail of dying men and animals behind them. On 4th September they staggered into the station of Suwayrkiyah, the last outpost of Medina territory. From henceforth they were under the domination of the Sharif of Mecca.

Suwayrkiyah proved to be similar to most desert villages, a mere straggle of huts and hovels, with a primitive but well-furnished *bazaar*, some date palms, and a few surrounding fields of wheat and barley. Burton purchased a sheep for a dollar, and some fresh dates, and a small celebration was held by his party which was only marred by the drinking water from the local wells which were strongly impregnated with Epsom salts.

The dry, parching *simoom* was blowing as the caravan took up its place on the following morning. This horrid wind, which closes the pores and prevents perspiration, is responsible for more desert deaths than anything else. Under its breath the eyes smart and sting, the ears throb, and the skin shrinks and cracks. As usual it seemed to affect the tempers of both man and beast. Camels moaned piteously as they took up their burdens and plodded forward through the scorching air, and among the pilgrims quarrels broke out in all directions, culminating in a fight between an Arab and a Turk. Here words soon led to blows ; the Turk struck the Badawi a heavy blow ; later the Badawi, biding his time, ripped open the Turk's stomach and left him gasping on the sands. A few compatriots fell out from the ranks of passing men and animals, wrapped the still-living man in his shroud and laid him in a shallow grave where the caravan left him to await death from thirst, jackals, or his wound. Burton could not help but look with horror on this scene, and contemplate what would be his own end were a wound to disable him.

The Baghdad contingent now split from that of Damascus and travelled ahead, as the fierce Wahabi mountain-men in the former were ripe for any sort of trouble. Under that hellish wind tempers were like tinder. An ancient Arnaut pilgrim, so decrepit that he could hardly stand, but with a rage like six lions, fell out with Mahsud and aimed a blow at him with a pole which missed the camel-man and caused the ancient man himself to measure his length in the sand. Mahsud was for murder, screaming : " Have we come to this that every old-woman Turk smites us ? " and he was only prevented from drawing and stabbing his doddering adversary by threats of being reported to the Pasha.

For four more days they followed the routine of the gun, travelling at night, in a south-easterly direction. After leaving Al Birkat, the ground took an upward tilt across a range of granite hills, cut by a deep *fiumara*. Camping here, they left at 6 a.m. on 9th September and, striking west, soon reached a large valley, where a general halt was called. Here they off-saddled, gathered in rows, and one of the most important ceremonies of the pilgrimage was performed.

This is the ceremony of Al Ihram, or the assumption of the pilgrim garb, specially carried for the purpose, and in which each pilgrim must enter the Holy City. Each man bathed therefore in a little *wadi*, perfumed himself, and was attended by a barber who shaved his head, cut his nails, and trimmed beard

and moustaches. The rigidly ordained costume consisted of
two lengths of red-striped white cotton cloth, one of which was
wound round the waist and loins, while the other was passed
over the back and body, exposing one arm and shoulder. No
hat must shade the naked skull from the sun. During this
period of mortification, which lasts until a final ceremony in
Mecca, the pilgrim is confined by a series of rigid prohibitions.
He may kill no game, nor even point an animal out for destruction, he must pluck no herb or vegetable, nor even a blade of
grass, smite no fly, nor give injury to any living thing large or
small. He must eschew amusement, and always scratch himself
with the palm of the hand rather than the finger, lest nail
uproot a single hair or destroy any vermin. The penalty for
any infringement of these rules, however minor, is the sacrifice
of a sheep.

Kneeling in their ranks, among the scattered rocks of the
hillside, the vast concourse of pilgrims now turned towards
Mecca and performed a two-bow prayer. Then from their
throats burst out a rough pæan of joy, the " talbiyah " :

> " Here I am ! [1] O Allah ! Here am I !
> No partner hast Thou, here am I ;
> Verily the praise and the grace are Thine and the Empire.
> No partner hast Thou, here am I ! "

Mounting once more they now struck south-westwards,
forming a picturesque scene under the declining sun. Led by
the tap of a kettledrum and a standard-bearer carrying a
flapping green crescent flag, the fanatic Wahabis rode in the
van, screaming, " Labbayk ! Labbayk ! " till the rocks rang,
while they wildly brandished spears, matchlocks, and daggers.
Clinging to them behind on their stirrupless wooden saddles
rode their fierce-eyed women, matted locks streaming in the
wind, and faces hidden by masks of wickerwork. Behind them
poured the spotless white figures of the rest of the caravan,
their skulls gleaming under the sun, some trotting on dromedaries, some swaying on asses, some staggering on foot. In
the centre of a sedately pacing guard glittered the magnificent
green and silver trappings of the Pasha's litter ; while the
wild Takruri, naked and filthy, hung like a cloud on either
flank.

Towards afternoon that same chill of foreboding which had
silenced the Medina caravan when approaching the passes of

[1] " Labbayk, allahumma, labbayk ! "

Sa'ad the robber-chief now fell on the whole assembly. A deep, black gorge of ill-fame loomed up ahead of them, and even the most fervent pilgrims grew silent as they entered the place.

As before their fears were justified. A mob of the Utaybah tribe, crouching behind boulders on both sides of the gorge, only waited for the caravan to be fairly in the middle before pouring down a volley which sent several pilgrims and their camels to the ground.

Instantly panic terror broke out. "Women screamed, children cried, and men vociferated, each one striving with might and main to urge his animal out of the place of death. At every matchlock shot a shudder ran through the huge body, as when the surgeon's scalpel touches some more sensitive nerve. The irregular horsemen, perfectly useless, galloped up and down over the stones, and the Pasha of the army had his carpet spread and debated over his pipe what should be done . . ."

At this moment, a truly magnificent sight for those who could appreciate it was provided by the Wahabis, who came galloping back from the van, full pelt, their tangled side locks tossing and the flaring matches in their hands casting a lurid glow over their fierce features. Dismounting, they drew their pistols and daggers and, led by a fearless young Sharif, swept up the hillside like a tongue of flame. The Utaybah fled, and Burton, who had primed his pistols but found he could do nothing, called loudly for his supper. His companions heard him in amaze. Sheikh Nur, exanimate with fright, could not stir a finger : the boy Mohammed with a face the colour of paper could only gasp, " Oh, sir ! "; and the surrounding pilgrims, thunderstruck at such temerity, exclaimed in horrified accents, " By Allah ! he eats ! "

The country through which they now passed was cracked and seamed by dark chasms and clefts above which steep precipices impended. Night fell and the caravan with yells of " Lab-bayk ! " which reverberated from rocky walls, the flash and banging of matchlocks fired to keep robbers and evil spirits at bay, and the flare and choking smoke of myriad torches leaping in the cavernous darkness provided an unforgettable scene. The way was pathless, and men and beasts slipped, clambered, and crashed in struggling heaps over the choking thorns and iron boulders.

Dawn discovered them reaching better country. They descended for an hour or so and found themselves approaching a deep depression known as the Valley of the Limes. Here, awaiting them on the right bank of a *fiumara*, from which could be glimpsed the far-off blue peaks of Taif, stood the green and gold tasselled tent of the Sharif of Mecca, who had ridden thither to meet his fellow plenipotentiary, the Pasha of the caravan. A brief halt was made while the pilgrims refreshed themselves with fruit and bread brought by troops of laughing Badu girls. Lying under the palms by the trickling waters of a stream the tired travellers relaxed for a moment before the last and most important stage of their journey.

And now as they wearily took the road again and evening drew near, a strange silence fell on the whole caravan, punctuated only by the occasional fanatic screams of " Here am I ! " A brooding, electric calm seemed to imbue the struggling masses, so that men spoke under their breath and urged their animals in silence. As darkness fell gently about plain and hills, all eyes were strained feverishly ahead for a first glimpse of the Holy City. None was rewarded, and night closed in on the caravan.

Burton dozed intermittently, but about 1 a.m. he was aroused by a wave of excitement sweeping down the lines.

" Mecca ! Mecca ! " screamed some.

" The Sanctuary ! Oh, the Sanctuary ! " moaned others ; and from all around suddenly broke out frenzied cries of " Labbayk ! " interspersed by sobs.

Looking from his litter Burton saw that the caravan had reached a break in the hills. Far below under the great canopy of the sky lay a wide plain, in which by the eerie light of the summer stars could be traced the outlines of a large city. Little else could be seen as they pushed their way downhill through a cutting in the basalt ridge, but the groans, gasps and hysterical weeping and screaming of the overwrought pilgrims continued without cessation.

Towards two o'clock they were feeling their way through the outer lanes of the city. Not a light seemed to greet them : but summer lightning flashing majestically above the Nejd hills guided their way. Presently the boy Mohammed pulled up his beast before a large crumbling house and sprang down from the litter to kick an Indian porter into wakefulness. The boy vanished, and soon from inside the building the unearthly wailing cry of " Lululu " [1] with which the Arab mother welcomes her lost children told that a family reunion was in progress. A few moments later the boy Mohammed appeared at the door and beckoned his guest inside. He had lost in an instant his cheeky impudence and was now the grave and courteously attentive host. Ushering Burton and Sheikh Nur into a large hall he had food set before them, and when they were satisfied ordered in cots from a neighbouring coffee house. On these the guests flung themselves in exhaustion to seek an hour or two of rest before their arduous pilgrim labours began at dawn.

§

With the first flush of light tingeing the yellow precipices and steeps around the town, Burton and Mohammed arose and performed the sacred ablutions. Then putting on spotless robes they pushed through the screaming mobs thronging the narrow streets, and approached the sacred Harim.

It was the culminating moment of the whole pilgrimage, and even the Englishman's steady nerve could not repress a thrill as they descended the two long flights of stairs from the doorway of the enclosure, traversed the cloister, and halted in sight of the Ka'abah itself. A strange emotion, a mixture of triumph, fear, and awe, swept over Burton.

" There it lay at last, the bourne of my long and weary Pilgrimage, realizing the plans and hopes of many and many a year. Fancy invested the huge catafalque and its gloomy pall with peculiar charms. There were no remains of graceful and harmonious beauty as in Greece and Italy, no barbaric gorgeousness as in the buildings of India ; yet the view was strange, unique—and how few have looked upon the celebrated shrine ! I may truly say that, of all the worshippers who clung weeping to the curtain, or who pressed their beating hearts to the stone, none felt for the moment a deeper emotion than did the Hajji from the far north. It was as if the poetical legends of the Arab spake truth, and that the waving wings of angels, not the sweet breeze of morning, were agitating and swelling the black covering of the shrine. But, to confess humbling truth, theirs was the high feeling of religious enthusiasm, mine was the ecstasy of gratified pride."

[1] The Arabs call this cry the " Zaghrata." It may be heard in joy and in sorrow, and even more stirring, as a background to the battle-cry " Allahu Akbar " when Moslems go to fight.

Pride, indeed, was perhaps the major emotion in the English-man's mind as he stood there in his long white robes contemplating the scene. He was one of the few Christians ever to stand upon this *sanctum sanctorum* of the Moslem faith. He had overcome the perils of the way, retained his disguise intact, and performed what was firmly believed to be the impossible. Had he not cause for pride ?

With that unerring delicacy which is one of the virtues of the Arab, the boy Mohammed had left his companion for a few moments, that in solitude the pilgrim might look upon the Holies and commune with his soul. Burton stood wonder-struck at the scene before him.

The Ka'abah, the supreme temple of Allah, the concrete expression of the whole Idea of Islam and the devotional lodestar of every Moslem on the wide face of the earth, is the very acme of stark simplicity, nothing but a huge, hollow, cuboid erection of grey granite, half covered with a ceremonial curtain of black, inscribed with prayers. It stands solitary, in the bowl of the mountains, unique and strangely impressive in the centre of an enormous open space backed by arched cloisters, beyond which gleam the gilded fretwork buildings of the town back by the forbidding hills.

This well-trodden open space is never empty, lines of beggars crouch on the outer fringe, flocks of holy pigeons fill the air with wings, and day and night without cessation through the cycle of years, chanting worshippers pace fervently round and round the Ka'abah in ritual devotion. Day and night, too, other worshippers sit waiting, watching, and praying, hoping that a time will come when for one moment the space is empty ; for it is believed that if ever a pilgrim performs the circumambulation alone, blessings, as the sands of the sea, will descend upon his head.

At this moment the whole space was a suffocating mass of bodies. The air rang with " Labbayks," murmured with prayers, and was rent with the sudden screams of the possessed.

" What a scene of contrasts," he noted. " Here stalked the Badawi woman in her long, black robe like a nun's serge and poppy-coloured face veil, pierced to show two finely flashing orbs. There an Indian woman, with her semi-Tartar features, nakedly hideous, with her thin legs encased in wrinkled tights, hurried round the fane. Every now and again a corpse, borne upon its wooden shell, circuited the shrine by means of four bearers. A few fair-skinned Turks lounged about looking cold and repulsive as their wont is. In one place a Calcutta Khitmutgar stood, with turban awry and arms akimbo, contemplating the view jauntily as those ' gentlemen's gentlemen ' do. In another some poor wretch, with arms thrown on high so that every part of his person might touch the Ka'abah, was clinging to the curtain and sobbing as though his heart would break. I saw a negro in a religious frenzy—a fine and powerful man as the numbers required to hold him testified. He threw his arms wildly about him, uttering shrill cries, which sounded like ' le, le, le, le ! ' and when held he swayed his body, and waved his head from side to side like a chained and furious elephant—"

Mohammed now appeared and, touching his companion meaningly on the arm, began to lead him through the long sequence of prayers and perambulations which custom demanded. Suffering intense pain from the burning rays of the sun falling on scorched naked heads and shoulders, jostled and suffocated by the throng of other worshippers, they performed their intricate genuflections, murmured their devotions and drunk with wry faces of the lukewarm bitter water of the holy well of Zem Zem, which caused their sins to fall to the ground.

They next approached the sacred Black Stone, which is built into one side of the Ka'abah, to perform the act of kissing it. It was surrounded by a mob of frenzied pilgrims who barred all approach until the boy Mohammed, calling on some stalwart Meccan acquaintances, cleared a way by sheer strength and hurled a number of screaming Badu from the place of honour. Burton was thus able to spend a full ten minutes over the much debated and little known object of Moslem veneration, and, while apparently ardently kissing it and rubbing it with forehead and hands, he was able to examine it narrowly, coming to the conclusion that it was aerolite.[1]

A few hasty prayers concluded a morning of labour which sheer exhaustion would soon have otherwise ended : and that evening Burton returned again to the Harim, in the vain hope of finding it empty. With a little caution and a concealed measuring tape, however, he was able to make a series of careful measurements, which he duly tabulated. The door of the Ka'abah itself was then shut, but a day or so later, Mohammed hastily informing him that it was open, he hurried to the Harim and obtained admittance. This was an act of extreme danger

---

[1] Burckhardt, *Travels*, vol. i. p. 250, considers it to be lava.

(shunned even by Burckhardt) for the officials within conduct a rigid examination of all entrants. Hoisted on the shoulders of two Meccans, he was raised up and pulled inside, and for the first time, perhaps, a tremor of fear shook his iron nerve. " I will not deny that looking at the windowless walls, the officials at the door, and the crowd of excited fanatics below, ' And the place of death considering who I was,' [1] my feelings were of the trapped rat description." But this did not prevent him from making a rigid examination of the simple but imposing interior and, during the prayer bows, scribbling his notes in pencil on the sleeve of his dress.

There now succeeded three days of extreme religious labour, all obligatory before he could put off his hateful *Ihram* and its restrictions. East of Mecca, six marching hours on the Taif road, lies mount Arafat. To this holy 200-foot mountain, renowned for its associations with Adam, the thousands of pilgrims dragged themselves on the day after their arrival to hear the famous Pilgrimage Sermon of the Standing, an imposing oration delivered by a preacher, mounted on a camel, from the extreme summit of the mount. Scores of pilgrims died by the way on this awful journey, Burton noting calmly how easy it is to die in these latitudes. " Each man suddenly staggered, fell as if shot, and after a brief convulsion lay still as marble."

The Sermon was followed by a journey to the Valley of Muna, where the pilgrims performed the ceremony of Stoning the Devil with seven stones, each man directing his stones at a small slab of suspended rock known by that evil name. Here the crush became so great that Burton had to use his knife to prevent himself being trampled underfoot. Next came the disgusting slaughter of several thousand animals, each pilgrim being required to sacrifice a sheep, and three hideous days while the blood-soaked valley sent up a noisome stench and clouds of flies circled above the rotting flesh. Finally the *Ihram* was cast off, the penances relaxed, and the ceremony concluded by an attendance at a sermon in the Harim.

It is fitting perhaps to conclude the brief narrative of Burton's stay at Mecca with his own description of that memorable scene.

[1] In spite of the law. See Burckhardt, *Travels in Arabia*, App. vii. As late as 1944 a Persian pilgrim was executed in the Holy City for defilement. Pilgrims who were present told the author the man was a simple lunatic, but fanaticism was so strong, the king was obliged to order his instant despatch.

" I stood wonderstruck by the scene before me. The vast quadrangle was crowded with worshippers sitting in long rows, and everywhere facing the central black tower ; the showy colours of their dresses were not to be surpassed by a garden of the most brilliant flowers, and such diversity of detail would probably not be seen massed together in any other building upon earth. The women, a dull and sombre-looking group, sat apart in their peculiar place. The Pasha stood on the roof of Zem-Zem, surrounded by guards in Nizam uniform. Nothing seemed to move but a few Dervishes who, censer in hand, sidled through the rows and received the unsolicited alms of the Faithful. . . . Apparently in the midst, and raised above the crowd by the tall, pointed pulpit, whose gilt spire flamed in the sun, sat the preacher, an old man with snowy beard. Presently he arose, took the staff in his right hand, pronounced a few inaudible words, and sat down again on one of the lower steps, whilst a Muezzin, at the foot of the pulpit, recited the call to sermon. Then the old man stood up and began to preach. As the majestic figure began to exert itself, there was a deep silence. Presently a general " Amen " was intoned by the crowd at the conclusions of some long sentence. And at last, towards the end of the sermon, every third or fourth word was followed by the simultaneous rise and fall of thousands of voices.

" I have seen the religious ceremonies of many lands, but never—nowhere—aught so solemn, so impressive as this."

§

The Moslem " Holy Week " was now over and, having accomplished his purpose, Burton prepared to leave for Jeddah. He sent his heavy baggage on as usual by Sheikh Nur (now Sheikh al Haji Nur), distributed a number of small money presents among his acquaintances, shook the dust of Mohammed's cheerless house from his feet, and with lightened heart trotted out into the desert accompanied by the boy Mohammed on a donkey. The short journey to Jeddah was accomplished without incident in one night, and once more the traveller gratefully inhaled the fresh air of the sea.

Not yet, however, was he quite out of danger. He was almost penniless, having only tenpence in cash ; and the camelmen were clamouring for their pay. He carried in a concealed pocket a draft from the R.G.S., and he decided to take the risk of applying to Mr. Cole, the British Consul, for help.

Three times a filthy, sun-blistered Afghan called at the consulate for an interview, sat patiently while the servants sneered and was turned away with a: "Let him wait." Finally he was driven to scrawl on a piece of paper: "Don't recognize me. I am Dick Burton, but not safe yet. Give me some money and take no notice of me": and was admitted to an astounded consul.

He secured a passage on board the S.S. *Dwarka*, travelling still as an Arab, and took the boy Mohammed on board for a tour of inspection. Perhaps his comparative safety made him momentarily careless and he let drop something which gave him away. But suddenly the boy Mohammed divined his secret. Coldly and politely he left the Englishman for the last time.

"Now I understand," he declared simply to Sheikh Nur as he headed his animal back on the Mecca road, "Your master is a Sahib from India; he hath laughed at our beards. . . ." And he rode out into the desert.

§

On 26th September 1853, the *Dwarka* slipped anchor and dropped down the channel, heading for Suez. As she crept out into the open sea, Burton's eye lighted on that bright, whitewashed dome, high above the harbour entrance, beneath which lies Eve, the Mother of the World, her right hand supporting her right cheek, her feet northwards, her head to the south, her lovely face turned in timeless sleep towards Mecca. Worn out with fatigue and heat, he could yet quote softly as that high white spot glimmered long on the fast-sinking Arabian coastline.

"I have been exposed to perils and I have escaped from them; I have traversed the sea, and have not succumbed under the severest fatigues; and my heart is moved with emotion of gratitude that I have been permitted to effect the objects I had in view."

Chapter Four

THE news of Burton's exploit soon reached England and for a
time his name was on everyone's lips. Strictly speaking his
achievement was little more than a *tour de force* ; geographically
almost negligible ; for the trouble at Medina had prevented
his doing more than set foot on the outer fringes of the " great
white blot." But this was forgotten. To have penetrated the
holy cities of Arabia in disguise was an adventure which touched
the imagination of every Englishman, and had the traveller
returned home there is little doubt that he would have been the
hero of the moment.

There were other rumours afloat, of course : scandal was
busy everywhere. Among other exploits attributed to him
were those of robbing a post-office in Cairo and basely murdering
an Arab who had pierced his disguise. These little fictions he
did not bother to deny : the only statement which he refuted
hotly was the one circulating in London clubs, that he had been
caught in a *harim* and castrated by the owner.

His absence lent encouragement to scandal. Had he
returned, he could have brushed this gossip aside with ease.
But he did not ; it was his first exhibition of that fatal indifference to public feeling which was to prove such a stumbling-
block in his career. Though worn out with the prolonged
fatigues of Arabian travel, England did not attract him. He
stayed in Cairo, putting together his notes for the projected
work : *A Pilgrimage to Al Madinah and Meccah*, and when his
leave expired he returned to Bombay.

Here he idled away a few months. But the restlessness and
freedom of travel were now in his blood. Military routine and
the social round irked his nature, and it was not long before he
was casting round for some new venture on which to try his
hand.

He found it in that strip of territory known as Somaliland,
bordering upon the dark confines of Abyssinia, an unmapped,
little-known patch on the East African coastline, upon which
Britain had already cast inquiring eyes.

As early as 1849 the Indian Navy had solicited permission from the East Indian Company to survey the coast and inland routes of Somaliland, and had received the following reply :

" If a fit and proper person volunteered to travel in the Somali country, he goes as a private traveller, the Government giving no more protection to him than they would to an individual totally unconnected with the service. They will allow the officer who obtains permission to go, during his absence on the expedition, to retain all the pay and allowances he may be enjoying when leave was granted. They will supply him with all the instruments required, afford him a passage going and returning, and pay the actual expenses of the journey."

This was incentive enough to the adventurous, and in 1851 the plans for a first expedition were drawn up by two naval officers. The idea was unfortunately dropped, and the project laid in abeyance. But the plans still lay to hand and attracted the eye of Richard Burton. It was this expedition that he planned to revive. Taking up the threads dropped by his predecessors he worked out a new plan of approach, as detailed as the information available allowed, and waiting a favourable moment laid it before Lord Elphinstone, the Governor of the Company. This discerning man approved it warmly, with the result that a letter asking permission was forwarded to the Court of Directors with his Lordship's recommendation enclosed. Their reply, received six months later, was favourable, and matters at once began to go forward in earnest.

Burton's plan was optimistic and bold. Briefly, it was to form a base at Berberah, and choosing a suitable caravan route strike south-westwards to the unknown Abyssinian city of Harar, thence turning south-east and cutting down to Zanzibar. For assistance, he determined to enlist the aid of three intelligent young officers on Indian service : Lieutenants Herne, Speke, and Stroyan, all skilled surveyors, geologists, and botanists.

This plan had the merits of boldness and thoroughness. Not only would it drive a wedge-shaped survey through a large tract of unknown country, but it would establish communication between two valuable ports and a wealthy inland city. Unfortunately the authorities at Aden, whither the expedition sailed, looked upon boldness as rashness. Outram, the Political Resident, convinced from long experience that he knew the Somal and his country, cast a disapproving eye on both the scheme and the enthusiastic young officers who had propounded it. To strike so boldly inland would be to court certain disaster, he told them ; caution must be their watchword. Their whole plan would have to be changed for something less ambitious and more safe.

Burton had perforce to submit, but not without a characteristic burst of sarcasm. " The insolent threats of the Somals have prepossessed this timid colony," he wrote scornfully. " For half a generation we have been masters of Aden, yet we are dared by the Badawin to come forth from behind our stone walls and fight like men. . . ."

But it was too hot to quarrel. Besides, the word of the Political Resident was law. A new plan was conceived, therefore, in which it was arranged that the party should split. Speke should proceed eastwards along the coast to a small bay, Bender Khor, from which he was to explore the watershed of the Wadi Nogal, prospect for gold, and purchase camels, and Herne and Stroyan were to stay at Berberah, inquire into caravan lines and collect geographical and meteorological data as a prelude to a closer survey. For Burton was reserved the post of danger. Travelling to Zeila in disguise, he was to make use of his knowledge of Arabia and title of Hajj to penetrate alone the city of Harar.

There were two routes connecting Zeila with Harar. The shorter of these was a five days' journey, striking directly south-west from Zeila, but passing through uncertain country where there was liable to be trouble with the tribes. The route eventually chosen was that running south along the coast, through territory of tribes dependant on Zeila, thence south-west through Gudabirsi and Girhi Somal country, and so to Harar.

If possible, this was a venture even more hazardous than his Pilgrimage to Mecca. Harar, the southernmost town of stone in equatorial Africa, set among the precipices of Abyssinia, a town with a language and culture of its own, inhabited by a people who hated the foreigner and attacked all who set foot in their territories, since they firmly believed an old legend that the first Christian to enter Harar would cause the downfall of that city, was an objective fit to daunt the most valiant. Ruled by a degenerate Moslem Amir and set in country thronged with marauding tribes who murdered not for plunder, but for the coveted feather of manhood, it had defied all previous efforts to reach it. A string of travellers including Salt, Stuart, Krapf,

Barker, and Rochet had all attempted it in vain. Could Burton succeed where they had failed ?

§

On the 29th October 1854, in the dress of an Arab merchant, Burton set sail from Aden with three native servants in an old half-decked *foyst*. Arriving at Zeila two days later he was greeted by the Governor, a fine Arab warrior whom he had met previously at Aden. The Governor was in the secret, so they had to meet as strangers, but he hospitably put a house at the Englishman's disposal and at the same time warned him that the expedition was doomed to almost certain disaster, as the friendship between Zeila and Harar had been broken off by the murder of the Governor's favourite, and the caravan road through the territory of the Eesa Somal was closed.

In spite of this warning, delivered with impressive Oriental fatalism, Burton went quietly about his preparations. A route was traced out, mules were ordered, and a search for a good Abban [1] was made.

The servants he had brought from Aden were a curious selection. They consisted of two Aden policemen, Hammal and Guled the Long, and Abdy Abokr, a rascally hedge-priest. Hammal was a coal-black, stout, and merry Somal with but one faculty beyond a certain bravery to recommend him, a brilliant gift of mimicry ; Long Guled, a gaunt skeletal creature over six feet high with shoulders parallel with his ears, was called " Long " for obvious reasons, to which his proud reply was always " Length is honour, even in wood " ; Abdy was a smooth-tongued dropper of proverbs, a goat-bearded creature of long back and stealthy gait, called for his general villainy and smattering of knowledge the " End of Time," [2] regarded with disfavour by Burton and only taken on the recommendation of the Governor of Zeila that he should be " looked on as a son."

After the many delays inevitable in the Orient, during which Burton assiduously cultivated his new personality, led the prayers in the Mosque, and made excursions into the neighbourhood on which he wrote copious notes, the expedition

[1] An Abban, or protector, is similar to the Arabian *rafik*, a man who contracts to lead travellers through the territory of his own tribe, handing him over on the borders to an Abban from the tribe adjacent.

[2] It is a Moslem belief that in the last epoch of the world the Moslem priesthood will sink into corruption.

was got into some sort of order. Mules and camels were collected and two stout female cooks were engaged and given the facetious names of Scherezade and Dunyazade after the famous beauties in the *Arabian Nights* : an Abban was also found in the person of one Raghe, a man of the Eesa Somal.

On the afternoon of 27th November 1854, the party clattered out of Zeila and headed due south, followed by a shout and a farewell discharge of shot from the Governor's matchlock-men. They made a vivid picture as they took the sand of the highway under the declining African sun. Foremost, bareheaded and clad in a clean white *tobe*, strode Raghe, the Abban, gripping a spear and shield ; next came the nodding camels loaded with baggage, and behind them rolled their drivers, the ponderous Scherezade and Dunyazade, their greased hair falling like spray about their shoulders, their faces shining with sweat and anxiety, walking heavily but strongly on bare feet and presenting those behind them with the sight of two gigantic pairs of buttocks, like natural cataclysms. " Each," wrote their amused and admiring leader, " looked like three women rolled into one : yet fat notwithstanding, they proved invaluable. They carried pipes and tobacco—for other folks' delectation, not their own—they led and flogged the camels, adjusted the burdens, and, most wonderful of all, could never be induced to ride. . . ." Silent and docile, they quietly did two-thirds of the domestic work of the party, never seemed to suffer from heat or cold, were happiest when listening open-mouthed to the more licentious of Burton's stories from the *Arabian Nights*, ever ready with a soft-voiced retort to any jest flung at them and readier still for a roll in the sand with any of the men who had the presumption and energy to take them. When really fatigued each would lie in turn on the ground while the other trampled on her back, kneading the flesh with powerful toes. From this operation both would rise refreshed.[1]

Behind these incomparable treasures rode the two Aden servants, lean and fat, in spotless *tobes* with red borders, and the unspeakable End of Time with a tongue like honey and a face like Judas Iscariot ; while last of all came the leader himself, a magnificent figure in white Arab robes and the bright green turban of the accredited Hajj, his big toes thrust through the iron toe-rings of his fine Abyssinian mule, a double-barrelled

---

[1] The author can testify to the benefit which can be got from this form of massage, particularly popular among Libyan Arabs, and called "tamseed".

gun across his lap and a brace of Colt pistols hanging from his
waist in home-made holsters. Five camels tied by their tails
completed the little caravan as it crept south-east across a
desolate plain towards the hills.

The country changed after the first day from a hard, stone-
less, alluvial surface, broken by tide reaches and boggy creeks
to a sea of yellow grass stubble, pitted with salt water pans
which lay parching under the scorching breath of the *simoom*.
Across this tough pasture land the caravan picked its way past
whistling Somal shepherds carrying in their arms the younglings
of the herds, or gripping their spears and driving lines of play-
fully biting camels to feed.

For the first day they kept in line with the sea, sleeping
within sound of its waters, but early next day they turned their
backs to the sun and struck inland where, after some hours'
marching, they made the village belonging to Raghe's kin; a
pre-arranged halting-place for the convenience of the Abban.
Here from a cluster of mud huts numbers of red-headed spearmen
swarmed round Burton muttering the suspicious "Faranj"
(stranger), and they began to deride his weapons until he raised
his rifle and with a charge of shot brought down a flying vulture
in a huddle of feathers. Screams of wonderment greeted this
exhibition, and, suspicions overcome, the spearmen came
clamouring for tobacco. Their importunity soon became unbearable. "Show not the Somal thy door, and, if he find it,
block it up," runs an Arab proverb, well known to the End of
Time, and Burton proved the truth of it during the all too long
stay among these rapacious savages What they could not beg
they stole, and the wily Abban, well pleased that his family
should profit while they might, delayed his party as much as
possible. Burton acceded to a short wait as a local tribe was
about to migrate and he wished to watch the phenomenon.

The wait was well worth the trouble. Rising before dawn
to the far-off shout of the Somal leader from a ridge top :
"Fetch your camels ! Load your goods ! We march ! " Burton
watched this ancient ceremony with intense interest.

"The spectacle was novel to me. Some 150 spearmen,
assisted by their families, were driving before them divisions
which, in total, might amount to 200 cows, 7000 camels, and
11,000 or 12,000 sheep and goats. Assisted by the boys, whose
heads were shaved in the cristated fashion, truly ridiculous,
and large pariah dogs with bushy tails, they drove the beasts

and carried the colts, belaboured runaway calves, and held up the hind legs of runaway sheep. The sick, of whom there were many—dysentery being at the time prevalent—were carried upon camels with their legs protruding in front from under the hide cover. Dromedaries laden with hutting materials and domestic furniture were led by the maidens : the matrons followed, bearing their progeny upon their backs. The smaller girls carried the weakling lambs and kids or aided their mammas in transporting the baby. . . ."

After a little difficulty in leaving Raghe's clan, who seemed to develop a constitutional dislike to seeing so much valuable plunder walk out of their hands still intact, a difficulty only overcome by Burton's promptness in displaying revolvers and threatening the dreaded evil eye, the party were able to leave late on Friday, 1st December. Forsaking the coast, they now struck due west, straight for the distant line of hills, and spent the first night at a water-hole.

The next day plunging into rolling countryside they received their first warning of danger. Towards evening they crossed the fresh trail of some 200 Habr Awal marauding horsemen. The broad line of hoofmarks threw the party into an instant confusion. Raghe prepared to run, Scherezade and Dunyazade clung to one another trembling, and what few teeth the End of Time possessed knocked together almost audibly in his head.

" What has slain you ? " cried Burton, angered at this cowardice, and lashing them with his tongue. The answer in the form of an old Somali proverb came from the pale lips of the End of Time, " Verily, O pilgrim, whoso seeth the track, seeth the foe ! "

No foe was seen, however, and that night they lay in the intense cold, covered in hides and clutching their weapons while they listened to the far-off roaring of the lions that infest the hills.

The next day, a long day of steady climbing, brought them to the confines of the Eesa Somal territory, and they entered that of the Gudabirsi. Here Raghe could go no farther, for between him and the Gudabirsi there was blood to settle and he dare not enter their lands. A new Abban was camped some three days' march away and two Gudabirsi had ridden to the border to escort the travellers with their letter of introduction to him.

They now quitted the rising maritime plain and entered the highlands proper. Their route lay among great rounded granite bastions streaked with white quartz, covered with the ubiquitous acacia tree and broken by incredible ravines of emerald green grass and luscious foliage filled with the flash of wings from varieties of beautifully coloured birds. Climbing slowly for three days they gradually reached an altitude of 3350 feet where the climate reminded Burton of southern Italy. Woodpeckers could be heard in the trees and the soft grass was starred with buttercups.

Here the long nights were passed round blazing fires while Burton, puffing at his pipe, told an entranced circle of listeners stories from the *Arabian Nights*. At this he was in his element; and he was to remember vividly in after years those long hours in the cold darkness of the Abyssinian highlands : the flickering light of the fire playing on the circle of eager faces, the deep silence broken only by the crackle of sparks and the distant roarings of lions or the chuckles of delight from the women at the story of the Porter and the Ladies of Baghdad, the groans of horror from the men at the trials of the betrayed King Shahryan. Sleep when it came was fitful, for it was well-known that the lions took a nightly toll of natives and when all had laid down to rest, the Somal guard leaning on his spear would face the outer darkness through the small hours whistling, singing, and talking to himself in different voices, as is the Somal fashion, to deceive plunderers into thinking that the guards were many.

By 21st December, the party had reached the border of the Gudabirsi and began to descend towards an enormous rolling plain of grass, the Marar Prairie. This plain, from lions and dearth of water, being almost uninhabitable, is considered as neutral ground by the surrounding tribes, who collect here in perfect amity to plunder travellers. A caravan was already waiting to make the dangerous passage and Burton's party joined it.

In one long line the pack animals guarded by spearmen and the imperturbable Scherezade and Dunyazade gripping pipes as weapons, they started off across the limitless sea of yellow grass. White-tailed *sigs* bounded before them and once or twice Burton caught a fleeting glimpse of that rare, ethereal creature, the oryx. Towards evening the lurking figures of lynxes and jackals appeared and, listening to the growing concert of the hunting lions, Burton reined to the rear to prevent stragglers. A young moon arose, turning the prairie into a

silver sea. Aroused by the sudden trembling of his mule, Burton
turned to see the stealthy figure of a large lion stalking them.
The crack of his rifle was the signal for the timid caravan to
start loudly reciting passages from the Koran, which they kept
up without ceasing until dawn.

Next morning, after camping in a local Kraal, they were
met by the son of the Gerad or governor of those regions, who
led them out of the sea of grass and up the gentle slopes along
the southern base of the Gurays hills. In a few miles the
landscape completely changed in character, and Burton, halting
to make notes, wrote :

" Before us lay a little Alp : the second step of the Ethiopian
highland. Around were high and jagged hills, their sides black
with teak and pine, and their upper brows veiled with a thick
growth of cactus. Beneath was a deep valley, in the midst of
which ran a serpentine of shining waters, the gladdest spectacle
we had yet witnessed : farther in front, masses of hill rose
abruptly from shady valleys, encircled on the far horizon by a
straight blue line of ground. Behind us glared the desert. We
had now reached the outskirts of civilization. . . ."

They pursued their way over gradually rising ground,
dotted with fantastically piled blocks of granite. An icy wind
was blowing which evoked from the miserable End of Time the
Somal proverb that " Heat hurts but cold kills." After a halt
at the Gerad's village, Wilensi, where they were hospitably
entertained by his wives, Burton determined to push on towards
Sagharrah, whither the Gerad himself had gone to settle a local
blood feud.

But now trouble began. First came the news that smallpox
was raging in Harar, and Scherezade and Dunyazade, fearing
for their charms, begged to be left behind. A quarrel also broke
out between Hammal and the End of Time ; the latter, whose
courage rose and fell in inverse ratio to the amount of danger
about, was now swelling importantly and declaring that he
commanded the caravan. One of the Abbans also refused to
go farther on account of the murderous reputation of the Harari,
and was dismissed with presents. Burton dealt with these
problems by arranging to dump all his major belongings at
this friendly village, leaving the two women to look after them,
packing the few needful articles of travel on mules, and pushing
swiftly forward with his mounted party, led by an old Badawi
Abban, Mad Said.

10 a.m. on the 29th of December saw them filing round the
northern side of a table mountain, through a lane fragrant with
dog-roses, and presently they dropped into a plain again and
after a ride of some fifteen miles reached Sagharrah about 4 p.m.
to be greeted by the Gerad in person.

The Gerad was a wiry six-foot Badawi with decided features,
a tricky smile, and an uncertain eye.   Burton, who was now in
pain from a sudden abdominal attack, looked at him doubtfully,
but, before he could begin to transact any business, was stricken
helpless by a bout of dysentery.

For two days he lay in a semi-coma while the life ebbed in
his body.   His host treated him with the utmost kindness,
sending to Harar for millet beer while his wife and daughters
sacrificed an expiatory sheep, and a flock of Galla Christians
gathered round his bed, weeping at the unhappy plight of the
stranger who had come so far only to die under a tree.

Possibly the wish to disappoint these wailers, aided by his
iron constitution and inflexible will, pulled him round.   At any
rate, without convalescing for a moment, he dragged himself
out of bed after a two-day nightmare, put on his best clothes,
and on 1st January 1855, an auspicious beginning to a new year,
sought an interview with the Gerad.

The meeting was pleasant but profitless.   Burton read aloud
the long letter of introduction from the Governor of Zeila, but
the crafty Gerad turned the subsequent conversation on to the
question of forts, in which he was interested.   Several times his
guest attempted to turn the talk into the matter of escorts,
but finally he gave up on the arrival of a group of Habr Awal
Arabs, friends of the notorious Amir of Harar who rode up,
dismounted, and politely plied the Englishman with questions.
They smiled with treacherous faces and, the moment Burton
was out of earshot, declared that he was a spy and must be
sent to Harar in chains.   Foiled by the Gerad, who answered
them with a curt refusal, they greeted Burton once more
with smiles, told him they would present his salaams to the
Amir, and rode off again leaving the whole party extremely
perturbed.

This was real danger.   To be dubbed a spy at the very gates
of Harar would mean disaster, and the expedition ending its
travels in the Amir's celebrated torture chambers.   The Habr
Awal were obviously riding now to get the Amir's ear.   Something must be done at once before matters went too far.

Burton now applied to the Gerad point blank for an escort, and was as straightly refused by that astute person who wished for no trouble with Harar. Go to Harar, was the tenor of his reply to Burton, and you are a dead man.

Checked here, Burton had to decide quickly. Calling his companions to him, he made them a stirring speech in which he declared that hitherto their adventures had been those of old women. Now was the chance to show that they were men. Who would ride with him to the forbidden city ?

The End of Time instantly declined, and was ordered to stay with the Gerad at Sagharrah, but Hammal and the Long Guled, seeing that their leader meant to ride alone if need be, rose in their shamed manhood and declared their willingness to accompany him, at the same time trying to turn deaf ears to the audible remarks of the bystanders that they were even now dead men. Mad Said was also persuaded to guide them, and with this small party Burton determined at once to push ahead.

But first he decided on a complete change of plan. To counteract the dangerous spy rumour, he determined to put aside his commercial disguise, and say instead that he was a Moslem emissary from the Political Resident at Aden. He therefore sat down and wrote a letter in English to the Amir of Harar as from the Resident, and proposed to deliver it in person with suitable speeches. This he hoped might counteract the spy rumours and give him some official protection.

He wrote a farewell letter, in case of accidents, to Herne at Berberah, leaving it with the End of Time, and then, stringently cutting down the baggage to a change of clothing, a book or two, a few biscuits, ammunition, and a little tobacco, he led the way on the morning of the 2nd January on the last stage to Harar.

They were now among the dark, mountainous sentinels of Abyssinia. Huge cliffs rose up on either hand like implacable barriers to the stranger, and all day and night showed the smoke and gleam of the many watchfires of the guardians of the passes. A long ride over gradually ascending hills brought them to the famous Galla pass, where a line of spearmen barred their way. Their baggage was inspected by the Chief who owned the pass, and after some palaver and a present or two they were reluctantly allowed to enter. Rounding the flank of a large mountain they entered the Amir's territory and were presented simultaneously with a panoramic view of Abyssinia. Halting and looking westwards, they could see about thirty miles distant, across a series of blue valleys and impending heights, a dark speck upon a tawny shelf of stubble—Harar.

Dropping in altitude again they passed through a rolling country that alternated between miles of enormous crimson-headed thistles and patches of ploughland where Galla peasants worked singing at their threshing. Now they drew close upon the heels of the treacherous Habr Awal, flogging their beasts in their haste to get to Harar. Seeing that they would be over-taken they sent a spurious message of friendliness to Burton, offering, if he would wait till sunrise, to enter the city in his train. He returned a polite affirmative but learned later that immediately on receiving it they had hurried ahead to gain a further night's march on him.

Once more he jettisoned his baggage, leaving all his instru-ments, journal, sketches, and other books with a Gorahi servant and orders that they should be forwarded to the care of the Gerad, as he determined to carry nothing into Harar but his firearms and a few presents for the Amir.

And now Harar drew nigh. By hard riding, the afternoon of the following day found them picking their way through the market folk returning from the city, and at 2 p.m. they halted in the shade of a huge tree and dismounted to take their first look at the forbidden city, among slim, naked-breasted women selling clarified butter and cotton.

There it lay upon a hill-top about two miles away, " the end of my present travel—a long, sombre line strikingly contrasting with the whitewashed towns of the East. Many would have grudged exposing three lives to win so paltry a prize. But of all that have attempted, none ever succeeded in entering that pile of stones. The traveller will understand my exultation. . . ."

But exultation must be tempered by caution. They were now on the brink of great danger. He made a quick sketch of the town while his servants bathed in a nearby stream, then remounting their jaded beasts they picked their way up the stony hillside. After an hour of scrambling up a rough path hedged with cactus they drew near the forbidding bastions of the city, and Burton's heart beat high.

The eastern gate was open and in its entry lounged a few surly matchlock-men and the usual idlers. Dark looks were thrown at the strangers as Mad Said hailed the warder. Some fingered knives and others the triggers of their guns, while others again broke out into murmurs of derision and shook their spears.

Burton sat immobile, his gun across his arm, while Mad Said sent the warder with a message that a deputation from Aden awaited the honour of an audience with His Highness, the Amir. Hammal and Long Guled sat fidgeting in their saddles while a crowd of passing Badu entreated them to desert their leader who was shortly to be executed.

For half an hour they sat waiting, a half-hour that required an iron nerve to support composure. Then the warder returned and insolently ordered them to dismount. They did so, but when he further demanded that they run across the threshold of the city,[1] Burton flatly refused and purposely sauntered in, staring with impudent sangfroid into the faces of the threatening mob.

Their guide led them up a rock-strewn street and so through an arch and into a large courtyard filled with Galla spearmen. Halting at a curtained doorway they were commanded to remove their shoes and hand over their weapons. Burton complied with the former but quietly concealed a revolver in his waistband, determined at the first sign of trouble to leap to the Amir's side and hold the weapon at his head. Bending, they passed quickly through the curtain and so into the Presence.

They found themselves in a large hall, hung with weapons, shackles, and instruments of torture, and filled with two lines of enormous half-naked Galla spearmen standing immobile and watchful. At the far end stood a group of courtiers in bright ornaments, and behind them, reclining on a divan, the Amir himself guarded on both sides by matchlock men holding flaring matches. As the Englishman followed by his two trembling servants entered, a deathly silence fell.

It was a moment for courage. He was alone ; he was in the hands of a Prince whose least word was death, and whose love of torture and fear and hatred of strangers was notorious. Moreover, by popularly believed legend, he was the fated instrument of their downfall. If they pierced his disguise and saw the European beneath, his fate would be certain. He must once more take the stage and act for his very life.

Marching slowly and with dignity through the lines of spearmen, he halted at the foot of the dais and, with an attempt

[1] A mark of particular humility and obeisance in the East.

at the nonchalant respect of a powerful emissary, declaimed in a loud voice :

" Peace be upon thee ! "

The silence which followed was broken by the sharp click of the Amir's finger and thumb as he made a signal and simultaneously extended a yellow talon to the Englishman. Two Chamberlains seized Burton's forearms as he bent to make his obeisance, but he could not bring himself to kiss that hand, " being naturally averse from performing that operation upon any but a woman's." He was then led to a mat facing the Amir and requested to sit.

The Prince of Harar was an etiolated youth of some five and twenty summers, thin bearded, yellow complexioned, and with the soft protruding eyes of the sadist. He was clad in crimson and lay on a low couch, from beneath the cushions of which there stuck out the handle of a scimitar.

Burton began by politely inquiring after his health, which was obviously bad, but the youth shook his head irritably and demanded an explanation of the stranger's errand. Burton replied with a long speech in his most flowery Arabic, declaring that he had made this long and dangerous journey with a message from the Governor of Aden and to see the light of His Highness's countenance, concluding with several efflorescent compliments calculated to touch the heart of the most obdurate Prince.

All eyes were now at the Amir. There was another threatening pause, and then across that etiolated little face there flickered a smile.

The Amir smiled graciously.

Instantly, as when an impending thundercloud discharges itself in blessed rain, the atmosphere in the courtroom relaxed in a series of sighs. Burton's hand dropped from his hidden pistol, and he knew now that he had succeeded.

A few moments later the Amir gave the signal to retire, and walking backwards from the room they left the dreaded Presence, accompanied by an obsequious Treasurer.

Outside, as if by magic, frowns had changed to smiles. They were led through narrow streets thronged with townsfolk to another palace of the Amir's which was put at their disposal. Here a frugal meal was served them and they flung themselves down on their couches, worn out with fatigue, but supported by the knowledge that they had overcome what had seemed the impossible.

§

For ten days Burton was immured in Harar, constantly watched by spies and well aware that the Amir was still debating his fate. He was intermittently interviewed by the Amir's Vizier and by a learned old Jami of the Ulema who questioned him closely in matters of theology. During this time all sorts of reports about him were circulating through the city, and the constant drain on his nervous system, together with the physical weakness of dysentery, made his life by no means a happy one.

He worked indefatigably, however, at a study of the town, populace and language ; Harar itself he found to be little more than a straggle of houses about a mile long and half a mile wide, surrounded by a wall pierced with five gates, and clustered about an ancient church with two ugly minarets.

Besides the suspicious and picturesque Harari, the populace consisted of Somal, Badu, and a number of other nationalities, most of whom came to call upon the stranger in his lodgings. A few days exhausted all the possibilities of the town and he began to long to depart.

But this was difficult. He could get no permission. Almost the Amir seemed to play with him as does a cat with a mouse, smiling graciously yet conceding nothing, and plying him always, through his servants, with keen questions as to the why and wherefore of his coming.

Burton began to grow desperate and planned to escape, a difficult operation for a stranger in a walled city whose gates were locked at sunset ; but it was imperative that he get away, the more so as it had just come to his ears that some Somal from the coast had just come into the city with the story that three Frankish brothers had landed at Berberah, that they were in the disguise of Arabs, and that one had gone to Harar to spy out the land while the others awaited him.

This was really awkward and it was obvious that a move of some sort must be made immediately. He had struck up some sort of theological acquaintanceship with the Jami, and now, by displaying his medical knowledge, playing on the fact that the old man had severe bronchitis and saying that he could send perfect cures from Aden, he was able to enlist this powerful ally on his side.

Another plea was made. The Amir hesitated ; then gave his grudging permission, and three days later, with a letter for the Political Resident and a special mule as a gift, the Englishman was allowed to depart unmolested.

Ill as he was with dysentery and worry, once outside those dread gates his cares seemed to flee. They passed out of the dark and stinking city, where dwelt suspicion, hatred, and death, into clear sunlight and freedom ; and for a moment, casting a brightening eye on the scene around him, as he rode rapidly eastwards, the traveller grew lyrical. " The dew hung in large diamonds from the coffee trees, the spur-fowl crew blithely in the bushes by the wayside ; never did the face of Nature appear to me so lovely."

Collecting the unbelieving End of Time at Sagharrah, they rewarded the Gerad and hurried on to Wilensi, where those titanic treasures, Scherezade and Dunyazade, shook with unrestrained delight. Here a halt of a week was made to lay in strength for the arduous desert march to Berberah, and, relaxing in the shade of this friendly village, Burton spent the time in compiling a vocabulary of the Harar tongue.

At dawn on the 24th of January the party started once more across the barren Marar Prairie with a caravan. Taking the Berberah route they plunged into desert on the other side and seven days later reeled into the city weak from starvation and having escaped death from thirst only by a miracle. After a brief recuperation Burton set sail for Aden where he was greeted with enthusiasm by the colony as being the first white man to break the dark spell over Abyssinia and come unscathed from the forbidden city.

§

This was achievement enough and he could have well afforded to rest on his laurels. But he was not satisfied : he had blazed a trail to Harar, and it was now necessary, he decided, to consolidate that trail with a larger expedition. Receiving the required permission from headquarters he once more enlisted the services of his bright trio of lieutenants, collected a party of forty-two men, and embarking on 7th April 1855, in the gunboat *Mahi*, for Berberah, led them to tragedy.

Landing at Berberah, which was almost empty as it was the season of the Fair, they pitched their tents in a line on the sand, Stroyan on the right, Herne and Burton in the middle, and Speke on the left, and prepared to await a cargo of instruments on their way from Europe. At this moment the gunboat was unfortunately called away, an act which was at once signalled by spies to the hills.

Just before dawn on the 19th of April, the Englishmen were awakened by a rush of feet and the screams of the speared and fleeing guards. Burton sprang up and called for his sabre, at the same time sending Herne to ascertain the force of the attack. Herne took a revolver, found that the camp was being assailed by some 200 Somali warriors, shot one who tried to brain him, and returned with the news that the guard had fled and the Somali were massing to attack the tents. Meanwhile Burton had gone to arouse Speke and Stroyan. Speke grabbed a revolver and ran to join Burton in his tent, but Stroyan fell speared in a dozen places before he had gone three yards.

The three remaining officers now crouched in Burton's tent and attempted to make some sort of defence. Burton stood gripping his sabre, while Speke and Herne, with the only pair of available revolvers, blazed at the shadowy figures in the doorway. The Somali meanwhile were running round the tent beating it with clubs, hurling javelins through the walls and tossing their long daggers under the sides. At length when the guy ropes snapped and the canvas threatened to collapse on the beleaguered men, Burton gave the order to sally, leading the way with Herne and Speke at his heels.

A mob met them in the doorway and instinctively gave back before the whirling blade of one of the finest swordsmen in Europe. Seeing what he thought was Stroyan's body lying on the sand, Burton cut his way towards it. At this moment a shout from behind him momentarily made him drop his blade and a spearman leaped in and transfixed him through the cheeks, springing back into the darkness before he could be cut down. Tearing at the firmly embedded weapon and half faint from pain and blood, Burton staggered in search of his comrades who had disappeared.

Herne's pistol was speedily emptied, but using it as a club he beat his way through the tribesmen, who, though shouting loudly : " Kill the Franks who are killing the Somali ! " for some reason let him pass. Speke, on the other hand, found his pistol jammed and was floored with a blow from a club. Three men pinioned him and left him to plunder, and he just managed to break free in time to catch the spear of a fourth who had crept up to slaughter him in his bonds. A succession of thrusts speared the unfortunate man in a dozen places through shoulder, hand, and thigh, and a final stab clean through the right leg made him leap maddened to his feet, dodge a hail of flung spears and totter out of range into the darkness and safety of the town.

In the cold light of dawn the three unfortunates met and sadly carried the gashed and battered body of Stroyan on to a native barque which had put in to their aid, and from which, a day later, it was committed to the sea.

Arriving at Aden, Burton's wound was attended to by a doctor who found that the upper jaw had been transfixed, carrying away part of his palate and four back teeth. Skilled treatment was urgent, and he accordingly left at once for England on sick leave, sad at heart at the loss of a gallant friend and the failure of a project which had started so well.

Chapter Five

THE four years since she had sailed so unhappily out of Richard Burton's life had dealt kindly with Isabel Arundell. From a jejune young lady she had matured into a woman of striking beauty and charm. In character she was still the impulsive, religious, and determined creature of Boulogne, but the school-girl longings had given way to a more positive ambition to do something in the world, and her desperate infatuation for a man who scarcely knew her had changed to an unswerving ideal love, less violent but more steadfast.

In Isabel's imaginative world Richard had pride of place. In the melancholy halls of her dreams, Richard sat in lonely majesty surrounded by all the emblems of Isabel's religious and superstitious leanings—omens, charms, numerological signs, holy medallions, and signposts of destiny—while at his feet she prostrated herself in selfless devotion. To love and be unloved —what could be more beautiful and sad ?

In the world of reality, she followed him tirelessly ; with little news of him beyond the reports in the newspapers, she yet endeavoured to follow his career with breathless interest. When news of his Mecca exploit had reached London she had wept with pride and hastened to her diary :

" Richard has just come back with flying colours from Mecca. I glory in his glory. God be thanked ! "

A few months later she notes :

" And now Richard has gone to Harar, a deadly expedition, or a most dangerous one, and I am full of sad forebodings. Will he never come home ? How strange it all is, and how I still trust in Fate ! "

At the time of his desperate fight at Berberah, his wounding and the murder of Stroyan, she was terrified by a series of horrible dreams. She saw Richard calling helplessly for her as he writhed on native spears, she watched him stretched in the desert under a blazing sun, dying from thirst, with his proud face upturned to the sky and his parched mouth calling faintly on her for water.

When the news of the tragedy and Richard's close escape reached her, she wrote :

" I felt it. Oh, I hope to Heaven he will not go back. How can I be grateful enough for his escape ? "

The coming of the Crimean War, however, lessened her preoccupation by absorbing some of her energies. For a time Richard slipped into the background while she begged for permission to go with Florence Nightingale and share the horrors of Scutari. She felt all the brave soldiers calling to her to minister to them, and saw herself, a second Lady of the Lamp, bringing comfort and hope to the shattered wrecks from Sevastopol.

Three times she applied for leave, and three times was refused on account of her youth and inexperience. She bombarded Florence Nightingale with letters. " How I envy," she wrote, " the women who go as nurses ! "

But it was in vain. Scutari was not for her ; and at length, reluctantly, she gave up the project.

Undefeated, she cast about for a scheme, any scheme, by which she could feel she was being useful, and decided that the next best thing to helping the dear, brave soldiers at the front, was to help their wives and destitute children at home.

So Isabel started a club, and called it the Whistle Club, because the members all carried tiny silver whistles. Then she changed her mind and decided to call it the Stella Club, in honour of the morning star—her star. And the Stella Club, comprising a number of other young ladies, got together and raised funds and busied themselves with helping the dependants of the Crimean warriors.

They started a soup-cauldron and a clothing collection, and took from the different barracks a list of the married women. Isabel went about ascertaining their true character and situations and told herself over and again that no difference must be made between them on account of religion.

Her own " beat " contained about a hundred women and some two hundred children. Here, she visited, wrote their letters for them, brought them clothes and titbits, and gave them much sound spiritual advice. " In many a soldier's home," she noted proudly in her diary, " my name is coupled with a blessing and a prayer." Then she adds : " Some people are a little hard on me for being the same to the fallen women as to the good ones. But those who are loudest in severity are generally the first to fall when temptation comes ; and who of us might not do so, but for God's grace . . . ! "

With the fall of Sevastopol, the Stella Club vanished, and Isabel became once more a young lady of leisure. A few weeks later, a solitary line in her diary shows the trend of her thoughts again.

" I hear that Richard has come home, and is in town. God be praised ! "

During the heat and languors of that summer of 1856, it became the custom of those society families unwillingly immured in London to catch a breath of fresh air and a sight of tropical greenery in the Botanical Gardens of Regent's Park. Here on any sultry morning between the hours of eleven and one o'clock were to be seen groups of young ladies escorted by mammas, tall-hatted young gentlemen, or the flare of military scarlet, pacing sedately beneath the rare trees, bending with studious assiduity and genteel cries of wonder over tropical plants, or sitting in the shade sketching, reading, and scribbling poetry.

Here, daily, during the hot weeks of that August came Isabel and her sister Blanche to walk and study, and it was here that Isabel's dreams were suddenly galvanized into reality. That Fate, she so firmly believed in, stepped in and magically waved its wand. Let her diary speak :—

§

" Miss Arundel, I believe ? "

Isabel and Blanche stopped. The blood flew from Isabel's cheeks. The voice was at her elbow.

" Don't say you've forgotten me. We met at Boulogne four years ago. Lieutenant Burton."

Yes, it was he. They turned to find him bowing and smiling from behind a black drooping moustache.

Remember him ! Isabel's heart beat suffocatingly while she spoke the conventional words of greeting. Her blue eyes searched his face timidly yet hungrily. Her hand trembled in his as he took it.

How he had changed ! While he spoke, with his eyes on Blanche, she examined him feature by feature. The hair was as black as ever and the jetty eyes as bright, but the suns of Mecca and Harar had burned and hardened his face. The lips, smiling conventionally beneath the heavy moustache, were fiercer, there were deeply scored lines about the eyes, the bones of his jaw stood out taut under the drawn skin, and upon his left cheek blazed a dreadful scar. She shuddered as she saw that long and jagged wound. That was where the Somal spear had gone in. Poor dear cheek! . . .

But he had turned and was chaffing her.

"Surely you won't chalk up 'Mother will be angry,' Miss Isabel?" he said, and Isabel noticed once again his curious laugh, soft and feline, bursting from between his shut teeth. His eyes were on hers. "Eyes that seem to look through you and beyond," as she had once called them.

In her confusion—it was strange that she, the cool, the self-possessed, should always behave like a schoolgirl in front of him—she dropped her book.

Burton stooped and picked it up. It was Disraeli's *Tancred*, the book of her heart. He asked her how she liked it and, when her wits and voice came back to her, she told him it was her favourite book. He begged permission to join them, and for an hour they paced the gravelled paths while he discoursed on Tancred the traveller and Tancred the man. Listening entranced to the slow drawl of his voice, Isabel mused on the strange twist of Fate that should have thrown a book and the living prototype of its hero together on her first meeting with him.

Isabel scarcely closed an eye that night. The next day she visited the Gardens again. This time she discovered Richard seated alone in the throes of a poem he was composing for Monckton Milnes. He got up with his soft, appraising laugh as she approached, and walked with her for a while, telling her something of his adventures and the plans he had for the future.

With the growing familiarity of contact, she began to lose something of her timidity. When he began to speak of Mecca, she caught him up, and for awhile discussed his exploit with a fluency of knowledge that intrigued him.

"Is it possible that you have read my book on the Pilgrimage?" he asked.

Her reply checked him momentarily in his stride.

"I have read every book you have written, Captain Burton."

He glanced at her with sudden interest, almost as if really aware of her for the first time.

"Not every one, surely, Miss Arundell? *Goa*, for instance, one of my earliest—and heaviest, I fear?"

" Yes, *Goa*," replied Isabel eagerly. " You should see my copy of *Goa*, Captain Burton. I have marked it on almost every page. And *Falconry in the Valley of the Indus, Vikram the Vampire*. . . . I treasure *Vikram* most. I used to read it over and over again at Boulogne. A wonderful book."

Richard's soft laugh thrilled her once more.

" The deuce, Miss Arundell ! I never knew I had a circle of young lady readers. I wonder at the courage of you. I aim at nothing purple in my writings. They are all facts. Facts, facts, facts, Miss Arundell. I love 'em. But you must read my *Kasidah*. I wrote it on my way home from Mecca. It's my declaration of Faith. I'm an agnostic, but if I lean at all, it's towards the Sufi'ism of the Moslems. Yet I hate learning. If a man's a man, he can stand upright and alone. It's different for a woman." He grinned at her with a sidelong glance. She knew he was speaking wickedly, but she could not help returning that smile. Then he said :

" But it is not all philosophy. There are some pictures in it, living pictures if I may say so. I composed 'em actually in the desert."

He began to quote gently :

" The hour is nigh, the Waning Queen walks forth to rule the later night ;
Crowned with the sparkle of a Star, and throned on orb of ashen light.
The horses neigh, the camels groan, the torches gleam, the cressets flare;
The town of canvas falls, and man with din and dint invadeth air ;
Slowly they wind athwart the wild, and while young Day his anthem swells
Sad falls upon my yearning ear the tinkling of the Camel-bells . . ."

He shook his head.

" Ah, those camel-bells, Miss Arundell. Once heard, you can never forget them."

He glanced down again at the pale face under the bonnet beside him, and found the blue eyes meeting his resolutely, almost ardently.

" I would I were a man, Captain Burton, that I might have done such things as you have."

His black eyes slowly and boldly appraised her upturned face.

" I'll wager there's not a man would second you, Miss Arundell. No, not a man ! "

She flushed and lowered her face while her heart beat loudly enough it seemed for him to hear it. Quickly she changed the subject and questioned him on his next project, her voice hurrying on as if to conceal her perturbation.

He replied to her questions with the enthusiasm of a man only too eager to discuss the subject nearest his heart. And on a seat under the trees he told her something of the great new expedition he was even then concerting to explore the Lake Regions of Central Africa. He told her of his hopes, of his plans, and something of the difficulties that awaited him in this most important expedition of his life.

" Intertropical Africa, Miss Arundell. A place of mystery and legend. The Veil of Isis. The very sources of the great Nile."

The Veil of Isis ! The poetic phrase caught her imagination. She glanced up at him to see his fathomless eyes ablaze with some inner light of their own, looking way beyond her at some goal visible only to his imagination.

" A hazardous expedition, Captain Burton."

" Aye, hazardous enough," he replied. " If half the stories the coast Arabs tell us, the interior is a dark and desperate place. It was too hazardous for poor Lieutenant Maizan, the only white man who has ever tried to enter."

" He turned back ? "

His lips curled in a mirthless smile.

" At Dege la Mhora the Wakamba caught him. They tied his hands and feet to a bamboo pole and slowly cut him in pieces during one long day. A gallant Frenchman and a barbarous piece of work. Inshallah, they'll find Dick Burton a tougher nut to crack."

She was shuddering with horror. The terse sentences had drawn for her a picture of poor Maizan too awful to contemplate. She saw the bamboo pole, the swaying helpless figure . . . and that helpless figure might be the man at her side. Even as he bent and began to draw a sketch upon a piece of paper on his knee, she sent up a little prayer to Heaven, a private, intimate prayer, straight from the heart : " God preserve him and keep him ! "

On a slip of paper he was drawing for her a rough map of Africa with the interior as he expected to find it.

" Not one big lake, one inland sea, as the ignorant native and Arab say, or as those dunderheads, Krapf and Rebman, believe, but a chain. A chain of linked lakes, and this big lake, Tanganyika. I am convinced it is the source of the Nile."

She took the map in her fingers and bent over it. But she did not see it.

" And you are leaving ? "

" In October, with Lieutenant Speke—Jack Speke who was with me at Berberah."

" Oh, I pray you will be successful and will return safely."

" Thank you, Miss Arundell. I will remember your prayer."

Isabel parted from him before her emotions became insupportable. When she got home, she wrote : " My mind is full of wonder and presentiment. I feel frightened and agitated . . ."

§

A fortnight later, in a secluded spot in the gardens, Richard led Isabel to a seat, slipped an arm about her and, rubbing his cheek on hers, said gently :

" I love you, Isabel. Could you do anything so sickly as to give up civilization ? And if I can get the Consulate of Damascus, will you marry me and go and live there ? Don't answer me now, because it will mean a very serious step for you—no less than giving up your people and living the sort of life that Lady Hester Stanhope led. Think it over and tell me when I come home from Africa, three years hence."

Isabel was long silent with emotion. It was, she thought (and wrote afterwards), just as if the moon had tumbled down and said, " You have cried for me so long that I have come." When at length she found her voice, she whispered :

" I do not want to think it over. I have been thinking it over for six years, ever since I first saw you at Boulogne. Oh, Richard, I have prayed for you every morning and night. My prayers followed you unknown to Mecca and to Harar. I would rather have a tent and a crust with you than be queen of all the world. And so I say now : ' Yes, *Yes*, YES ! ' "

His arm tightened about her, with his other hand he tilted her lowered chin. Then he swept her up into all the terror and ecstasy of her first kiss.

With his mouth against her cheek, he murmured :

" Your people will not give you to me. I am considered a bad lot, a mocker without religion, and even worse things. I am no match for a pure young girl like you."

" I belong to myself," whispered Isabel. " *I* give myself away. I love you, Richard." And she turned on him all the glory of her dark blue eyes.

She rushed home, and falling on her knees before the little shrine in her bedroom poured out her soul in wonder and happiness. Then, to her diary she confided : " I would have suffered six more years for such a day, such a moment as this. All past sorrow was forgotten in it. All that has been written or said on the subject of the first kiss is trash compared to the reality. Men might as well undertake to describe Eternity." Then in a burst of reaction. " Providence and Fate must decide my future. I feel all my own weakness and nothingness. I am as humble as a little child. Richard has the upper hand now, and I feel that I have at last met the master who can subdue me. The load of shame, wounded pride, and unrequited affection is lifted from my brow and soul. He loves me—that is enough to-day."

§

It was about as strange a love-match as could possibly be conceived. Here was a man of violence and unbelief, a man who looked on women as primarily instruments of pleasure, whose *affaires* were notorious and none too savoury and whose whole sexual logic was bound up in the exotic polygamous tenets of the East he knew so well allying himself to a virtuous, young Catholic girl, whose faith, greater almost than her love, coloured her whole life. Here was a man whose estate was trifling, his pay less, his life in continual jeopardy in distant places, and his hopes of financial stability, at least for some years, non-existent, offering himself to a partner of delicate upbringing, accustomed to the comforts of comparative wealth and security.

Was ever such a strange union conceived ?

What was this invisible yet very powerful bond which had drawn them together, springing apparently from nothing mutual in circumstance or outlook ? On Isabel's part it seems perhaps more clear. Richard wielded over her that strange magnetism which so many had felt and most had found distasteful. It was a power of which she was quite aware and which worried while it stirred her.

" Whatever the world may condemn in him of lawless actions or strong opinions, whatever he is to the world ; he is perfect to me," says the diary. " I would not have him otherwise than he is—except in spiritual matters. This last point troubles me. When I am in his presence, I am not myself—he makes me for the time see things with his own eyes, like a fever or a momentary madness ; and when I am alone again, I recall my own unbelief and ways of thinking, which remain unchanged, and am frightened by my weak wavering and his dangerous but irresistible society . . . I have no right to love a man who calls himself a complete materialist, who professes to acknowledge no God, no law, human or divine. And yet I love him purely, passionately, and devotedly ; there is no void in my heart ; it is at rest for ever with him . . ."

She loved him, she believed in him, her Catholic training had taught her how to shut her eyes to what she ought not to see—and she had ambition. Ambition, indeed, is perhaps another answer to the question of what bound them together. " I worship ambition," confesses Isabel, and adds, " it is infamous the way half the world live and die and are never missed . . ." Of Richard she writes : " I know his hobby is reputation."

It did not seem to occur to her that that same vain pomp might be the source of his affection for her ; that in her and her powerful family connections he saw a possible string to those aloof and disapproving " powers that be." Indeed a misguided ambition seems to be the only logical explanation of Richard's side of the affair. Marriage without money would be the last thing of value to him at that stage of his career. What was there in Isabel beyond " beauty and affection," those two virtues that were all he asked of women, to differentiate her from any of the numerous women he had chased to bed without ever a thought of marriage. More witty, more beautiful women, he must have met many. Then why should he have chosen Isabel ?

§

For the present, until Richard returned from Africa, three years hence, the engagement was kept a secret. For three more years, except to her most intimate friends, Isabel would have to nurse her love in silence.

Burton called at the Arundell house, where he was received on the footing of a casual Boulogne acquaintance. Mrs. Arundell took a natural dislike to him, but her husband, like Isabel, fell completely under his curious spell. " I don't know what it is about that man," he told a friend, " but I cannot get him out of my head ; I dream about him every night."

For a few weeks Isabel trod on air. Daily, in the moments he could spare from his work, she met her Richard ; daily she swore undying affection, talked of the time when they would be in the desert together, under one tent, with one crust between them, and nightly on her knees she poured forth her thanks before her little shrine and filled pages and pages of her diary.

If constant prayer and intercession could help the Central African Expedition, then constant prayer was theirs, and as earnest of her good wishes she presented Richard with a medal of the Blessed Virgin and insisted on his wearing it as a protection against the savages.

" Take away the gold chain," was his reply. " They will cut my throat for it out there."

In return, he gave her a little poem (copies of which he had already distributed, *sub rosa*, to several other women friends) and which she put in a bag and hung over her bosom.

> I wore thine image, Fame,
> Within a heart well fit to be thy shrine !
> Others a thousand boons may gain,
>   One wish was mine—
>
> And now I see a glorious hand
> Beckon me out of dark despair,
> Hear a glorious voice command,
>   " Up, bravely dare."
>
> She pointed to a grisly land,
> Where all breathes death—earth, sea, and air !
> Her glorious accents sound once more :
>   " Go, meet me there ! "
>
> Mine ear will hear no other sound,
> No other thought my heart will know.
> Is this a sin ? " Oh pardon, Lord !
>   Thou mad'st me so."

September 1856.   R. F. B.

As the fateful day of Richard's departure drew near, Isabel steeled herself to bear it. Her part was doubly difficult as she could only see Richard clandestinely and must treat him as a casual guest before her family.

On 3rd October they met as usual and arranged to see one another the following day. Richard seemed unusually tender.

The same afternoon he paid a formal call on Mrs. Arundell at Montagu Street. Isabel was going that evening to see *Pizarro* at the theatre, and she begged him to accompany them. He replied that he would be there if pressure of work would permit it. He appeared strangely agitated and rose to take his departure after only staying an hour. As he left, Isabel remembering, the tryst of the following day, called after him jokingly, " I hope we shall see you on your return from Africa." Then she ran out on to the balcony and surreptitiously blew him a kiss.

That evening she sobbed all through *Pizarro* at the miseries of Cora. Richard never appeared. She returned to bed feeling strangely restless and uneasy. In the early hours of the morning she dreamed that Richard entered her room, bent over her, and gave her a cold farewell kiss.

She sprang out of bed and ran screaming to a brother's room, where, flinging herself on the floor, she cried : " Richard is gone ! I know it ! I know it ! I saw him in a dream ! "

The rest of the night she spent betwixt sobbing and dozing in an armchair. The morning post brought confirmation of her fears. In a letter to her sister, covering one enclosed to herself, he told her of his secret departure.

As usual, unable to say good-bye, he had left London the previous evening and embarked from Southampton at two o'clock in the morning. He begged her forgiveness, and swore that they would meet again in 1859.

Isabel took his letter up to the privacy of her room and abandoned herself to sorrow, retiring to her bed for three days. She forgave him for leaving her so abruptly, but wished that her last memory of him could have been less formal. To her diary she cried :

" I beg from God morning and night that Richard may return safe. Will the Almighty grant my prayer ? But I will not doubt, whether I hear from him or not."

And later : " I have been trying to make out when it is midnight in East Africa, and when the morning star shines there, and I have made out that at 10 p.m. it is midnight there, and the morning star shines on him two hours before it does on me.

" God rest him and keep him in those perilous places ! "

She had three years to wait. But was that too long to a woman who would have to prepare herself to live an adventurous life ? She would have much to do.

When she was on her feet again she forgot her sorrow in a multitude of occupations. She began to study Arabic, she read many books of travel, tried her hand at cooking, and had lessons in fencing.

To a friend coming upon her in the midst of her leaping and parrying with as much speed as a crinoline would permit, she replied with sublime simplicity :

" Why ? To defend Richard when he and I are attacked in the wilderness together."

Isabel was nothing if not thorough.

Chapter Six

To explore the unknown regions of central Africa ; to discover the very source of the Nile. What an undertaking ; what an achievement ; and how much a problem after Richard Burton's own heart.

Since Ptolemy first fired the imagination of the western world in A.D. 150 with the postulation that two giant lakes, buried in central Africa among the fabled Mountains of the Moon, gave birth to the great river, geographers had speculated upon and explorers attempted to solve this age-long mystery.

Yet up to 1850 the mystery was almost as deep as ever. Travellers had penetrated south-eastwards along the Blue Nile to its source in Lake Tana, and the White Nile had been traced southwards from Khartoum to Bahr el Ghazal and some short distance up the tributaries. But beyond that point the maps were silent ; a vast unknown country peopled with legend lay farther south. The dark womb of the Nile stream remained as deep an enigma as ever.

In 1855, however, the first few gleams of light began to penetrate the darkness from the south-east. Two German missionaries, Krapf and Rebman, who conducted a primitive mission station near Mombasa, startled the geographical world by publishing a map based on reports received over a considerable period from natives and Arab traders who had penetrated the interior. From these reports, they had placed, inland some 1000 miles from the coast, a vast inland sea, as large as the Caspian, and shaped like a great leech or slug. This they stated was called by the Arabs the Sea of Ujiji, and by the natives the Lake of Umyamvezi (or Lake of the Moon Mountains) ; and this they placed in their map as the possible true source of the Nile.

Nor was this all. The very Mountains of the Moon themselves began to emerge from the mist of legend into solid fact. For, pushing inland in 1848, Rebman had looked out one morning from a rise in the matted jungle to see far on the western horizon a great peak rearing its head in the sky, its base skirted in mist, its slopes shimmering in snow. He got no nearer, but a year later Krapf, pushing farther, not only confirmed Rebman's discovery, but caught a glimpse of a further giant (Kenya) towering in the centre of a low range. " Snow on the Equator ! " wrote Rebman. Æschylus had spoken of " Snows where Nile is born." Were these the fabulous Moon Mountains, and did their snows feed the Nile ?

The problem remained unanswered for several years. In England the publication of Rebman's map was received mostly with derision. Paris was more broadminded and presented the industrious Germans with a gold medal. Lieutenant Maizan made a solitary attempt to follow in their footsteps and was murdered before he had travelled more than a few miles. And at this point in 1856 central African exploration had come to a standstill.

§

But if English travellers and geographers were in the main sceptical about giant lakes and snow-covered mountains on the equator, Burton was not among them. He had pondered long on the Nile mystery and that vast blank space on African maps. And a study of such diverse writers as Herodotus, Pliny, Bruce, Sonnini, and Lacerda, together with the modern travellers Rebman, Krapf, and Ehrhardt, had led him to a definite theory that a vast lacustrine system must be the source of the Nile ; and he was convinced that an expedition striking inland from Mombasa or Zanzibar would have every hope of success in finally clearing up the mystery.

Once again, on his return from an abortive period of service at the base in the Crimea, he put himself in touch with the R.G.S., and with the assistance of the influential old explorer, Admiral Back, received their sanction for an expedition and a grant to the extent of £1000.

He next enlisted the services of Lieutenant John Hanning Speke, the Indian officer who had been wounded with him at Berberah. His choice of Speke was based on two reasons—the young man was a brilliant surveyor and botanist, both qualifications which Burton lacked, and, secondly, Speke had lost at Berberah upwards of £500 of personal property, and his leader, who felt partly responsible, realized that some recompense should be made for the loss. A third companion was arranged for, Doctor Steinhauser, M.O. for Aden, and a personal friend of Burton's. He was to have accompanied the expedition in his official capacity, a fact which might have saved much of the subsequent tragedy and bitterness, but at the last moment sickness prevented him, and Burton and Speke had to go alone.

In October 1856 the two men embarked at Southampton for Bombay, where they both had to report before permission from the Company for a proper furlough could be received. There, Burton's friend, Lord Elphinstone, came to their assistance. He procured for them a two years' furlough, and a naval sloop which, knowing the impression it would be sure to make on oriental minds, he provided specially to take the explorers to Zanzibar.

Burton's orders from the R.G.S. were briefly : " The great object of the expedition is to penetrate inland from some place on the east coast and make the best of your way to the reputed great lake in the interior . . ." Thence he was to continue at his own discretion.

§

On 19th December 1856, with a salute of guns, they swung into Zanzibar harbour and disembarked. They found the Arab city, then flourishing under the rule of the Sultan Sayyid Mahid, to be a small and stinking place, crammed with slaves and ivory, and a hotbed of intrigue between Europeans, Americans, and Indians. Assisted, however, by the British Consul, Colonel Hamerton, they established themselves in comfortable quarters, called upon the Sultan and were favourably received, and began to lay plans for the expedition.

Unfortunately they had reached the East African coast at the wrong season for interior travel and they were strongly advised to defer their expedition until the wet season had set in, and to utilize the interval in the three months' coastal trip to examine the coast towns and receive their " seasoning " of fever.

Burton determined, therefore, to proceed up the coast to Mombasa and call upon Rebman, the last member of the famous Mombasa mission. He called this trip a " preliminary canter " and hoped that during it they would both receive those doses of seasoning fever which had to be suffered before acclimatization could begin.

In this expectation he was more than rewarded. After a run, via Pemba Island, to Mombasa and a visit to Rebman who, with his gallant wife, lived some fifteen miles in the interior, they continued up-coast to Pangani, whence they made a brief excursion inland to the forbidden territory of Fuga, and followed this by a hippopotamus shooting trip up the Pangani River. Returning from the latter they were stricken with so terrible a bout of fever that, when the Zanzibar boat came to fetch them, Burton was completely helpless and had to be carried, semi-conscious, on board, while Speke staggered along the quay, supported under both arms, with a face the colour of a guinea.

The succeeding four months at Zanzibar were spent pre-paring for the expedition, obtaining passports from the Sultan and letters of marque to Arab trading-stations in the interior, engaging an escort, leaders, and guide, arranging for porters, and purchasing not only provisions and tackle but the vast quantities of beads, iron rings, wire, and cloth, the only currency in the interior, which would have to be carried with them.

No small hindrance was placed in their way by the attitude of the Arab traders. These, fearful that the expedition was an attack on their trade territories, intrigued with might and main to prevent the departure. They preyed upon the credulous minds of the escort with hideous stories of the interior, offered shoddy goods to the expedition at exorbitant rates, and worst of all, tried to make a " corner " in native porters to prevent the expedition from hiring any, with such success that, on landing at the mainland, out of some two hundred men necessary for the journey only a paltry thirty-six could be obtained.

Owing to the diplomacy and firmness of the British Consul, however, all serious obstacles were smoothed away, an escort from the Sultan's private army was hired, and a corvette, the 18 gun Artemise, put at their disposal for transport to the mainland.

The escort consisted of eight Beloch mercenaries and a caravan leader, a half-cast Arab named Said bin Salim, who, sorely against his will, was impressed by the Sultan into service. He was soon to show his quality. Two negro gun carriers accompanied the party, Sidi Bombay and Sidi Mabruki, and two Goanese personal servants from Bombay.

Accompanied by a rascally Banyan named Ramji, Said bin Salim preceded the party to the mainland with instructions to obtain 170 porters. He succeeded in obtaining only thirty-six. The consequence was that when the expedition arrived at Kaole, the starting-point, on 17th June 1857, most of the heavy baggage, including an iron boat in sections for lake navigation, had to be left behind.

Difficulties began almost from the moment they set foot on the shore. First, the Beloch escort and their Jemadar, or leader, had no sooner landed than they were set upon by their compatriots, who, determined to save them, terrified them half out of their wits by more stories of the horrors of the interior.

One man, who had been to Umyamwezi, or said he had, declared that nothing short of 100 guards, 150 guns, and several cannon would enable them to overcome the perils of the interior, which included cannibals who killed their victims by staking them head downwards over ants' nests, the fierce Wagago tribe who practised mutilations, pygmies who shot poisoned arrows out of trees, rhinoceros which slew 100 men at a charge, herds of elephants, and voracious hyenas.

" And who is he (Burton) that he should reach Ugogo ? " was the general question.

Burton managed to quiet the cravens by hiring a further five Beloch soldiers and ten armed slaves furnished by Ramji at exorbitant rates. He also engaged a medicine-man and bribed him to cast a fair augury for the expedition.

Their route lay along the tiny, winding caravan road, of which they knew nothing except the names of the principal stopping-places ; and they were armed with three letters of introduction to Arabs, both particular and general, in the interior. Burton further carried round his neck an *etui* which contained his diploma from the Sheikh of Mecca and a bag of dried chestnuts which, for some superstitious reason, he always wore on his person.[1] He also carried, as a further insurance, Isabel's medal of the Blessed Virgin.

§

Armed spiritually at all points, but otherwise terribly undermanned, the first British Central African Expedition, after innumerable delays, false starts, and halts, left Bomani for the interior on 1st July 1857.

Its departure had little of the romance usually associated with such ceremonies. Certainly a party of Beloch came to see them off and fire a prodigious salute which set the thirty donkeys kicking madly ; but Burton and Speke were far too occupied in flogging, cajoling, wheedling, and ordering the sulky

[1] It was found in one of his pockets after his death.

Beloch escort, malingering slaves, and lazy porters into moving themselves at all to have any historical reflections. Speke, with his pale, arrogant face, bright golden hair and beard, rode in the van on a donkey, while Burton, dark almost as the Arabs themselves, took up the rear. The Beloch were posted two to a donkey, one to drive, the other to lead, and Ramji's armed slaves, or his " sons " as he ambiguously called them, took up the centre round the three score porters. A blood-red Moham- medan flag flew in the van, the Union Jack in the rear, and the whole caravan, appallingly unequipped as both travellers were to find to their cost,[1] struck westwards along the track to the accompaniment of the monotonous thumping of a drum, the howls and screams of well and ill wishers, the yells of prancing witch-doctors, and the thunderous discharge of matchlocks.

They were soon plunging knee deep through stinking swamps matted with mangroves roots thickly clustered with huge fresh-water oysters, and broken with higher levels of red sand, on a route running parallel with the eastern bank of the Kingani river. The road was a mere straggling path, passing now through thick patches of razor-edged grass or tangled jungle, now through plains broken here and there with rest huts and fetish cairns built of skulls and bones.

They were soon in the dangerous Uzaramo country, and at their first halt at Nzasa they were approached by three headmen from local villages, asking if the white men's journey was peaceful or one of revenge for the murder of Lieutenant Maizan. On being given a small tribute and told that the mission was a peaceable one, a huge war drum that stood ominously in the centre of the village was removed and a ceremonious dance by native women took its place. But already the Beloch escort was quaking and Burton began to eye them askance.

He had a further taste of their quality the following day when, half-way between Nzasa and Kiranga Ranga, the second stage, a loud bellowing and feverish agitation in the van brought the whole caravan to an abrupt halt and set the Beloch blowing furiously on their matches and yelling for priming powder. Send- ing a messenger forward, Burton learned that the cause of the trouble was a line of Wazaramo [2] spearmen thrown across the

[1] Burton had £1000 for this expedition. Twenty years later Stanley on the same route found £20,000 scarcely enough.
[2] For convenience it should be explained that, in the Swahili tongue, the name for a region, a tribe, and an individual is indicated by a different prefix. Thus Uzaramo—the district ; Wazaramo—the tribe ; Mzaramo—the man.

road, who were demanding *honga* (tribute) on pain of death.
Speke, through the medium of Bombay, his gun carrier, was
haranguing them and the fierce-eyed, chicken-hearted Beloch,
who could have blown them out of existence with one volley,
were looking furtively for avenues of escape while outwardly
making preparations for a valorous defence. On Burton's
party coming into view, the Wazaramo wavered, then stood
aside to watch them pass, a proceeding which sent Beloch
bloodthirstiness up to boiling-point and led them to boast that
at a word they would take the country and make Burton a
Sultan.

During the first week, crawling slowly along from station
to station, their nights were cheered by the distant thunder of
the *Artemise's* evening gun which was carried clearly across the
miles of jungle. For a while it lingered with them, a reminder
of the civilization they were fast leaving behind ; then it
ceased altogether. But as they struck deeper into the unknown country, a new sound grew out of the west, a throbbing,
impatient drumming, often coming from three directions at
once. The naked porters heard it and muttered to one
another, rolling their eyes ; the Beloch swore and fumbled
with their matchlocks ; the white men listened curiously. For
days and nights it continued until they reached the safer
district of Khutu. It was the signal drums of the Wazaramo
constantly noting the movements of the white men entering
their country.

By now they had fallen into the proper routine of an East
African caravan and day succeeded day with monotonous
regularity. At 5 a.m. the camp would be roused from sleep,
prayers said, and breakfast consumed. An hour later Burton
and Speke would commence the hardest task of the day—getting
anybody to move. Porters crouched over the fires bathing their
faces luxuriously in smoke, the Beloch would be singing spiritual
songs and gobbling roast mutton, the " sons " of Ramji would
still be snoring loudly. For over an hour the usual wheedling,
cajoling, and beating would go on until at last some semblance
of a move was being made. Shouts would now begin to fill the
air :

" Kwecha ! Pakia ! Pakia ! Hopa ! Hopa ! Collect pack !
Set out ! Safari ! Safari leo ! A journey, a journey to-day ! "
would be accompanied by bellows of laughter from the porters
and cries of : " I am an ass ! I am a camel ! " Horns would

bray, bells jangle, drums beat, men shout, whistle, and sing, and gradually in twos and threes the long straggling line would assemble.

Followed a long pause while deserters were counted and their packs laden on to any who could be intimidated or bribed into carrying them. As usual in Africa, the strongest carried least while the weak staggered along with double loads : the Beloch refusing to carry anything and even the " sons " of Ramji only a small personal parcel each.

When all was ready, the guide raised his blood-red, tattered flag and took the van where, followed by a stark-naked man beating a kettledrum, he marched forward in all the dignity of scarlet broadcloth, monkey-skin head-dress, flaunting a bunch of crane feathers, and insignia of his office—a fly-flapper made of leopard tails. Behind him would pour the unruly mob of porters, each coal-black and stark-naked except for a girdle of goat-skin. From the buttocks of each protruded a wooden three-legged stool, strapped there for use in damp weather, and in their greasy mops of hair waved bunches of crane, jay, or ostrich feathers. Armed with spears, bows, and knobkerries and balancing their big loads of cloth and beads on their heads, they moved in fits and starts along the jungle trail, the myriads of little bells attached to their arms and legs sending up a perpetual tinkling.

Next, supposedly guarding them, but in reality loafing, deserting, or squabbling, came the " sons " of Ramji, armed with cumbrous Tower muskets and dressed in strips of rag ; marching, braying loudly on kudu horns to lend an exaggerated impression of the size of the caravan to any intending plunderers. Behind them again came the Beloch, led by the Jemadar and overlooked by Said. Clad in tattered white which threw into strong relief their bearded half-caste faces, they would ramble along in a body, ready to start at the wagging of a straw, each attended by a personal slave and some women camp-followers. Each was armed with a matchlock and his body hung with a profusion of powder-horns, smoking-matches, balls, and wadding. Each would make the slightest glimpse of a sparrow or hedgehog an excuse to blaze away in a cloud of smoke ; and each almost invariably missed.

The white men either walked, rode on asses, or, when overcome with fever, were carried slung in hammocks, each attended by a gun carrier and a Goanese boy.

The march was attended by a constant uproar, which increased in volume on entering a village. Here some bellow : "Hopa ! Hopa ! Go on ! Go on ! " Others : "Mgogolo ! A halt ! " Others again : "Food ! Food ! Don't be tired ! The kraal is here ! Oh, we see our mothers ! " while others imitated the sounds of birds and animals to attract admiration.

As night falls, after innumerable rests during the day, they halt, build fires and cook, and only when they have secured the best places for themselves and fed comfortably do they think about the comfort of their white employers. At length, as the moon rises and throws a light over the whole jungle scene, they crouch round the fires, listening to the jungle sounds—the yell of the baboon, the scream of the leopard, the roar of the lion, or the cough of the hippo—and crying out the name of each in turn, until some jungle cry more eerie than the rest sets them shouting "Ghosts ! " and crouching closer to the flames . . . while in their tent the white men write their notes, or try to snatch a little sleep.

§

On 5th July, the caravan reached the malarious plain of the Kingani River, known by the Arabs as " The Valley of Death and Home of Hunger." Fever now began to attack the two men, and Speke for a while could scarcely sit his donkey. One of the " sons " of Ramji attempted to desert, but was brought back by the muzzle of a gun, and the whole party plunged into a dense tangle of bush and thorns, whence, lashed with bitter rain and wind, they began a descent into the dark, malodorous bottom. That night they slept intermittently in a hollow and woke to a morning of such misery with rain, wind, and miasmatic mists that fresh attempts at desertion continued all through the day.

Leaving Sagesera, they marched on over a low plain, both the Europeans now heavily stricken with fever and barely able to attend to their own wants, let alone superintend the caravan. At a trunk road, where several caravan routes met, they were halted and thrown into confusion again by a company of haughty Wazaramo who barred the way armed with bows and arrows upon which the poison was still wet. In spite of loud threats and prodigious, empty preparations by the Beloch, they coolly stood their ground until paid *honga*, when they vanished into the bush to signal by drums to chiefs farther along the route.

Troubles came thick and fast. Said went down first with fever, slaves ran away and had to be followed, the Beloch grumbled and wanted to turn back, and Burton, carelessly sleeping in a damp place, arose to find himself seriously ill.

" I arose weak and depressed, with aching head, burning eyes, and throbbing extremities. The new life, the alternations of damp, heat, and wet cold, the useless fatigue of walking, the exposure to sun and dew, and, last but not least of morbific influences, the wear and tear of mind at the prospect of imminent failure, all were beginning to tell heavily on me."

They were now approaching the ill-famed village of Dege la Mhora, where, eleven years previously, Maizan the Frenchman had been tortured to death by the Wazaramo. Burton, knowing the native mind, was determined to make a halt at this village to show that his caravan had no fear ; for to show fear would be to invite trouble. Said and the Kirangozi, however, to whom fear was as natural and constant as any other emotion, protested vigorously, and, on being defied, tried every device they could think of to dissuade their leader. They suggested that the village should be hurried through at dawn before the inhabitants were awake and, on this failing, they next halted at a small village some distance from the place of terror, declared loudly that it was Dege la Mhora, and were only exposed when Burton, whose knowledge of the Wazaramo tongue was growing daily, questioned the headman.

They reached Dege la Mhora to find war drums thumping, the village cleared of women, and a double line of archers and spearmen waiting in ambush, ready to fill the air with poisoned arrows at the cocking of a matchlock. The trembling Said called an instant halt and, when the headman came stalking forward to inquire if it be peace or war, clung to Burton like a woman. On learning it was peace, however, the headman dismissed his guard, called off his ambush, and benignly accompanied the caravan to its next stage, while a troop of his spearmen secretly dogged every foot of their passage. With this unpleasant and invisible escort, they marched hurriedly to the banks of the Mgeta River, the boundary line between Uzaramo and Khutu, which they crossed with such haste that a gun carrier dropped Burton's double-barrelled elephant-gun in the deepest and most irreclaimable part of the river.

In safer regions now they pushed on towards the highlands of Duthumi, a long, plum-coloured range of hills, spreading along the western horizon. Fighting their way through leopard-infested jungle, swamp, river, and plain, weakening daily from poor diet and constant attacks of fever, they reached Duthumi only to collapse helpless and lie prostrated for a week with fever.

For three days Burton tossed on a vermin-infested pallet, in a wild delirium which obsessed him with the idea that he was two persons, each opposing and thwarting one another. During the hot, tortured nights he was surrounded by ghastly visions, hag-like men and women with heads protruding from their breasts, serpents oozing in slime, and horrific animals. Speke, even worse, had a fainting-fit strongly resembling sun-stroke, which seemed permanently to affect his brain.

For a week both men were incapable and, when they recovered sufficiently, Burton was aware of a change in his companion. Speke had lost the alacrity of a subordinate, he grumbled frequently and complained of neglect, and he sat brooding over grievances to which he would not give tongue. For long the seeds of dislike and envy must have lain dormant in him ; now the miasma of African fever was helping them to blossom into the hatred that was to warp both their lives, damage Burton's career, and send Speke to what was probably a suicide's grave.

But that was not yet. Meanwhile both men pulled themselves together and, staggering weakly, reorganized the caravan, sent messengers back to Kaole with reports and a brief account of their progress for the R.G.S., also an urgent request for medical stores and accessories, many of which seem to have been overlooked.

On 24th July, feeling strong enough to advance, and aided by some fresh slaves hired from a passing Arab trader, they struck once more along the trail, and plunged into a country of singular desolation and ugliness.

" Crossing a steep and muddy bed, knee-deep even in the dry season, we entered fields under the outlying hillocks of the highlands. These low cones are not inhabited ; they are even more malarious than the plains, and the woodage extends from base to summit. Beyond the cultivation, the route plunges into a jungle, where the European traveller realizes every preconceived idea of Africa's aspect ; at once hideous and grotesque. The general appearance is a mingling of bush and forest, which, contracting the horizon to a few yards, is equally monotonous to the eye and palling to the imagination. The

black, greasy ground, veiled with thick shrubbery, supports
in the more open spaces screens of tiger and spear grass, twelve
and thirteen feet high, with every blade a finger's breadth. The
footpaths are crossed by lianas, creepers, and climbers, thick
as coir cables, frequently crossing one another like network.
The earth, ever rain-drenched, emits the odour of sulphuretted
hydrogen, and in some parts the traveller might fancy a corpse
to be hidden behind every bush. To this sad picture of miasma,
the firmament is a fitting frame : a wild sky, whose heavy,
purple nimbi chased by chilling gusts, dissolve in large-dropped
showers ; or a dull, dark grey expanse, which lies like a pall
over the world. In the finer weather the atmosphere is pale
and sickly ; its mists and vapours seem to concentrate the rays
of the oppressive ' rain sun.' The sensation experienced at once
explains the apathy and indolence, the physical debility, and
the mental prostration that are the gifts of climates which moist
heat and damp cold render equally unsalubrious and uncomfortable. That no feature of miasma might be wanting to
complete the picture, filthy heaps of the rudest hovels, built
in holes in the jungle, sheltered their few miserable inhabitants,
whose frames are lean with constant intoxication, and whose
limbs, distorted by ulcerous sores, attest the hostility of Nature
to mankind.

"Such a revolting scene is East Africa from Central Khutu
to the base of the Usagara mountains." [1]

On 25th July, having crossed this terrible region as quickly
as possible, they reeled into Zungomero, the principal town of
the eastern regions, a great slave mart, and centre of traffic.
They had taken four weeks on the journey from the coast—
almost double the usual time, and thirty-six Wanyamwezi
porters, who had prudently preceded them from Kaole, so as
not to travel in the dangerous company of white men, and were
waiting, had almost given up hope of seeing them, now rushed
forward with yells of delight to indulge in a wild dance of
greeting.

§

Zungomero, lying in the path of the up and down caravans,
was crowded with Arabs and slaves carrying ivory from the
interior. Low mud Arab huts sprawled about its streets among

---

[1] *The Lake Regions of Central Africa* (Clowes 1860). All subsequent quotations, in this section, are from this book.

the clustering native hovels, with here and there a long ware-house belonging to the traders. It was built on a large plain of black earth, shadowed on three sides by towering hills, and so damp and miasmatic as to be excessively dangerous to health. The demoralized natives lived almost entirely on intoxicating grain beer, and were fat, ulcerous, and lazy. The *Cannabis indica* plant grew with profusion and the peculiar screaming cough of the *bhang* addicts was heard everywhere.

Slave caravans, huddled in the great central square, were a piteous sight, causing even the hardened Europeans to wince. Long strings of naked, diseased, and starving natives—men, women, and children—were yoked neck to neck with heavy poles, and driven by whips wielded ruthlessly by half-caste overseers. Captured in remote villages in the interior, or sold by starving parents, they were being hastened to the coast for sale. Scores would die *en route*, many from smallpox, more from starvation and flogging, the most from the spears of the overseers, whose custom it was to establish no precedent by leaving a living slave behind; lameness, sickness, childbirth, a single slip and fall by the wayside—all being settled by the spear, even the babe in arms being speared and thrown away so that the mother could carry more ivory.

All night long the surrounding country was full of the shrieks, explosions, and lurid flames of local raids, where the debased Wakhutu race set one village upon the other and sold their captives to the passing caravans.

In Zungomero, the drunkenness, drugs, and licentiousness of the natives drove the Beloch to extremes. They disgraced themselves by raping some women, stealing poultry, and quarrelling violently with the slaves. Thoroughly disgusted, Burton nearly dispatched them home. But he remembered that though useless as guards, being cowardly, treacherous, and erratic, they had a value, psychological, if not real, among the tribes of the further interior. They must be borne with as best could be for the sake of the expedition.

Five fresh porters were now engaged, bringing the complement of the caravan up to 132 souls and the Jemadar, who had squandered his advance pay in Zanzibar upon the purchase of a boy slave for amorous dalliance on the march, found that custom had staled, and now exchanged him for a girl slave amid an uproar of laughter and the innuendoes of his friends.

§

The vapours of Zungomero soon stirred the fever already circulating in the travellers' blood, and they hastened to leave the unhealthy spot before they succumbed.

So feeble that they could scarcely sit their donkeys, almost completely deaf, and with oscillating vision, they started off on the second stage of the journey on the 7th of August 1857, and for five hours struck across the black plain towards the looming range of the Usagara mountains. A scene of incredible desolation lay all round them. For miles the country had been raided, the inhabitants dragged into slavery, and villages razed to the ground. Nothing now remained but a few stinking corpses, the blackened ruins of huts, and hordes of great vultures.

About noon they reached the foothills and began to climb out of the damps, vapours, and miasmas of the maritime plain. Spirits rose automatically with the invigorating mountain air, and almost hourly the travellers felt fresh life flowing through their veins.

In spite of constant bickering between the Beloch and the " sons " of Ramji, good progress was made upwards. But they were not to be spared trouble long. A new horror now appeared in the shape of slave caravans, hurrying coastwards, stricken by smallpox. As these approached with their long lines of yoked slaves and flogging overseers, the travellers were appalled to see : " men staggering on blinded by disease, and mothers carrying on their backs infants as loathsome objects as themselves. The wretches would not leave the path, every step in their failing strength was precious ; he who fell once would never rise again ; no village would admit death into its precincts ; no relation or friend would return for them, and they would lie till their agony was ended by the raven and vulture, the hyena and the fox. Under these circumstances, as might be expected, several of our party caught the infection ; they lagged behind and probably threw themselves into some jungle, for the path, when revisited, showed no sign of them. . . ." A line of bloated corpses, black and crawling with maggots or clean picked into shining skeletons, showed where the disease had already ravaged several caravans.

To add to their troubles, the donkeys began to die, then in quick succession several of the Wanyamwezi porters disappeared with smallpox, and the Beloch became hysterical with fear in case they would catch it. The travellers were now on the summit of chilly Usagara and were passing through a country broken with dry ravines and so swept by smallpox as to be almost unbearable. " The corpses of porters were even more numerous . . . our Moslems passed them with averted face and with the low ' *la haul* ' of disgust, and one decrepit old Wanyamwezi porter gazed at them and wept for himself." Provisions were growing scarce. The country was barren, and as if to add the finishing touch to their difficulties, several important surveying instruments were found to be broken by the carelessness of the porters.

At Zonhwe matters came to a head. The Beloch mutinied for more food. Three days' provisions had been supplied at Zungomero to carry them over to the next provisioning place, and they had stuffed themselves with the whole three days' supply before the first day was over. They were now marching on lean bellies, and blamed Burton for it. The Jemadar, a one-eyed scoundrel with a perpetual frown, called a council in which, speaking loudly so that Burton would overhear, they worked themselves up to a fever pitch. One declared he would take " that man's life," if it meant chains for the rest of his days, another complained that " in all Nazarenes there is no good." The climax occurred when, spurred on by his comrades, the Jemadar approached the half-deaf and tottering Englishman and accused him of starving them.

" I told him not to eat abominations (i.e. talk nonsense), upon which, clapping hand to hilt, he theatrically bade me to repeat the words. Being prostrated at the time by fever, I could only show him how little dangerous he was by using the same phrase half a dozen times. He then turned fiercely upon the timid Said and vented the excess of his wrath. . . ."

A few minutes later, with loud threats and curses, the whole escort deserted in a body and marched back the way they had come.

The " sons " of Ramji, assembled by their leader, swore eternal faith, referred to the recalcitrant Beloch as " dogs and sons of dogs," dispersed, and were then overheard discussing similar tactics. Desperately the two Englishmen determined to pin their faith in the Wanyamwezi porters, bury their baggage, and strike on alone. Burton gave orders for a general departure, the porters picked up their loads, when suddenly the whole mob of Beloch came trooping penitently back again.

Burton ignored them pointedly, gave the order to march, and for the whole day took not the slightest notice of them. In the evening, by which time he hoped the lesson had sunk into their infantile minds, though scarcely able to stand with weakness, he publicly harangued them in the argot of the Cairo *bazaars*. They came forward penitently, one by one, took his hand, and begged forgiveness, attributing their conduct to immoderate indulgence in opium and women. They swore to reform—an oath which was kept only as far as Ugogo.

Altogether they were a miserable scarecrow band. "Their constitutions, sapped by long residence at Zanzibar, were subject to many ailments, and in sickness they were softer than Indian Pariahs. Under the slightest attack of fever they threw themselves moaning upon the ground; were soon deterred by the sun from bringing up the rear, and by night they would not keep watch, even when in actual danger of robbery. As men at arms, one and all deserved to wear the wooden spoon: I saw the whole garrison of Kaole firing for an hour, without effect, at a shell stuck on a stick, distant about a dozen paces. . . ."

With the breach temporarily healed, the expedition pushed on again to Muhama, which they reached on the 19th August and laid in stores for a long desert march ahead of them. Down caravans, riddled with smallpox, were still passing them on their way to the coast, an even more desolate country lay ahead, and, to make the nights even more restless, a new terror in the form of hyenas began to attack them. Creeping up while man and beast slept, these voracious brutes would make a sudden spring, give one slashing bite with their huge jaws, stripping the entire quarters off an ass or tearing half the face off a man, and then leap back into the jungle and vanish.

They were now traversing the grass plains of the Myombo River valley. Beating their way through forests of canes they came upon village after village razed to the ground, the paths strewn with nets, drums, pestles, and fragments of furniture, with here and there a corpse, and here and there a live villager who was lurking in the jungle, not daring to revisit the wreck of his former home, and who fled on seeing the strangers.

A desolate and hideous country, defiled by the hand of man and warred upon by nature. Plagues of ants beset the caravan by day, and at night dense armies of red ants, enormous pismires, tsetse flies, and dangerous mosquitos made life a constant torture.

They were now drawing near the looming 5000-ft. Rubeho range, and halting to make a survey, they discovered more instruments had gone wrong. The only pedometer had broken down, two chronometers had stopped without reason and a third had its glass broken and the second-hand wrenched from its face by the clumsy Goanese. For a few observations they utilized it by counting the ticks, then finally it broke down too and they had to have recourse to the old method of splitting a 4-oz. rifle ball, suspending it from a string, and using its pendulum motion as a watch while they took local and Greenwich time by the sextants.

Entering the Usagara country (25th August) they began the ascent of the valley of Mukondokwa, shaking so badly with fever that for two days they crawled on " physically and morally incapacitated of any exertion beyond balancing ourselves upon the donkeys. . . ." As they climbed, the nights became freezing cold, and icy winds and sleet pitilessly lashed the naked porters. To add to their discomfort they had entered the region where the dreaded Wahumba tribe live, and all day and night, until Inenge, the little settlement at the foot of the towering Rubeho, was reached, they hurried forward without a murmur and at a speed which was set by no one so much as the Beloch.

At Inenge they found a large Arab caravan with some 400 Wanyamwezi porters halted. Civilities were exchanged, some donkeys and packing rope bartered, and a female slave called " Don't know " of Herculean proportions and brazen lungs purchased for six cloths and a coil of wire. She was a regrettable choice. Her name rather than " Don't know " should have been " Don't care." Given to one of the sturdiest of the Khutu porters she at once exhausted him and proved herself physically capable of receiving the entire caravan. Never backward in such matters, the Beloch led the way to oblige her, were followed by the eager " sons " of Ramji and the porters, who pursued her one by one into the bush. The result was turmoil, and " Don't know " became such a menace to peace that she was gladly sold again for a few measures of rice at the earliest opportunity.

The Arab leader of the other caravan, impressed by Burton's letters and diploma, proved a sympathetic and helpful source of information. Not only, on hearing of the mutiny, did he lecture both the Kirangozi and the craven Beloch, but he delayed his own journey two days to superintend the expedition's preparations for crossing the Rubeho. He dispensed valuable tips about Ugogo and Ujiji, and placed at Burton's disposal his house in Unyanyembe. Letters, diaries, and maps were entrusted to his care for transmission to the consul at Zanzibar, and Burton saw him depart with regret. "It had really been a relief to hear once more the voice of civility and sympathy."

It was a welcome respite before the great labour in front of them. Ahead towered the great Rubeho, its slopes running steeply up to the sky. "Trembling with ague, with swimming heads, ears deafened by weakness, and limbs that would hardly support us, we contemplated with a dogged despair the apparently perpendicular path, and the ladders of root and boulder, hemmed in with tangled vegetation, up which we and our starving, drooping asses were about to toil. On the 10th of September we hardened our hearts and began to breast the Pass Terrible. . . ."

No sooner were they out of Inenge and bending their backs to the wearisome climb, than war whoops broke out all over the mountainside, from behind every boulder sprang a man, and a Wahumba ambush that had been waiting for the caravan to clear the village swept down upon the latter in a plundering raid.

Dashing down, sometimes only a few yards from the caravan, of which they took little notice, they swept into the village like a black flood armed with spears and axes. From the straggle of huts far below rose the screams of the slaughtered and the smoke and flames of fires. To have attempted to give aid would have been suicide. Speke was so weak that it required three men to hold him up, and Burton tottered along on the arm of one. The asses fell continually, and every few yards up the precipitous ascent the porters flung themselves panting on the ground while the Beloch groaned that they were dying. In this manner, and by clinging to their supporters, the summit of the Pass was reached in six hours, though not without the loss of several donkeys. At the top the whole party flung themselves down among aromatic flowers and lovely grass to recover. Burton exclaimed on the beauty of their surroundings, but Speke could not reply. The last few hundred feet of the ascent he had climbed in a complete coma.

Speke grew steadily worse and a few miles farther on fell

into a dangerous delirium. For two nights he swore, cursed, and screamed at Burton, becoming so violent that it was necessary to remove his weapons. Then he fell into a death-like trance.

Meanwhile, in their usual contrary fashion, the Beloch were bellowing to march, saying that the great height was too cold for them. Speke could scarcely be moved as Burton feared that at any moment he might expire, but a hammock was rigged up for him, and, supported by two porters, accompanied the party on the downward descent from the Rubeho. Rain lashed them ceaselessly, accompanied by driving mists and hail, until they reached warmer regions where Burton could call a halt, muster the porters, and examine their loads.

To his dismay he found that an oufit calculated to last a whole year had been half-exhausted in three months. Theft, desertion, and the prodigal *honga* handed by the timorous Said to any clamouring spearman had sadly depleted the store. They had enough to carry them to Unyanyembe, but no farther. After that they must wait for the heavier caravan that was supposed to follow them from Kaole.

Continuing on their way again, they debouched on the plateau of Ugogo ; a coarse, arid country of dry scorched grass and withered cane stubbles, which gave place, as they dropped closer to the district town of Ugogi, to deep ravines of red stone fringed with feathery mimosa and bottomed by lush grass, mud, and water.

The 19th of September saw them straggling into Ugogi, the central stage which wiseacres in Kaole had prognosticated they would never reach. Three days were spent at this half-way district between the coast and Unyanyembe. Dry, warm, and fertile, it was nearly 3000 feet above sea-level, and a paradise after the pitiless region of Usagara. Tribally it was a no-man's-land. The Wasagara claimed the ground, but Wahehe and Wagago lived there in comparative amity and were periodically plundered by the Warori. Here, while laying in provisions for the next march, Burton managed, for the sum of four cloths per man, to engage the services of fifteen more Wanyamwezi porters. This stroke of good fortune was most opportune, as the donkeys were now reduced to only nine, and most of these were useless.

In this healthy air constitutions improved again. Speke was able to get about and, though still partially blind, went out to shoot for the pot, returning home, to the delight of the Beloch, loaded with guinea fowl, partridges, and young buck.

On 22nd September they took the road again, leaving Ugogi behind them and striking off across the waterless track through the Ugogo country. The scenery soon changed and " the road wound over a grassy country, thickly speckled with calabashes. As the villages and fields were left behind, the land became a dense, thorny jungle, based upon a sandy, red soil. The horizon was bounded by gradually trimming lines of humpy, outlying hill, the spurs of the Rubeho range, that extended like a scorpion's claws westward, and the plain, gently falling in the same direction, was broken only by a single hill-shoulder and by some dwarf descents. As we advanced through the shades, our difficulties increased ; thorns and spiky twigs threatened the eyes, the rough and rugged road led to many a stumble, and the frequent whine of the hyena made the asses wild with fear. . . ."

In a little the country changed to brackish pools of water and rolling tundra spotted with hundreds of game. Elephants roamed in herds, giraffe cantered delicately across the stubble, and scores of species of wild buck leaped off in clouds of dust on the approach of the caravan. The Beloch and the " sons " of Ramji spent all day firing in all directions with a prodigious waste of powder and shot. No one hit anything and tempers were vented in a general beating of the women.

The intermittent nagging of the drums was now in their ears again, as the Wagogo from afar watched the entry of the strangers into their country. They were in dangerous regions once more, and that evening the Kirangozi, before allowing them to break for camp, clambered on to a convenient boulder, flung a warning hand towards the west where the drums were mumbling, and cried :

" Listen, O ye whites ! and ye children of Sayyidi ! and ye ' sons ' of Ramji ! hearken to my words, O ye offspring of the night ! The journey entereth Ugogo !—Ugogo. Beware and again beware (violent gesticulations). You don't know the Wagogo, they are —s and —s (he stamps). Speak not to those Washenzi pagans : enter not into their houses (he points grimly to the ground). Have no dealings with them, show no cloth, wire, nor beads (speaking with increasing excitement) Eat not with them, drink not with them, and make not love to their women (here the speech became a scream). Kirangozi of the

Wanyamwezi restrain your sons! Suffer them not to stray into the villages, to buy salt out of the camp, to rob provisions, to debauch with beer, or to sit by the wells! Beware, beware, beware. . . ." And thus for half an hour while native mouths hung open and native eyes rolled slowly in their sockets in the direction of the far-off drums.

His peroration was wise. In Ugogo the watchword was force. Among the Wagogo the unpleasant *honga* used sparingly by the other tribes began in earnest. A number of powerful chiefs ruled the district and each chief levied on travellers a heavy tribute. Nor dare the latter refuse it.

By the Kirangozi's experienced suggestion a middle route was taken through the hundred-mile stretch of Ugogo. It lay, unlike other routes, through the districts of only four chiefs, and they reputed the most powerful and honest. Even so, with their depleted stocks, the journey would be ruinous.

The following day they fell in with an Arab caravan travelling in the same direction, which gladly agreed to accompany them through the dangerous region. The journey now became a parade which would have been laughable in any other situation.

" From the day of our entering to that of our leaving the country, every settlement turned out its swarm of men and women, boys and girls, some of whom would follow us for miles with explosions of Hi !—i !—i ! screams of laughter and cries of excitement, at a long, high trot—most ungraceful of motion ! —and with a scantiness of toilette which displayed truly unseemly spectacles. Vainly the escort attempted to arrest the course of this moving multitude of semi-nude barbarity. . . ." At night when camping they would enter Burton's tent to squat and stare at him, remarking loudly on his peculiarities, nor, unless he himself turned them out, could anything move them—the Beloch not daring to stir a finger and the " sons " of Ramji on being ordered to do their duty slunk off muttering to Burton to remember that these men were Wagogo.

At Kanyenye, the district of the most powerful of the Wagogo chiefs, they were detained four days and consistently bled of cotton and wire by the drivelling and decrepit old chief. It was useless to refuse, for a word from the old man would have raised 500 spearmen, and Burton was convinced that at the slightest sign of attack the escort would bolt and he would have no one to stand by him but Speke.

Several of the porters were persuaded to desert by the Wagogo and only with difficulty recovered; and they were just about to move on again out of that inhospitable area when a large down caravan appeared, led by an Arab who greeted Burton warmly. This kindly man not only made them a present of a donkey—their thirty beasts had been now reduced to five—but he obligingly waited a day for them to complete reports and arrange diaries and maps which he offered to carry to the coast for them.

On the 10th of October they left Kanyenye and struck across elephant country with sadly depleted stocks. Porters began now to desert in numbers, donkeys fell exhausted, Speke was made helpless by another attack of fever, and the Kirangozi, by trying to rush them past a settlement without paying *honga*, nearly led them to massacre.

The next stage was Khokho, where they halted to lay in provisions for four marches and pay the usual heavy *honga*. They left here after five days only to plunge into a hellish district of tangled jungle and bog whence swarms of gadflies, bees, and tsetse flies attacked them by day, enormous pismires invaded the tents and bit them mercilessly at night, and hyenas attacked the asses, leaving one so gashed that it had to be destroyed. Here fifteen Wanyamwezi porters incontinently vanished, leaving their loads to be carried by the rest. At Tura, the next settlement, where they were mulcted of nineteen cloths, they managed to hire some porters from another caravan.

Speke now became so ill that, in order to continue the march, Burton gave him his own donkey and, though himself so weak that he could just stand, rather than use valuable goods by being carried by the porters, elected to walk unaided through the torrid jungle.

As usual the Beloch rushed ahead, followed by the "sons" of Ramji, who in a few hours had drained the water provisions of every drop. Behind them alone and in tatters staggered their leader, without a mouthful of water to comfort him. Several times he fell and lay gasping by the side of the trail, very near his end, and each time some passing porter, kinder than the rest, helped him up and onward. Reaching a point where the Beloch were themselves resting, he asked for water, and was refused until he drew his pistol and demanded it. A few moments later the faithful Sidi Bombay, who had seen Speke into the next camping-place, returned in hot haste leading the ass and bringing food and drink to the beleagured man. It was a typical example of Beloch behaviour.

For another day they continued across this waterless country, so thick with elephant and game. Then reaching with relief the boundary of Ugogo, they halted to recoup and count their resources.

§

They were now on the borders of Unyamwezi, Land of the Moon, far-famed in legend, never before seen by white men ; and sick and dispirited though they were, they could not help a sense of achievement and anticipation as they crossed the desert called Mgunda Mkhali, and reached the boundary.

Entering the great forest of Rigwa, whose tangled depths cut off Ugogo from Unyamwezi, they toiled for days through a fetid twilight, their path barred by creepers, lianas, and thick brambles. More porters deserted, the Beloch murmured, and leopard and hyena dogged the footsteps of the few exhausted asses. Here and there where villages dotted the route, people swarmed from their huts, drums were beaten frantically, and hordes of naked men and women, their bodies dripping with sesamum and castor oil, ran after the caravan screaming " Beads ! Beads ! "

Entering a large village, they halted and were entertained for the night under a wall-less roof where Burton had to suffer " a mob of starers that relieved one another from morning till night and made one feel like the denizen of a menagerie."

Seven days later, the 7th November 1857, and the 134th day of their march, they prepared to enter Kazch,[1] the Arab settlement and caravan meeting-place of Eastern Unyamwezi.

To make their arrival impressive, they halted in the forest and changed into their best clothes, polished their arms, hoisted a new flag, and marched across the plain towards the town. They entered " with floating flags, booming horns, muskets ringing like saluting mortars, and an uproar of voice which nearly drowned the other noises ; we made a truly splendid and majestic first appearance. The road was lined with people, who attempted to vie with us in variety and volume of sound. Advancing, I saw several Arabs standing by the wayside, they gave the Moslem salutation and courteously accompanied me for some distance. . . ."

[1] Subsequently called Tabora by Stanley, and now known by that name.

Among these Arabs was one Snay bin Amir, an Harisi, an upright and resolute man, agent of an Indian merchant, and to whom Burton bore a letter from the Sultan of Zanzibar. Burton sought him out, when the requisite courtesies had been observed, and was received with kindness and such generous hospitality, both by him and his friends, that he exclaims : " Striking, indeed, was the contrast between the open-handed hospitality and hearty goodwill of this truly noble race, and the niggardness of the savage and selfish African—it was heart of flesh after heart of stone. . . ."

Kazeh, in the district of Unyamwezi, was, like Zungomero in Khutu, the great meeting-place of the up and down caravans. From here their routes radiated as far as Lakes Nyanza and Tanganyika, Uganda, Urori, and Zanzibar. Though a place of indifferent climate, it was a pleasant resting-place after the perils and hardships of the road.

Here the expedition was detained from the 8th of November until 14th December 1857 ; and in spite of the unfailing kindness and hospitality of the Arabs, the delay was a continual trial of patience. On the morning after their arrival, the whole troop of Unyamwezi porters vanished : the Kirangozi begged a furlough of fifteen days to visit his family, and the Beloch and " sons " of Ramji, left unsuperintended, began their usual round of excesses.

On 14th November, heralded by a twilight darkness, the wet season burst over the Land of the Moon with torrents of rain and hail. Fever followed inevitably, and in twos and threes the caravan began to go down. This type of fever seemed more virulent than any other. The two Goanese boys went down with it first, one of them lying unconscious for three days ; they were followed by the intemperate Beloch who collapsed in a body. Porters were almost impossible to hire, Said the caravan leader revolted and had to be brought to heel. Indeed, were it not for the help of Snay bin Amir, it is doubtful if the expedition could have continued. For a week Burton himself lay at death's door until, revived somewhat by the application of the crude but effective Arab remedies, he managed to pull himself together.

At length, determined that further delay would be his finish, even if not the finish of the expedition, he dragged himself out of bed and dispatched the grumbling Speke ahead to make a camp. On the 15th December, driving the recalcitrant Beloch with his tongue, while he lay with reeling head in a hammock carried by slaves, he followed his subordinate.

Halting at Yombo, they made a two days' stay while they scraped together as many provisions as could be obtained. Here, the change of altitude so far cured Burton of his fever that his normal propensities returned and he was able to take particular note of the Yombo women—" who would be deemed beautiful in any part of the world." Sitting among them smoking, he noted their faces as : " purely Grecian ; they had laughing eyes, their figures were models for an artist, with ' *Turgide, brune e ritondette mamme*,' like the bending statue that delights the world." But Yombo was only a brief and pleasurable respite. Twenty porters were hired here, five of whom immediately deserted with their hire. Pushing into the thick, green jungle, from which sun and rain drew a perpetual reeking steam, they headed for Msene, which they reached on the 30th.

Very different was Msene from Yombo, and a striking example of the variety of African temperament. This latter village was a veritable sink of debauchery. The dance drum was never silent in the market-place, both men and women lived in a perpetual state of drunkenness, and copulating and pederastic couples lay night and day in the open streets. The effect on the Beloch can be imagined. They rushed into this Elysium like wild bulls and could only be dragged away with difficulty. Twelve days were spent in the unpleasant spot, and Burton's anxiety and weakness brought on the fever again.

He grew steadily worse, and at Kajjanjeri was so far gone that Speke feared the worst, and the sufferer himself became resigned—though even that did not prevent his accurately recording his sensations.

" My extremities began to weigh and to burn as if exposed to a glowing fire. The whole body was palsied, powerless, motionless, and the limbs appeared to wither and die ; the feet had lost all sensation except a throbbing and tingling as if pricked by a number of needle points ; the arms refused to be directed by will, and to the hands the touch of cloth and stone was the same. Gradually the attack seemed to spread upwards till it compressed the ribs. . . ." But the onset of death could be regarded with equanimity. " I was easily consoled. If one of us was lost, the other might survive to carry home the results of the exploration. I had undertaken the journey with the resolve either to do or die. I had done my best, and now nothing appeared to remain for me but to die as well. . . ."

For ten days he lay in a coma, while the iron constitution which had overcome Sindian, Arabian, and Somaliland fevers fought to overcome this insidious Equatorial ague. On the eleventh day he returned to consciousness and gave the order to march. Suspended in a hammock, his extremities still numb,[1] he took control once more ; and only just in time. A few days later, Speke went almost completely blind with a fever attack, fell off his donkey, and had to be led helplessly along.

Speke blind and exhausted, Burton numbed and almost semi-conscious, still they continued at a crawling rate through thick jungle and hills. On the 8th of February, after paying exorbitant *honga* to a riverside chieftain, they crossed the Malagarazi River, and at once entered a howling wilderness, cut by swamps. Rain beating pitilessly on them made matters worse and the sudden desertion of five Wakhutu porters added to the confusion.

On, almost at their last gasp : February the 10th found them, scarcely moving, making the perilous passage of the Ruguvu River. Not a sign of habitation or man could be seen, and every few miles a big swamp of black mud had to be negotiated. To add to the dismal scene, overhead black storm clouds rolled in battalions.

The next day, a far glimmer stealing up on the western horizon began to rouse interest and speculation. As they marched towards it, it resolved itself into a long line of sky-blue cliffs with summits gilded by the filtering sun. A day later and it was towering above them and, feeling their way through tall screens of waving grass, they began the ascent.

Laboriously they climbed through sharp spear grass, tangled bramble, and boulder. Porters groaned with weariness, donkeys staggered and fell dead, the Beloch flung themselves down every few yards and said they would go no farther.

They reached the summit. A breeze met their faces, and a few moments later (13th February 1858) occurred one of the historic moments in central African exploration.

" As we entered a small savannah, I saw the leader running forward and changing the direction of the caravan. I followed him. Presently he breasted a steep and stony hill, sparsely clad with thorny trees ; it was the death of my companion's

---

[1] It was a year before he could properly walk again.

riding ass. Arrived with toil—for our fagged beasts now refused to proceed—we halted for a few minutes upon the summit.

" ' What is that streak of light which lies below ? ' I inquired of Sidi Bombay.

" ' I am of opinion,' quoth Bombay, ' that it is *the* water.' "

" I gazed in dismay ; the remains of my blindness, the veil of trees, and a broad ray of sunshine illuminating but one reach of the Lake had shrunk its fair proportions. Somewhat prematurely I began to lament my folly in having risked life and lost health for so poor a prize, to curse Arab exaggeration, and to propose an immediate return, with a view to exploring the Nyanza. Advancing, however, a few yards, the whole scene suddenly burst upon my view, filling me with admiration, wonder, and delight. . . .' "

Emaciated, dizzy, and half-blind with fevers, their clothes in tatters, and their possessions reduced to a bare minimum, the two first Europeans gazed down upon the mighty breast of Tanganyika. The sight before them was sufficient recompense for all their tribulations.

" Below and beyond a short foreground of rugged and precipitous hill-fold, a narrow strip of emerald green, never sere and marvellously fertile, shelves towards a ribbon of glistening yellow sand, here bordered by sedgy rushes, these cleanly and clearly cut by the breaking wavelets. Farther in front stretch the waters, an expanse of the lightest and softest blue, in breadth ranging from thirty to thirty-five miles and sprinkled by the crisp east wind with tiny crescents of snowy foam. The background in front is a high and broken wall of steel-coloured mountain, here flecked and capped with pearly mist, there standing sharply pencilled against the azure air ; its yawning chasms, marked by a deeper plum colour, fall towards dwarf hills, which apparently dip their feet in the wave. . . . The eye falls upon a cluster of outlying islets, speckling a sea horizon. Villages, cultivated lands, the frequent canoes of the fishermen on the waters, and, on a nearer approach, the murmurs of the waves breaking upon the shore give a something of variety, of movement, of life to the landscape. . . ."

Thus the great sea of Ujiji to the eyes of the explorers. " Truly it was a revel for soul and sight," cries Burton again. " Forgetting toils, dangers, and the doubtfulness of return, I felt willing to endure double what I had endured ; and all the party seemed to join me in joy. My purblind companion found nothing to grumble at except the 'mist and glare before his eyes.' Said bin Salim looked exulting—*he* had procured for me this pleasure—the monoculous Jemadar grinned his congratulations and even the surly Beloch made civil salaams. . . ."

With hearts warmed by achievement, the whole party hurried down the inner slope and reached a little waterside village of grass huts. Here Burton was able to hire a large canoe in which they embarked the following day, and began coasting along the eastern shore of the lake.

After a three hours' hard paddling through breath-taking scenery of sweeping mountain, yellow beaches, and green jungle, over the smooth surface of the lake broken by boats of naked fishermen who shouted a greeting, " Hai, hai ! " gambolling hippopotami, and hundreds of whirling flamingos, they pushed through a thick matting of reed and water-weed to the Ujiji landing-place, a mass of shingle littered with boats and tumbledown sheds.

No sooner did they set foot on shore than the hills echoed with shouts, and scores of Wanyamwezi natives rushed from their huts, flung themselves down to the water's edge and stood bawling with excitement, their eyes bulging from their heads at the sight of the first white man they had ever seen.

Assembling themselves and advancing towards the town itself, the usual uproar of tom-toms, horns, screams, and piercing whistles burst out round the caravan, and reaching the *bazaar* they were almost mobbed. A few Arabs met them here and directed them to their quarters, a verminous building, where, too exhausted even to look around, they flung themselves down on filthy pallets to recover a little from their fatigues.

They had marched over 800 miles and been eight months on the road.

§

Recovery at Ujiji was painfully slow. At first the damp, cold lake climate did not seem to agree with the sick men. It rendered them listless and liverish and without the strength or will-power to throw off their complaints. Burton lay prostrate for two weeks, unable to read or write and too shaky to go out and converse. Speke, less groggy on his feet, was still half-blind and suffered from a curious facial spasm, owing to a beetle that had pierced his tympanum, and which, becoming embedded in wax, caused a gnawing pain and twisted up his mouth in a manner which made eating or speaking almost impossible.

Nor was their situation helped by the behaviour of the chief of the local tribe, the Wajiji. Convinced by native logic that men who came into his land without a trade or business that all men might see, but came seemingly to spy out the land with strange instruments to test its worth for conquest, suspected and distrusted them from the first. He remained, even when supposedly helping them, a perpetual thorn in their side, intimidating the Beloch, claiming *honga* before he would perform even the common courtesies of his tribe, and spreading doubtful reports about them round the lake.

Ujiji, itself, at that period was little more than a cluster of miserable huts at the lakeside, with an Arab *bazaar*, a few Arab storehouses, fish stalls, and canoe beaches. The local tribe, the Wajiji, had all the ferocity of the Wagogo mixed with the debauchery of the Wakhutu. Except for the lake fishermen and small traders, the remainder of the population spent most of its time drinking *pombe* and smoking *bhang*; lying half the day drunk, the rest coughing up its lungs in hemp smoke.

As soon as they were in a fit state to move, the two men began preparations for an exploration of the lake, and particularly its northern head, where Arab traders who had penetrated some distance in the direction informed Burton they had felt the influence of a large river draining northwards. A Swahili came forward and declared that he had actually seen this river, and that it issued from the lake at the extreme north.

Could this be the Nile ? Both men were excited and hastened preparations for the journey. But the journey was dangerous. The tribes to the north of the river were antagonistic to travellers. They attacked all who approached, and some were cannibals. Kannena, the Wajiji chief, when asked to accompany them as guide, with his men as escort, made such a show of fear that he had to be offered a fabulous bribe.

Speke was sent off to an Arab trading post across the lake to hire the only boat which would be of use to them—an Arab dhow, while Burton organized the expedition and planned the route.

A month later Speke returned empty handed, and with a wild story that he had discovered the Mountains of the Moon.

He had failed in his attempt to get the dhow ; but fortunately during his absence Burton had been able to hire one from an Arab for 500 dollars.

Preparations were completed, and on 9th April at 4 p.m., led by the surly Kannena in a tattered red turban, a number of his men bearing salt, their wives and children, together with two of the Beloch, Burton and Speke embarked in three boats and turned northwards, with the British flag fluttering over those waters for the first time in history.

For hours they glided close to the eastern shore, across calm waters of a translucent dark green, in which the hippos rose like sea serpents all round them. At each turn of the coast, fresh beauties revealed themselves. Wooded hills of green grass swept sharply down to the lapping waters, their heights crowned with luxuriant foliage and tree blooms whose perfume filled the air. Small villages clustered in little coves, their huts surrounded by palm groves and yellow mimosa. Along the edges of the shore huge dog-faced monkeys swung in the trees and called to one another, while iridescent lizards slipped in and out of the undergrowth. Overhead turtle doves swept in droves, kingfishers flashed like blue lightning, wild geese in pairs, and, higher in the empyrean, eagles hovered like tiny specks.

As usual with the negro, progress was not possible without din. Bursts of speed in which paddles were dashed in the water, splashing everything in the boat, were followed by periods of rest and loud conversation. The paddling was accompanied by " a long, monotonous, melancholy howl, answered by the yells and shouts of the chorus, and broken occasionally by a shrill scream of delight from the boys. The bray and clang of the horns, shaums (native clarinets), and tom-toms, blown and banged incessantly by one or more men in the bow of each canoe, lasts throughout the livelong day, except when terror induces a general silence. At times they halt to eat, drink, and smoke ; the *bhang* pipe is produced after every hour and the paddles are taken in whilst they indulge in the usual screaming, convulsive whooping cough. . . ."

Discomfort to this mode of travel was added by the fact that, for fear of crocodiles, no dung or offal is thrown overboard, everything being tossed into the hold, where, under a hot sun, the stench grew momentarily worse.

Thus they coasted as far as the village of Wanfanya, a Wajiji settlement of foul hovels, where they halted two days and the two Beloch escort deserted, terrified by the tales of horrors awaiting them up the lake.

Alone now with the Wajiji the two white men continued to Ubwari, and from thence, after heavy *honga* payments to Muri-vumba, a filthy spot, full of crocodiles, mosquitos, and a tribe of disgusting cannibals who lived on offal, carrion, and raw human flesh.

Uvira, their next stop, was one of the biggest trading centres on Tanganyika, lying on the north-west side of the lake and feeding the caravans which radiate from here. Here the lake had shelved in breadth to a distance of only seven or eight miles. Uvira was looked upon by the Arabs at that time as the *Ultima Thule* of lake travel, farther north the tribes were too dangerous to visit. Burton was determined to push on, however, buoyed up by the wondrous hope that the great river ahead was the veritable source of the Nile.

On the 26th of April, however, their hopes were suddenly and irrevocably dashed to the ground. A visit from the local Sultan of Uvira brought direct information about the river at the head of the lake. This river, known as the Rusizi, did not, the Sultan declared emphatically, flow out of the lake, but into it ; and could therefore by no means be connected with the Nile stream. Numerous bystanders, among them Arab merchants who had daringly penetrated to the mouth of this river, confirmed him. The Nile dream had vanished.

It was a sad ending to their high hopes. But Burton determined even so to explore the river and lay down the limits of the lake. His boatmen, however, flatly refused to go a foot farther, declaring that, if the white men did not value their lives, they did themselves.

Without boatmen, they were helpless, and there was nothing to do but turn back.

For Burton that slow journey back to Ujiji was a long-drawn-out torture. Ulcers had broken out all over his mouth so that he was unable to chew and could scarcely speak, and for nine days he had to sit in a half-waterlogged canoe with no back rest, knee-deep in filthy water, and in the company of a crew of stinking and verminous paddlers, several sick children and slaves, a goat, and all the garbage of native travel—gourds, spears, broken vases, revolting food, and excreta.

Health improved, however, when on 14th May the rainy season ended in Unyamwezi and for once cool mornings, clear sunshine, and cold nights, after the six months of rain and cloud, sent health and strength back into the tired and dispirited bodies of the travellers.

But health brought no cessation from anxiety. Their stock of trade goods was now dwindled almost to nothing. A few handfuls of beads, a few *shukkas* of cloth, and a dozen or so coils of wire were all that remained of the caravan. The Beloch had to be paid, food gathered for the 260-mile trek back to Unyanyembe, and a sufficiency of goods kept to settle the *honga* levied by the trade route chieftains. No word had come from Snay bin Amir at Kazeh, nor even a rumour of the appearance of the caravan of fresh stores which had been arranged to be sent from Zanzibar.

Matters were getting desperate, for nowhere might one have starved with greater ease than in the fertile central Africa of those days. On 22nd May, however, while half-hearted preparations were being made by Said bin Salim to get some sort of caravan together, the usual clatter of musket shots announced new arrivals at Ujiji, and with relief and joy they watched their long-delayed caravan arrive with an escort of four of the " sons " of Ramji, a bundle of letters and journals, and the medical supplies asked for at Khutu. For the first time these men who had been twelve months away from civilization learned of the Indian Mutiny, of which three years before Burton had warned an apparently unheeding government.

Burton had by now completed his report on the district, and, as no further purpose could be served in staying, four days later, replenished in provisions and strength, the caravan left Ujiji for the homeward march. As they climbed the declivity behind the town and halted at the top to look back, Burton was aware of a curious presentiment that this would be his last sight of the waters he had discovered. He felt, and not for the first time, what he describes as " the strange, inexplicable melancholy which accompanies all travellers in tropical countries. Nature is beautiful in all that meets the eye ; but she is a syren whose pleasures pall, and one sighs for the rare simplicity of the desert. I never felt this sadness in Egypt and Arabia ; I was never without it in India and Zanzibar. . . . ."

Long he paused, looking out across the scene while the caravan behind him fidgeted to start. " I shall long remember the morning of the 26th of May which afforded me the last sunrise spectacle of the Tanganyika lake. The charm of the scenery was perhaps enhanced by the reflection that my eyes might never look upon it again. Masses of brown-purple clouds covered the quarter of the heavens where the sun was about to rise. Presently the mists, ruffled like ocean billows, and luminously fringed with Tyrian purple, were cut by flung rays, whilst from behind their core, the internal living fire shot forth its broad beams, like the spokes of a huge aerial wheel, rolling a flood of gold over the light blue waters of the lake . . . and a soft breeze, the breath of the morn, woke the waters to life. . . ."

It was a sad and beautiful farewell, and one that was to linger with him often through the troubled years ahead.

§

The return journey was hampered by the usual quarrels and alarms. There was not a Beloch and scarcely a porter who had not squandered his substance in Ujiji on the purchase of slaves. Most of these miserable wretches managed to desert before very far, leaving their baffled owners cursing with helpless rage ; one little slave girl who became lame and could not march, was carried by her owner the Kirangozi until he got tired, laid her down, then cut off her head rather than that she should be left for others. With quarrels, bickering, and constant alarms and excursions after their property, there was scarcely a man who could give his proper attention to the disposition of the caravan. Progress was thus unavoidably slow, and it was not until 20th June, after twenty-six days of toilsome, uneventful travel, that they reached Kazeh.

Here they stayed for three months and here occurred the first real break with Speke and what was subsequently to prove possibly the greatest blunder of Burton's life.

During their first halt at Kazeh, Burton, in conversation with Arab merchants, had learned of the existence of another and even larger lake than Tanganyika lying fifteen or sixteen marches to the north. Careful questioning elicited enough information for this unknown water to be laid down in a crude map, which was forwarded to the R.G.S. It now only remained for someone to make the journey to this water, actually verify its existence, and, if time permitted, survey it.

That someone had now to be chosen and the task accomplished.

Speke's version of the affair is that, on pressing Burton to make the journey, the latter refused, saying, " he had done enough and he would do no more." Speke thereupon begged to be allowed to go on his own, and Burton, after some demur, was forced at length to agree. Burton put obstacles in his way, but he overcame them. To Speke, therefore, lies the credit of the whole expedition, as without his constant pressure and alacrity nothing would have been done.

Burton, on the other hand, throws a different light on the question. There was, he argued, much work to be done at Kazeh, not only in organizing the caravan for the long march to the coast, but also in completing the detailed report he was making of the region. For the former, Burton's presence was urgently necessary, since Speke knew no Arabic and almost all the work had to be done in that language.[1] Moreover, Speke was disliked by the Arabs owing to his behaviour. " His presence in Kazeh," says Burton, describing how he himself gave Speke the orders to march to Nyanza, " was by no means desirable." And stung to retort by Speke's insinuation, he makes a sarcastic reference to " Anglo Indians who are ready to take offence when it is least intended, who expect servility as their due, and whose morgue of colour induces them to treat all skins a shade darker than their own as niggers. . . ."

So there we have the two sides, for what they are worth, and judging them in the light of sharp tempers, liverish constitutions leading to nagging irritability, brains giddy with fever, and minds chafing under a too long proximity of temperaments of totally different calibre, it is difficult to find the truth.

But whatever that truth is, and it will never be known, there can be no doubt that in letting Speke leave alone on the trip up-country Burton was making what proved to be a tragic mistake in his career. All other considerations should have gone by the board with such a prize at stake. On that march Speke discovered the Victoria Nyanza and returned confident that he had found at last the true sources of the Nile. Subsequent history proved Speke to be right (though at the time, as in the case of his ludicrously placed Mountains of the Moon, he had not nearly enough data to guarantee his assertion), and thus the honour of the greatest geographical discovery of the nineteenth century was snatched at the last moment from the man who had tried so hard and done so much to deserve it.

Speke was away three months, made a plucky march to Victoria Nyanza, roughly mapped the lower limits of the lake

---

[1] Travellers who have spent long periods in a primitive country with a companion who is ignorant of the language will sympathize heartily with Burton.

and returned with his jubilant report. Burton, who had spent the interval in his usual careful cataloguing and note-taking for his proposed book on the region,[1] also preparing for the homeward journey, greeted him coolly. He acknowledged the achievement of Speke's march but denied that on Speke's data he could assert the discovery of Nyanza as the true source of the Nile. Speke's temper flared up, Burton, never slow to be roused, retorted, then both men pulled themselves together with the knowledge that to quarrel openly in those lands was to set a dangerous example. For the moment the subject of the Nile sources was dropped. Preparations were made for departure and, on the 20th of October, they quitted Kazeh for the homeward route.

Burton was ill and Said bin Salim, who had been deputed to produce some porters who could support him in a hammock on the march, secured three bearers characteristic of his usual skill, viz. a tottering old man, a knock-kneed boy, and a notorious skulk. After one march they collapsed, and their unfortunate load had to have recourse to the expensive method of hiring bearers from village to village.

At Ilanga, whither they had had to struggle through a biting east wind, Speke was stricken almost to death with fever. Lodged in the only dwelling available, a verminous cow-house exposed to the full force of the east wind, he fell into a sort of fit, deliriously crying that hordes of tigers, leopards, and other carnivora were harnessed with iron hooks and dragging him over the ground, while a crowd of giants, devils, and demons stripped the sinews and tendons from his legs. " Frame fixed and rigid, eyes glazed and glassy," noted Burton, who assiduously nursed him, " he began to utter a barking noise, and a peculiar chopping of the mouth and tongue with lips protruding, that completed the terror of the beholders. . . ." This passed and once more he fell into delirium in which he raved and screamed at Burton. With the release of his pent-up subconscious, the appalled Burton was made for the first time

---

[1] *The Lake Regions of Central Africa.* Possibly one of Burton's greatest difficulties during the expedition had been the constant labour in sickness or health of maintaining the compendious volume of data he collected on every region he passed through. No subject is left untouched, no detail too irrelevant not to be pursued to its end. The *Lake Regions* is a complete *vade mecum* to central Africa : and the brilliance and accuracy of Burton's reports may be gauged when it is stated that during the first World War, in various phases of Eastern warfare, his notes on trade routes and geographical features, even after a lapse of half a century, were often the only reliable information obtainable.

really aware of the secret resentment, envy, and hatred Speke
had been nurturing for him silently for years. Episodes long
buried floated before his delirious eyes. He cursed Burton for
cheating him of the supposed money owing for his Appendix to
Burton's book on the expedition to Harar.[1] Once more he was
fighting at Burton's side outside the tent at Berberah, and
Burton was ordering him not to step back or the Somal would
think they were running; and he raved at Burton for thinking
him a coward. Over hundreds of little unimagined details and
trivialities of the march which he had remembered and stored
up he now poured his fury. Then he came-to and, convinced
that he was approaching dissolution, wrote a farewell letter to
his family. His agonizing spasms, however, now began to pass
off and presently he could call exhaustedly to his companion,
" Dick, the knives are sheathed ! " [2]

Eight days later he was sufficiently recovered to move and,
with him slung in a hammock like the still-numbed Burton, the
party continued their journey.

They now, with extra slaves and camp followers, amounted
to a caravan of 158 souls. By 3rd November they had reached
the Tura wells and begun the transit of dreaded Ugogo. This
was accomplished without accident, except for the usual exorbitant *honga* demands. But even so a general terror pervaded
the party through these regions, so much so that the simple
glare of some harmless M'gogo boy was sufficient to set the
Beloch's teeth chattering.

By the 7th of December, however, they were out of Ugogo
and safely ascending the slopes of the Usagara mountains,
where at the first halt a typical African example of thanks-
giving occurred. Burton amusedly records it as an instance
of the native mind. By the fire the following dialogue takes
place :

" The state, M'dula (i.e. Hajji Abdullah) ? "

" The state is very (well) and thy state ? "

" The state is very (well) and the state of Spikka (Speke) ? "

" The state of Spikka is very (well)."

" We have escaped the Wagogo, white man O ! "

" We have escaped, O my brother."

---

[1] An account of Speke's work on the coast while Burton was making the
journey inland, so full of inaccuracies that Burton had to edit it considerably
before printing. The book made no money.

[2] It was a severe attack of the *Kichyomachyoma*, or " Little Irons " fever.

" The Wagogo are bad."

" They are bad."

" The Wagogo are very bad."

" They are very bad."

" The Wagogo are not good."

" The Wagogo are not at all good."

" They are not at all good."

" I greatly feared the Wagogo, who kill the Wanyamwezi."

" Exactly so."

" But now I don't fear them. I call them b—s and b—s and I would fight the whole tribe, white man O ! "

" Truly so, O my brother."

And thus for hours until Burton's ennui would turn to marvel.

By the 12th of December they were crossing Usagara and scrambling through stormy red hills belted with thorn scrub and forests of wild fruit trees, among which gazelle darted and rhino grazed. Dawn of Christmas day discovered them crawling along the steep banks of the Kikaboga River, whose turbulent waters had to be forded three times. Thence they dropped down into Khutu.

Through Khutu the usual troubles again beset them, porters ran away, asses died, the Beloch mutinied, and fever dogged their footsteps, and it was not until 20th January that they left the province and entered dangerous Uzaramo. Five days later they crossed the yellow M'geta River, and the 30th of January saw them joyously greeting the first mango trees which heralded the coast.

On 2nd February they reached a little rise and saw the sea. " We lifted our caps and gave ' three times three and one more.' The 3rd of February saw us passing through the poles decorated with skulls [1]—a sort of negro Temple Bar—at the entrance of Konduchi."

The long and arduous journey of the first Central African Expedition was over.

That same evening, the Beloch and the " sons " of Ramji were packed off to the island, and six days later Burton and Speke followed them.[2]

---

[1] Presented by Burton later to the Royal College of Surgeons.

[2] I am omitting as irrelevant Speke's later charges that Burton had cheated the Beloch of their pay, or Burton's reply and the long acrimonious correspondence that ensued between Burton and the India Office. Interested readers will find the correspondence printed in the Appendix to the *Lake Regions*.

§

Returning to Aden, Burton lingered there long enough for Speke to precede him to England by some two weeks. Although on parting, the latter had made a promise to await his principal's arrival before getting into touch with the R.G.S. Speke was no sooner landed than he hurried to the Society, levelled his charges against Burton, stated his own case, and obtained the sanction from the Society for a new expedition to explore his new lake, the Nyanza, with himself as head and Burton excluded.

Burton returned to find John Hanning Speke the lion of the season, himself treated with reserve by the R.G.S. and positive displeasure by the Government, and the usual crop of ugly rumours floating about concerning him.

To their behaviour he turned what was at least outwardly an indifferent shoulder, but Speke's assertion that Nyanza was the Nile source he contested hotly, and he produced a thesis, backed by several eminent geographers, laying the claim to Tanganyika.

The battle of the Nile source was waged for years, in actual fact until Stanley and Livingstone made their final discoveries. But the battle of Speke and Burton was of a more personal nature than a mere argument over a patch of water. Strong passions were stirring in both of them. The rest of the story is told in a few words.

In September 1864 the controversy reached such a height that the two men were prepared to meet one another on the platform and fight it out face to face. It was arranged that they should meet at the British Association meeting at Bath that year.

Laurence Oliphant, the author and friend of Speke, mischievously conveyed to Burton, whom he disliked, a remark of Speke's that if Burton appeared on the Bath platform, he, Speke, would publicly kick him. Burton's retort was, " Well, that settles it ! By God, he shall kick me ! "

On the morning of 13th September the two men met for the first time for years. They were to speak that afternoon, and an onlooker noted that Speke's face had a curious look of " sorrow, yearning, and perplexity. . . ." After a while he began to fidget a great deal, and exclaimed half-aloud, " Oh, I cannot stand this any longer ! " He rushed from the building.

The afternoon arrived and Burton stood waiting on the platform with his notes in his hand when a hasty message was brought into the building. Speke, while out shooting only an hour after leaving the platform, had " accidentally " shot himself dead in the field.

Burton staggered visibly on the platform, then sank into a chair with his face working. " By God, he's killed himself ! " [1] he exclaimed. When he got home, he wept bitter tears, repeating over and over again the name " Jack ! Jack ! . . ."

§

Speke discovered the Nile source and Burton failed. Yet in a sense Burton's was the greater achievement, for it was he who laid down the road for that discovery and all that came after it. In his own words :

" I went into a country ignorant of it, its language, trade, manners, and customs, preceded only by a French officer who was murdered directly he landed. Without money, support, or influence, lacking in the necessaries of life, I led the most disorderly caravan that ever man could gather together into the heart of Eastern Africa and discovered the Tanganyika lake. I brought home sufficient information to smooth the path of all who chose to follow. I opened the line to Englishmen and they had but to follow me."

[1] The general theory at the time was that Speke's death was accidental. But he was a careful and experienced shot and one who would by instinct never put himself in jeopardy when carrying a weapon. Posterity will be inclined to believe that Burton was right.

Chapter Seven

In the spring of 1858 Isabel returned to England with her sister and brother-in-law from a continental tour, which she had hoped would help her to forget the pangs of the long separation from Richard. It had not succeeded. At Nice she had sat for days, either fiddling with a little portable shrine and bric-à-brac that had been touched by the Pope, from which she wafted continual prayers across the Mediterranean, or moping in her window, looking with vacant blue eyes towards the South. " My windows look over a little garden where an African tree is, and the sea beyond, and beyond that again Africa and Richard." In Genoa she found no pleasure in the excursions her party arranged. She could only scribble in her diary : " I am all alone and Richard's place is vacant in the opera-box, in the carriage, and everywhere. Sometimes I dream he came back and would not speak to me, and I wake up with my pillow wet with tears. . . ."

She returned home in a dismal state of mind. Richard was expected back that year and, as the months lengthened, her despondency increased till it gave way in a burst of hysteria which drove her into a Norwich convent with the determination to take the veil. Here she remained several weeks a prey to religious doubts and fears, wondering whether Richard's delay was a punishment from Heaven or merely a tribulation sent to try her, and covering the pages of a private journal with devotional thoughts. The outlet to her emotion eased her a little. After all, was not courage one of Richard's virtues and should it not be one of hers ? She thought better of taking the veil, came out of her retreat, and travelled to London to find John Speke, returned alone from Africa, the hero of the hour in London society, and around the name of Richard, whose whereabouts were still unknown, a little sea of unpleasant murmurs rising.

While Speke was being fêted evrywhere, the usual rumours were cropping up about his leader. People spoke not openly but by suggestion. Why was Burton lingering ? Why had

Speke gone to the R.G.S. alone and received the sanction for a new expedition in which Burton's name was omitted ? Why did Speke mention his leader with such hesitant reserve ? Was it true that porters had been cheated of money, Burton's nerve had failed him on the journey, and he had shirked the expedition to Nyanza ? [1]

With tigerish ferocity Isabel defended him. He was too great for the petty world of society to understand. Envy, jealousy, dislike—were these not always the rewards of genius ? Richard was perfect, there was none to equal him.

But where was he ?

The days passed. Then, forwarded from Zanzibar, undated and unsigned, there came to her a single slip of paper in the familiar hand.

To Isabel :

That brow which rose before my sight
    As on the palmer's holy shrine ;
Those eyes—my life was in their light ;
    Those lips—my sacramental wine ;
That voice whose flow was wont to seem
    The music of an exile's dream. . . .

A radiant happiness pervaded Isabel. At last she knew that all was well. For a while the sun shone ; then as the time drew near there came another cloud of doubts. When, in a newspaper note she read of Richard's expected return, her misgivings flooded her again, and in her diary she wrote that she felt " frightened, sick, stupefied, dying to see him, and yet inclined to run away. . . ."

A day later she called upon a friend, who happened to be out, and while waiting and musing over Richard's return she heard a ring at the door-bell below. A moment later she heard a familiar voice in the hall asking if the servant knew of her address. Then the door opened and in limped Richard himself.

" For an instant we both stood dazed. I felt so intensely I fancied he must hear my heart beat and see how every nerve was overtaxed. . . ." But only for an instant. With a glad cry Richard extended his arms, and she rushed into them, all thought forgotten in a first passionate embrace.

[1] In writing this section of the book, I applied to the R.G.S. for leave to examine the correspondence of the Burton–Speke controversy. The secretary of the Society refused, saying he thought " no useful purpose could be served " by reviving this matter. I could well imagine a sardonic smile from Mortlake at this reply.

But to her young vigorous body she pressed a sapless, shrunken form ; and, holding him at arm's length a moment later, Isabel scanned him with horror and pity. The sturdy, black-browed, alert young man who three years earlier had marched out of her life so full of health and confidence, had become a mere framework of himself. Disillusionment had bent his spirit, and twenty-one attacks of fever had broken down his iron constitution. He was still partially paralysed and blind ; with protruding eyes, lips shrunken back from the teeth, hair streaked with grey and an emaciated figure on which the brownish yellow skin hung in bags.

At that all her young love, her strength, her confidence surged out to meet him. He was hers as never he had been before. The shock of meeting her had set him tottering on his feet and, taking his arm, she helped him down, and into a cab. For hours they drove round the Park, speaking little, yet drawing strength from one another. Then, cherishing and comforting him, she gradually drew from him his story until some of the bitterness began to go out of his voice. With her arm through his, she clung to him, gazing up at him with her limpid blue eyes full of such adoration that his spirit revived, and gradually he turned to speak of the future. In a world of misunderstanding, distrust, and ingratitude, the glory of a love that could say " he was still—had he been ever so unsuccessful, and had every man's hand been against him—my earthly God and King, and I could have knelt at his feet and worshipped him . . ." was perhaps almost full compensation.

§

Never was a man more in need of the sympathy that from this solitary quarter was lavished on him. London's reception of the great traveller was but lukewarm compared with that which had been showered on the opportunist Speke. In some quarters he was shunned ; scientific societies treated him with reserve ; and government departments heartily disliked him.[1] To the usual crop of stories and rumours about him he turned

[1] Not unnaturally. His strictures on the Indian Government relating to its measures for protection in the Red Sea, sent to the R.G.S. for forwarding to the proper quarter, had drawn a terse reply stating that the " want of discretion, and due respect for the authorities to whom you are subordinate, has been regarded with displeasure by the Government." But this was not his worst crime. The massacre of Christians at Jeddah, the following year, proved that his strictures were right and that the Government's laxness was to blame. To have anticipated this was unforgivable.

the usual deaf ear ; considering them not worth refuting ; and quite unaware of the great damage they invariably did him.

During the remainder of that year he concentrated on completing his *Lake Regions*, made short trips to the Continent, and then, as if finally making up his mind, returned to Isabel and asked her to marry him at once.

Isabel wavered, then ran to her parents. Her father liked Richard, but Mrs. Arundell as violently disliked him. In him the latter seemed to see concentrated all the worst vices of human nature. Burton was a Protestant, was notorious, penniless, and without prospects, being fairly universally discredited. Religious reasons apart, what possible sense or propriety could there be in such a union ? Isabel demurred, defended Richard on all practical points, but found him indefensible against a vigorous Catholic on matters spiritual. Torn between her filial and devotional love and the sensual worldly affection she had for Richard, she remained in a quandary of indecision from which Richard's plea that they should elope together at length stirred her. She refused ; and once more, with a promptness which seemed as if it had only been waiting for an excuse and without saying good-bye, her lover vanished. Behind him he left a letter saying he had gone to North America and would not be back for nine months. " Think well over our affair," he wrote, and he reminded her that he was past forty while she was nearly thirty, that it was ten years since they had first met and three since he had proposed to her. He was giving her nearly a year in which to make up her mind. When he returned he would expect an answer ; and if that answer was " No," she would never see him again.

Isabel, who should by now have become accustomed to such behaviour, was overcome. The correct thing to do under such circumstances was to be prostrated—and prostrated Isabel became. She retired to bed and wrote her mother an inchoate letter of several thousand words which must have made the old lady's head ache. Then she fell into a temporary decline.

§

Meanwhile Richard, after a tactless [1] departure in his usual cloud of secrecy, was crossing the Atlantic. His destination

---

[1] The Speke controversy was beginning to swing round in his favour. Influential friends, including wealthy Lord Houghton, were speaking of subscribing towards an expedition for him to lead to Africa on his own. People were inquiring after him ; and he chose this auspicious moment to vanish.

was Salt Lake City, headquarters of the Mormons, which he was hoping to visit and examine for the same reasons that he had visited Mecca. His familiarity with the polygamy of the East, a system which he often violently defended, had aroused in him an intense interest to see the result of its application in the West. Stories of Mormonism, both comic and horrible, were constantly reaching England. Burton decided to discover for himself what truth lay in them.

On 7th August 1860, after an uneventful voyage and cross-country journey, he reached St. Joseph, Missouri, where the expedition proper began. Here he took wagon, and in the company of a U.S. officer, a judge, a state secretary, and a marshal, crossed the river and fell into the so-called Emigration Road.

They were prepared for all emergencies. Nebraska was a battlefield in which three columns of soldiers were desperately struggling to keep the Comanche, Kiowa, and Cheyenne Indians at bay. Wild stories of murdering and cannibal emigrants were in the air, and informants in New Orleans swore that Salt Lake City was a murder den. "They are shooting and cutting one another in all directions," was the gist of their warnings. "How can you expect to escape?"

It was not long before Burton had a chance to undergo some of the suffering and danger experienced by the emigrants. Passing from the wide rolling expanse of Emigrant Way, his party reached a wide pitted prairie land across which could be seen toiling several emigrant wagons. On closer acquaintance these proved to consist of troops of half-naked, semi-starving proselytizing women dragging children and camp impedimenta slowly and painfully behind the wagons on the long trek to the Rocky Mountains. If they were a danger, it was only that of transmitting vermin or disease.

Burton's own route, covered uncomfortably in the stifling, rattling wagon, crossed Platte Bridge, Diamond Springs, and Sweetwater. Nights were spent in filthy shanties inhabited mostly by Irish settlers with broods of children, bugs, and flies. Food consisted more often than not of roast mutton hacked off a putrefying carcass and boiled in tallow. Rarely could a cleanly and satisfying meal be had. Indians followed the wagons in gangs pilfering and begging.

Reaching the Rockies and making a toilsome ascent they at length reached the top, where they halted for a while and Burton

saw far below him Salt Lake City spread out on the plain.
Scenes reminiscent almost of the Mecca pilgrimage, when
first the pilgrims sighted the Holy City, greeted his eyes as the
emigrant wagons topped the rise and their miserable members
saw the Mormon city below. They gave vent to the emotions
long pent up in their bosoms by " sobs and tears, laughter and
congratulations, psalms and hysterics. . . . It is indeed no
wonder that the children dance, that strong men cheer, and that
nervous women, broken with fatigue and hope deferred, scream
and faint. . . ."

Descending to the city, which lay in a valley surrounded
by mountains, Burton's party halted at the only hotel, where
they were civilly received. Burton had made the journey
dressed in an old English shooting-jacket, wide-awake hat,
buckskins, and pistol belt. He now changed into black frock
coat and stove-pipe hat, specially brought for the purpose, and,
with the assistance of a useful acquaintance picked up on the
journey, went out to examine the city and see something of
Mormon Society.

His first impressions were favourable. The city was well
laid out, irrigated, and drained, and each householder possessed,
in addition to a house and couple of acres in the city, a large
suburban allotment of from five to ten acres.

The people themselves seemed sober and industrious until
one knew them well enough to see behind their barrier of heavy
reserve, where their temperament was found often to be cold-
blooded and treacherous.

Their general character seemed to be exemplified in their
leader, the dictator Brigham Young. Securing the necessary
introduction, Burton called upon him for an interview, which
was granted.

He found the Prophet a large-framed bucolic man of fifty-
nine, with courteous manners and an easy discourse on all matters
except religion. It was difficult at first to believe that behind
this veneer lurked a ferocious spirit and indomitable will-power
that would stop not even at murder to attain its desires. They
spoke of general matters first, the Prophet expressing interest
in Burton's Tanganyika expedition. When the latter turned
to the subject of Mormonism, however, Young retired into his
shell; and upon Burton's applying for admission into the
Mormon Church (a ruse to obtain an insight into their customs),
he accompanied his downright refusal with a : " No, Captain,

I think you have done that sort of thing before." Burton
pleaded, saying that after all he had travelled several thousand
miles to join a colony which was "sensible enough to
permit polygamy." Young retorted with questions about the
Pilgrimage to Mecca. This was Burton's *congé* and, after a
little further talk, he left.

Burton's verdict on the Prophet was, under the circumstances, a fair and just one, which subsequent history was to
prove correct. Non-smoker, teetotaller, eater of baked potatoes
and buttermilk (how he was able physically to satisfy his large
female *harim* on such a diet must remain one of the strongest
evidences of his divinity), Burton found him a man of even,
placid temper, "his manner is cold, in fact, like his face somewhat
bloodless ; he impresses a stranger with a certain sense of
power. . . . He has been called hypocrite, swindler, forger,
murderer—no one looks it less. . . . The arts with which he
rules the heterogeneous mass of conflicting elements are indomitable will, profound secrecy, and uncommon astuteness . . ."
with none of "the weakness and vanity which characterize the
common uncommon man. . . ."

In the intervals of examining this amazing colony, its
churches, its *harims*—Young's famous Bee House, where he
kept some twenty wives, reminded the traveller of nothing so
much as a large English hunting stable—he made excursions
in the district, visiting the so-called Dead Sea or Salt Lake,
whose reputed buoyant properties he tested characteristically
in a painful bathe ; and the police quarters at Camp Floyd,
where a few companies of men were supposed to guard the
Mormons whom they cordially detested.

In the city itself, life soon began to pall. A peculiar "Moslem
gloom" hung over everything ; women were in seclusion ;
austerity of morals and conversation was the keynote. It
needed only the clandestine advances of an amorous Mormon
woman to decide him that, after a stay of three weeks, it was
time to move. On Thursday, 20th September, in the company
of a none too reputable party, including several renegade
Mormons, they left the city of the plain and entered dangerous
Indian country on the 580-mile trek to San Francisco. The
Sierra Nevada was crossed in a howling blizzard, from which
the caravan fell into country ravaged by Comanches. Aided
by luck and a modicum of bluff, for they passed several smoking
encampments raided by the Indians, they reached San Francisco

on 1st November, without incident.   Here Burton shipped homeward through the Panama, after a nine months' journey across the American continent and a covered distance of about 25,000 miles.[1]

§

On Christmas Day 1860 Isabel was staying with relatives in Yorkshire.   There was a large house-party gathered, and she had been asked to sing.   Someone propped up the music with a copy of that morning's *Times*, and as Isabel bent forward to scan the music a single announcement from the printed newspaper behind it caught her eye.

" Captain Burton has arrived from America."

Overcome, she excused herself and retired to her room.   She sat up all night packing and wondering how she could get away. Two letters from Richard, delayed and bearing unmistakable signs of having been opened by her relations, hardened her heart.   She contrived a telegram to herself, left the house in a flurry of snow with her usual piles of baggage and hurried down to London.

Burton met her with a calmness that checked the transports she had prepared for him.   He spoke to her with finality : there would be time for kissing afterwards.

" I have waited five years.   Our lives are being spoiled by the unjust prejudices of your mother, and it is for you to consider whether you have not already done your duty in sacrificing two of the best years of your life out of respect to her.   Now you must make up your mind to choose between your mother and me.   If you choose me, we marry and I stay ; if not, I go back to India and return no more.   Is your answer ready ? "

And Isabel replied :

" Quite.   I marry you this day three weeks, let who will say nay." [2]

§

Isabel found plenty of people to say " Nay " ; Mrs. Arundell being quite the loudest.   Isobel was obliged therefore to plan a little subterfuge into which all the family except her father and

---

[1] The result of this journey was the publication of *The City of the Saints*, 1861, from which the extracts in this section were taken.

[2] This romantic version of the meeting is Isabel's ; but something similar must undoubtedly have been said.

mother entered. She fixed the marriage for Wednesday, 23rd January 1861, the date of the Espousals of Mary and Joseph, and only changed it to the 22nd on Richard's earnest representations that twenty-three was an unlucky number ; then feeling weighed down by happiness and guilt she rushed to Cardinal Wiseman for advice.

After a solemn conversation, the Cardinal sent for Richard and invited him to sign a document containing three pledges :

(1) Isabel should be allowed free practice of her religion.

(2) Any children must be brought up to be Catholics.

(3) The marriage must be solemnized in a Catholic Church.

Richard signed, and preparations immediately went ahead.

Isabel now began a period of prayer and devotion. To her confessional book " Lamed " she confided :

The principal and leading features of my future life are going to be :

" Marriage with Richard.

" My parents' blessing and pardon.

" A man child.

" An appointment, money earned by literature.

" A little society.

" Doing a great deal of good.

" Much travelling."

This programme was followed by a carefully tabulated series of rules, entitled : " Rules for my guidance as a wife." The more important of which were :

(1) Let your husband find in you a companion, friend, and adviser, that he may miss nothing at home, and let him find in the wife what many other men fancy is only to be found in a mistress.

(2) Make his home snug. If it be ever so small and poor, there can always be a certain *chic* about it. Attend much to his creature comforts ; allow smoking or anything else ; for if you do not, *somebody else will.*

(3) Improve and educate yourself in every way, that you may enter into his pursuits and keep pace with the times, that he may not weary of you.

(4) Be prepared at any moment to follow him at an hour's notice and rough it like a man.

(5) Do not try to hide your affection for him, but let him see and feel it in every action. Never refuse him anything he asks.

(6) Never confide your domestic affairs to your female friends.

(7) Hide his faults from *everyone* and back him up through every difficulty and trouble, but with his peculiar temperament advocate peace whenever it is consistent with his honour before the world.

(8) Never permit anyone to speak disrespectfully of him before you ; and if anyone does, no matter how difficult, leave the room. Never hurt his feelings by a rude remark or jest.

(9) Never ask him *not* to do anything—for instance with regard to visiting other women, or anyone you particularly dislike ; trust him and tell him everything, except another person's secret.

(10) Do not bother him with religious talk, be religious yourself and give good example, take life seriously and earnestly, pray for and procure prayers for him, and do all you can for him without his knowing it, and let your life be something that will win mercy from God for him. You might *try* to say a little prayer *with* him every night before laying down to sleep and gently draw him to be good to the poor and more gentle and forbearing to others.

(11) Never open his letters nor appear inquisitive about anything he does not volunteer to tell you.

In order that her parents should have no suspicion of what was taking place, Isabel had arranged that it should be said that she was going away to visit friends. At nine o'clock on Tuesday, 22nd January 1861, she ran up to her parents' room for a final farewell. Both blessed her in happy ignorance and she was so overcome that when she was outside the room she had to kiss the door. Driving to the house of friends, she changed her travelling dress for a fawn confection with a black lace cloak and white bonnet, then, clutching a friend's hand, she was driven rapidly to the Catholic church in Warwick Street.

Richard was standing on the steps in a rough shooting-coat and puffing furiously at a black cigar. If he wished to turn back, as some say he did, it was now too late.

They made a striking couple as they entered the building, where a deputy of Cardinal Wiseman awaited them. The dark Arab cast of Richard's face and the tall square figure in its rough tweeds were a perfect foil for Isabel's brown-gold, blue-eyed, buxom beauty. Spectators watched in admiration as the great traveller led his bride up the aisle, but there were those who wondered at the result of this strangely ill-assorted union.[1]

The ceremony over, they drove to a friend's house in Welbeck Street for the wedding breakfast, and thence walked to Burton's bachelor chambers in St. James's. Their baggage had preceded them. Once inside, Isabel gave one glance at the rooms littered with books, MSS., Eastern bric-à-brac, and weapons in which he had lived, then she shut the door and flung herself into his arms.

He was hers at last.

That evening Burton sat down and wrote to his new father-in-law a characteristic letter.

> My dear Father,
>
> I have committed a highway robbery by marrying your daughter Isabel at Warwick Street Church, and before the registrar—the details she is writing to her mother.
>
> It only remains for me to say that I have no ties or liaisons of any kind, that the marriage was perfectly legal and respectable.
>
> I want no money with Isabel; I can work, and it will be my care that Time shall bring you nothing to regret.
>
> > I am,
> >
> > Yours sincerely,
> >
> > Richard F. Burton.

Mr. Arundell received the news of the marriage with pleasure. His wife never forgave it. To the end of her life she declared, " Dick is no relation of mine "; and she steadfastly refused to believe any good of him.

§

Burton refused a honeymoon, considering such things " indelicate exhibitions," and he almost immediately applied himself to the task of completing his book on the Mormons, *City of the Saints* (1861). For a few weeks Isabel was deliriously happy; then she settled down and began to take serious stock of the situation.

On liquidating their joint debts, Burton discovered their sole assets to be a lump of capital, worth £4000, the income

---

[1] His sister, Eliza, did not approve; and her daughter summed up the union as on his part " as serious an imprudence as when he sent Speke alone to search for the Victoria Nyanza." *Life of Captain Burton*, Georgiana Stisted.

from which, together with his half-pay, brought in about £350 a year; a sum which for two extravagant people was utterly inadequate. It was obvious that he must cast about for lucrative work. His books barely paid for themselves, his prospects were nil. What should he do?

He was still in the Indian army, and in the ordinary course of events would have returned to Bombay with his wife, rejoined his regiment and settled down once more to the routine of army life.

But India was impossible. Incredible though it might seem after his subsequent exploits, the reverberations of the Karachi affair still hung in the air. He knew from private advice that headquarters had not forgotten, and that, so far as Indian service was concerned, an ineradicable black mark stood against his name. Hopes of promotion, with such prejudice against him, were almost none.

A friend suggested the Consular service, for which his qualifications admirably fitted him. But Consulship in a sense meant retirement, and Burton did not want to retire. Yet, what else was there? For a while he considered it and hesitated. Then urged on by Isabel, he wrote tentatively offering himself for a post. Isabel got into touch with influential friends, Lord John Russell was approached, and the result was a letter from the Foreign Office offering him what seemed the worst Consulate on record; that at Fernando Po, on the West African Coast, with a salary of £700 a year.

Burton as usual thought he saw his enemies behind the offer and laughed sardonically. Fernando Po, called unofficially the " Foreign Office Grave," the cemetery of almost every Consul who had been there, was a fitting place for one of England's most hated men. " They want me to die," he exclaimed. " But, by God, I intend to live just to spite the devils ! "

In replying, accepting the offer, he made but one plea, and that for Isabel's sake.

" My connection with H.M.'s Indian Army has now lasted upwards of nineteen years, and I am unwilling to retire without pension or selling out of my corps. If, therefore, my name could be retained upon the list of my regiment—as, for instance, is the case with H.M. Consul at Zanzibar—I should feel deeply indebted . . ."

He would also be able to retain the half-pay that would help to smooth Isabel's path at home.

This letter was forwarded to India by the Foreign Office where, as he must have half-expected, only too glad to be rid of him, they promptly struck his name off the Army List and swept his whole nineteen years' service into oblivion.

Coldly furious, yet resigned, he turned his back on his active military career and rarely spoke of it again, except to refer with bitter sarcasm to the " office rats of Bombay."

§

One rare friendship, and from a quarter least expected, came in this awkward and uncertain period to gladden his heart. He had for some time been a regular visitor at Fryston, the Yorkshire mansion of that dilettante patron of the 'sixties, Lord Houghton. To Fryston was invited all that was brilliant, witty, and new in contemporary life. Here poets rubbed shoulders with generals, and politicians with the brightest products of the London or Paris *ateliers*. It was Houghton's mischievous delight to mix his gatherings so that the most incongruous persons were brought in contact. At the famous Fryston round dinner-table the oddest of personalities were set beside one another, and their host would watch their behaviour with all the sensations of a benign and roguish Puck.

He must have contemplated a meeting between the burly explorer and Orientalist, Richard Burton, and the sprite-like, effeminate little poet, Algernon Charles Swinburne, with the complacent thrill of an artist bringing off a *chef d'œuvre*. Two such opposite and incompatible types it would be difficult to find. Swinburne was lured down to Fryston by the promise of an opportunity to read de Sade's *Justine*, which had given vice a new name, and there young, intolerant poet and soured, middle-aged traveller met.

But Houghton's amusement turned to amazement. Unbelievably, here two bizarre personalities ran together and fused. Something in each man seemed instantly to call to the other. Perhaps it was the same vigorous courage, fanatic hatred of the conventional, and love of the scabrous ; perhaps it was Burton's admiration of perfect literary artistry compared with his own cumbrous flounderings, and Swinburne was attracted by Burton's intense physical magnetism, so at variance with the poet's own frailty.

The week-end was one of the most successful ever held at Fryston. Swinburne forgot the delicious torments of *Justine* in listening to the stories from Burton's own great erotic knowledge. In turn he delighted the traveller with recitations of some of his unprintable squibs. Rossetti, Palgrave, Froude, Petherick, and the Kingsley's were there. In the drawing-room Swinburne and Rossetti gave extracts from their latest poems, and Burton sat cross-legged on a pillow, read Omar Khayyam alternately in English and Persian, and raised his head to chant a Call to Prayer to a circle of entranced ladies. Palgrave must have been amused : we are not told what Froude or the Kingsley's thought. Swinburne and Burton talked together incessantly, and only one person watched their growing friendship with distress. Isabel disliked Swinburne on sight. She guessed, if she did not know, the tastes which attracted Richard to him, and the reason for the covert winks and sly remarks which passed constantly between them. She watched each vie with the other in shocking the ladies, knowing that this was Richard's fatal weakness and that Swinburne was encouraging it. And when they returned to London and Richard began to take Swinburne on a round of dissipation (which nearly shattered the poet's already weak health), she redoubled her prayers for him.

But she said nothing. It was part of her laborious policy of wifehood never to criticize Richard, even to herself. She suffered in silence, trying hard to forget what was really only a pinprick in her new-married life. Fortunately the two men could meet but rarely and, with Burton's increasing social engagements, less and less.

§

Isabel could not accompany him to the deadly climate of Fernando Po and, while the few remaining months of his leave sped by, she tried to forget the inevitable parting as best she could. They plunged into a round of society ; or rather Isabel led, dragging the unwilling Richard after her. Her friends watched with amusement as, radiant and gushing, Isabel led this morose-looking ogre across drawing-room floors ; wondering what such a vigorous, handsome, well-bred girl could see in a penniless eccentric of forty, with few friends, a bad reputation, and no status except that of a third-rate Consulate on some desolate coast.

But Isabel was above noticing strictures. She was playing a new part for the first time in her life, and enjoying it thoroughly. Her Richard was to be a Consul ; very well, then, he should not lack for a good Consul's wife. With that wonderful energy of hers, she moved mountains to raise and secure her social status. She pestered Lord John Russell until he secured her a " drawing-room " ; then she got herself presented at court so that her social position at foreign embassies should be secure for all time. She prodded Richard into asking Lord Houghton to induce Palmerston to give an evening party, of which she was to be the bride of the evening. She gave " at homes " in Richard's bachelor rooms and conducted throngs of young ladies round his trophies while she descanted on her future life with him in the desert. For seven months she was in heaven. She was always to look back on this time as the happiest in her life. " Even if I had had no other, it would have been worth living for."

But the time for parting came only too soon. In August, Burton had to leave for his Consulate. Isabel accompanied him to Liverpool in an agony of desolation. There was only one consolation. They had arranged a half-way meeting-place at Madeira, where she could meet him for holidays and leave. But even this could not help to assuage her grief at parting and her gnawing fear " knowing he had Africa at his back he would do more of those explorations into unknown lands."

At Liverpool she clung fiercely to his arm, choking back the tears manfully, and he, who hated good-byes, made her promise that, if he allowed her to accompany him on board, she would not unman him by crying. Pluckily she promised, followed him below, unpacked his bags, settled his cabin, and arranged his things.

Then came the agony of farewell. " My whole life and soul were in that good-bye . . . I found myself on board the tug which flew faster and faster from the steamer. I saw a white handkerchief go up to his face . . . I then drove to a spot where I could see the steamer till she became a dot. . . ."

That little figure in its waving crinoline with fluttering handkerchief was Burton's last sight of England for another eighteen months.

Chapter Eight

WITH the discovery of Tanganyika, Burton's career as explorer and pioneer was virtually finished. He was to make other expeditions, but they were now to be always restricted by the leading-strings of wife or consular duty. No more was there to be that rare and precious joy of breaking new paths in distant countries, alone and accountable to none. A new life lay before him, civilian and comparatively unadventurous; and henceforth his books seem to reflect it. They lose the *joie de vivre* that make Mecca and Harar so infectious; they take on the added solidity and complexity of the student. In them, narrative seems to become a mere thread on which to string enormous loads of data. They are the work of a man in retirement; the traveller turned scholar.

He faced his new task with energy and determination; energy to overcome the problems before him, determination to succeed in this career, even though failure had dogged the last one.

His first emotions on reaching Fernando Po were, he confesses, suicidal. The little Spanish island off the Gold Coast seemed to be nothing but a death-trap. At that time the only part inhabited by the Spanish colonists was the lowlands round the harbour, a region as unhealthy and dangerous from tropic damp and rotting vegetation as that in a fetid marsh. Cholera, dysentery, and enteric stalked through the town and, within a few weeks of his arrival, yellow fever swept away seventy-eight out of the 250 white men in the colony. Santa Isabel, where the Consulate, a stifling, wooden structure with corrugated iron roof and frameless windows through which stole perpetually the stench of the rotting refuse in the harbour, stood, was reminiscent of some Goya purgatory.

" Pallid men were to be seen sitting or lolling languid in their verandas, and occasionally crawling about the grass-grown streets, each with a cigarette hanging to his lower lip . . . breakfast and dinner were frequently enlivened by the spectacle of a something covered with a blanket being carried in, and after due time a something within a deal box being borne out on four ghastly men's shoulders. Strangers fled the place like a pestilence; sailors even from the monotonous 'south coast' felt the *ennui* of Fernando Po to be deadly—gravelike . . ." [1]

Burton decided to try the effects of height, moved his Consulate several hundred feet up the hill-sides above the town, and was rewarded by an instant improvement in health. He erected a new building, called it Buena Vista, and settled down to his duties.

Two important ones required instant attention. The first was the behaviour of the town negroes who, grown familiar with Spanish " poor white trash," treated the remainder of the colony, including Burton's predecessor, with an insolent familiarity very damaging to consular prestige. Burton's cure of this evil was instant and absolute. A big buck nigger, sent to try the new Consul's mettle, strode into the Consulate one day, clapped the Consul on the back, made a joke with him; and next instant found himself flying head first through the nearest Consulate window to land amid shrieks of delight from the native boys.

With the second evil, that of visiting ships, he was equally abrupt. The policy of captains putting in at Fernando Po with cargoes was to unload as quickly as possible and put out to sea again before the fever-stench took too close a grip of their nostrils. Thus merchants had no time to reply to their correspondence, mails were delayed, and trade was seriously hampered. An examination of the shipping contracts showed that captains were obliged to stay in port " eighteen hours daylight " in order to take on the mails. The previous Consul had evidently overlooked this. Burton put the document on his desk and, when the next captain hurried in, the following dialogue is reported to have taken place.[2]

" Now, sir, hurry up with my papers. I want to be off; going to clear out."

" Oh, you can't go. I haven't finished my letters."

" Oh, damn your letters, sir. I'm off."

" Stop a bit," said Burton, still *piano*, " let's have a look at your contract. It says here you must stop eighteen hours daylight."

" Oh yes, but nobody has ever enforced that; the other Consuls have never bothered about it."

[1] *Wanderings in West Africa*, 1863
[2] *Life of Sir Richard Burton*, Isabel Burton, 1893.

" The more shame for them," said Burton. " Now are you going to stay ? "

" No, sir, not I."

" Very well then." Here Burton must have risen with that sudden, disconcerting, feline grin. " I am going to the Governor's and I am going to shot two guns. If you leave *one minute* before your time expires, I shall send the first gun across your bows, and the second slap into you. I am a man of my word. Good morning ! "

§

Burton's consular jurisdiction was found to extend over the whole Bight of Biafra ; and after the first spell of work was over, he was able to make numerous expeditions along the Gold, Slave, and Grain Coasts. A journey to Abeokuta, in the company of a naval mission, was succeeded by one to the deathly Bonny River region, where torture was a cult and men and animals nailed to trees in hideous agony offended the eyes of the traveller, and attested to the tastes of the people.

Recuperative holidays were also taken in the lovely Cameroon mountains, which rise sheerly from the sea nineteen miles from Fernando Po on the mainland. Here Burton was the first man to scale the topmost peak, 13,370 feet high, where he built a memorial cairn of stones, concealing beneath it, we are told, a torn page of *Punch*.

With welcome breaks like these he was able to keep his health and stave off the decimating yellow fever which many at home had believed would kill him. His literary work comprised a number of pamphlets and monographs to the R.G.S. and two voluminous books of record, *Wanderings in West Africa* (Tinsley, 1863) and *Abeokuta and the Cameroons* (1863). He also collected the material for a book on the Gaboon country, *Gorilla Land*, which was to appear later (1875).

Thus the first eighteen months of his Consulate passed : so happy that he was able to write : " Life, as an American missionary remarked, is somewhat primitive at Buena Vista, but it is not the less pleasant. An hour of work in my garden at sunrise and sunset, when the scenery is equally beautiful, hard reading during the day, and after dark a pipe and a new book of travels, this is the *fallentis semita vitae* which makes one shudder before plunging once more into the cold and swirling waters of society—of civilization . . ."

§

But, if he was happy, there was another at home who was
not. To Richard, during the tranquil days at Buena Vista,
there came from England a little poem :

> Oh, when wilt thou return, my love ?
> For as the moments glide,
> They leave me wishing still for thee
> My husband by my side ;
> And ever at the evening hour
> My hopes more fondly burn,
> And still they linger on that word,
> " Oh, when wilt thou return."

Isabel, living with her parents in London, was fretting
constantly. Grass widowhood did not sit well on her active
and affectionate nature. It was not the inaction that galled her,
for she had plenty to do. Commissions of various sorts came
from Fernando Po by almost every mail. She fought unsuccess-
fully against the Bombay Government's edict to strike Burton
off their list ; she arranged his book on the Mormons (largely a
defence of polygamy) for the press ; she sent and received a
constant flow of books, pamphlets, and MSS. She also had the
unpleasant task (given her most foolishly by her husband) of
taking over some Napoleonic relics which had come into the
hands of Burton's family,[1] and a complete set of Richard's
works to the Royal Family at the Tuileries. She was refused
an audience and returned home in an ignominy that was none
of her fault. After this setback—a shattering blow to one with
her social aspirations—she pined all the more for Richard and
with her spirits lowered by an attack of diphtheria fell into one
of her declines. Then, realizing that to behave thus was not
worthy of her husband, she arose, went to the Foreign Office,
and burst into tears upon the shoulder of Sir Henry Layard,
who was so touched at this piece of diplomacy that he obtained
a four months' leave for Richard and had it dispatched the same
afternoon. A few weeks later (December 1863) Richard was
home.

Their meeting was a happy one. Christmas was spent at
Fryston with Lord Houghton and at Wardour Castle and Garswood, Yorkshire, with Isabel's relations. The following month

---

[1] Burton's uncle, an army surgeon, had been present at Napoleon's death on
St. Helena, and had secured a lock of hair and a drawing of the Emperor.

they decided that Isabel should accompany Richard part of the way back to Fernando Po, for a long holiday *en route*.

Isabel's diary prattles gaily on this holiday. They embarked in an ancient steamer at Liverpool and ran almost instantly into the "biggest storm that was ever known." While Burton was helping at the pumps and Isabel lay *in extremis*, a drunken naval officer burst into her cabin and lay rolling about in several inches of water on the floor. Richard returned, hurled the officer outside by the scruff of the neck, and rather brutally told his wife that the captain had remarked they could not live long in such a sea: to which Isabel could only reply feebly, "Thank God it will be over soon." Immediately, she records, Burton turned on her in a fury. "I shall never forget how angry he was because I was not frightened, and gave me quite a sermon . . ."

Reaching Madeira, they spent a few weeks there and then continued to Teneriffe, where Isabel had her first taste of the campaigning she had so longed to do with her husband. After a tour of the island, they ascended the Peak, at first on horses and then on foot, Isabel towed by a guide with a red *cummer-bund* round her waist. They reached the top on Passion Sunday, and here Isabel, in petticoat and blouse—she had shed all other garments on the way—persuaded the Catholic guides to let her say Mass, while all knelt except Richard, who looked on, smoking a cigar, as if watching some native rite.

At Orotava they lived a whole month " in the wilds among the peasantry . . . no trammels of society, no world, out of civilization, *en bourgeois*, and doing everything for ourselves, with the bare necessaries of life." Isabel was idyllically happy; this surely was the wild and lawless life spoken of so frequently by Mr. Disraeli. Settling down together, they fell into that routine that was to become familiar to Isabel during the next twenty-five years. "We rose at seven, cup of tea, and toilet. Then came my domestic work (Richard had plunged into literature at half past seven) . . . Breakfast at ten, write till two (journals and diaries kept up, etc.), dinner at two; then walk or ride or make an excursion; cup of tea on coming in, literature till ten, with a break of supper at eight, and at ten to bed; a delightfully healthy and wholesome life, both for mind and body . . ."

But the little cloud always looming on the horizon grew gradually larger. Richard's leave drew to its close; and after a clinging farewell at Santa Cruz, Isabel returned to England while Richard turned his face once more towards the vapours of Fernando Po.

§

During the early months of 1864 Burton's consular duties were enlivened by an expedition that in some ways was not unreminiscent of the journey to Harar. This was a diplomatic mission to the negro kingdom of Dahomé and a visit to its king, Gelele, with messages and presents from the British Foreign Office and the Sovereign.

For some years Dahomé, situated between Abeokuta and the Grain Coast, had presented a difficult problem to Her Britannic Majesty. A pagan and semi-civilized country under the sway of a despot king to whom, by state law, all men were slaves and women wives, it had attracted the attention of humanitarians by its wholesale export in slaves, by the severity of its warfare, carried on against neighbouring countries, by a highly trained army of Amazon women soldiers, and by its yearly religious ceremonies, known as Customs, which were made the excuse for human sacrifice on a large and revolting scale. Few Europeans had penetrated to Abomey, its capital sixty miles in the interior, but those who had done so brought back appalling stories of what they had seen. At the Customs, some said, as many as 2000 men and women were slaughtered in a day ; others told of canoes paddled down deep trenches filled with blood, pyramids of skulls, cannibal orgies, and other nightmares. Many of these stories were obviously second-hand fabrications told to gullible Europeans by slave-dealers who wished to deter them from entering the country : but sufficient positive facts had been obtained to justify a naval mission to the capital, a year before Burton's departure, which had brought back accredited accounts enough to make any stiff-collared English gorge rise.

And so to their Consul in the Bight the Foreign Office turned with instructions to call upon the king and endeavour by soft words backed by steel to turn him gently from his profession of slave-dealing and his religion of human slaughter. One very positive instruction was given : " You should, if possible, stipulate with the king before proceeding to Abomey that there should be no human sacrifices during the time of your stay in his capital, and you will, under any circumstances, decline to sanction these sacrifices by your presence, if they should unfortunately take place whilst you are in the country . . ." [1]

It was no easy task, as no one knew better than Burton ; but he entered upon it with alacrity for he was always pleased of an opportunity to study native tribes, and was aware that this chance would be an unparalleled one. He embarked on the 29th November 1863 on H.M.S. *Antelope*; a touch of comedy being added to his departure by the arrival of an urgent request from Isabel, who was viewing the expedition with concern, to accompany him from England with a magic lantern containing Old Testament scenes which she was convinced with her oratory would soften the savage heart of Gelele and turn his thoughts towards the Church of Rome.

Whydah, the Dahoman port, was reached on 5th December, after a halt at Lagos to pick up a medical officer, Mr. Cruick-shank ; and an official landing was made through the surf amid the customary salute of muskets. The party was received on shore by a headman led by a Kru-boy carrying a Union Jack, followed by five hammocks and a guard of six armed Kru-men in brilliant red caps. Here they were joined by a native Wesleyan minister, a Mr. Bernasko, who knew the language and had visited the interior.

A halt of eight days was made at this miserable native port, where the only signs of commerce were a few tumble-down European liquor factories, while the Commission waited for the arrival of the king's messengers from Abomey with the royal permission for them to proceed. These at length arrived, two eunuchs bearing the credentials, a shark and a lion stick, decorated pieces of wood attached to crude effigies of fish and beast, hammered out of silver dollars.

With these, the party left Whydah on 13th December and turned north-eastwards through luxuriant but untilled country. The Mission now consisted of nearly a hundred souls, and included body servants, interpreters, fifty-nine porters, and thirty hammock men. Among the goods carried was a large crate containing the presents sent to the king from England. These, chosen by the Foreign Office, on whose authority we do not know, consisted of :

One 40-foot circular crimson silk-damask tent with pole complete.

[1] Foreign Office, 20th August 1863.

One richly embossed pipe with amber mouthpiece in Morocco case.

Two richly embossed silver belts with lion and crane in raised relief in Morocco cases.

Two silver and partly gilt waiters in oak case.

One coat of mail and gauntlets.

The journey of Abomey, a mere sixty miles, took six whole days ; little time was available for marching as several hours had to be spent at each of the native villages *en route* attending festivities and speeches.

" At every village, even where only two dancers could be mustered, upon us was the ceremony inflicted. Advancing in our hammocks, which were preceded by men capering, firing, and shouting songs of welcome, we saw the Caboceer (Chief) prepared to receive us in state. Shaded by a tattered and battered old white calico umbrella, he sat upon a tall Gold Coast stool, with a smaller edition cut out of the same block supporting his naked feet. Our seats were ranged opposite the Caboceer—mine in the centre, Mr. Cruickshank's on the right, the missionary's on my left, the interpreters behind, and the rest anywhere . . ." Then began interminable hours of dancing, speech-making, and rum-drinking. The principal dance of Dahomé was the decapitation dance, in which the performer went through all the gestures of sawing off and exhibiting the head of an enemy. When exhaustion terminated these inspiring efforts, the chief would then approach the Mission and bow low to Burton, shouting that : " If I ordered him to jump (suiting the action to the words) jump he must ; if told to fly (fluttering his arms) he must become a bird, and if sent beneath the earth (smoothing the dust with his hand) he must go there . . . The speeches were delivered with an immense vehemence of voice and gesture ; at times a screaming question was addressed to the bystanders, who replied with a long-drawn groan of general assent and applause . . ." [1]

Proceeding like this through the long, hot days, they at length reached Henvi, a midway station, where they met the outposts of Gelele's famous warrior women, the Abomey Amazons. These *androgynes*, who far outstripped the effeminate men of the country in valour and efficiency, were nearly six feet tall, immensely broad and very powerfully developed.

[1] Extracts in this section are taken from *A Mission to Gelele, King of Dahomé*, 1864.

They were dressed in skirts and tunics, carried heavy muskets and knives, walked with a military roll, and only betrayed their sex by the bulging of their breasts. As soldiers they were feared the length and breadth of the Gold Coast; they were apparently immune from pain, fought with the ferocity of tigers, and gave no quarter. Their profession demanded of them a strict celibacy except towards the king, to whom they were official wives. But celibacy being difficult in 90 degrees F., no fewer than 150, at the time of Burton's mission, had been found pregnant and were being tried by the king at a special inquiry outside the capital. From this few would escape, and most of their paramours would die.

The country changed as they approached the last stages of the journey from rolling grassland and jungle to settlements built of reddish clay, the dust from which lay over everything like a bloody and ominous pall.

Towards the end of the sixth day, a little tinkling bell heard along the narrow path warned them that they were nearing the dread king's neighbourhood. Instantly the entire native escort dived into the jungle and lay with their faces hidden while a troop of women preceded by the bell-ringer came down the path. The Englishmen looked on astonished at this disruption of the caravan by a handful of women; but on inquiry were informed that the women were the king's personal slaves, and that no man, on pain of death, might look at them. Tinkling warning-bells were now heard everywhere as the party approached the court, and little groups of women could be seen in all directions moving through grovelling groups of men. Small temples appeared by the wayside exhibiting hideous little images with enormous phalli that dripped realistically in perpetual baths of palm oil; human skulls and jawbones lined the houses, and the Dahoman national flag, a decapitated head, a red knife, and a torn heart on a white background, fluttered from roof-tops.

A few yards farther on they were met by a deputation from the king and formed into a procession for entry into the royal presence.

" All our party then formed file, led by a youth carrying the king's cane, which had reached us at Whydah, and by the solemn eunuch. . . . Mr. Hilton (a native interpreter) preceded the hammocks with the flag of St. George, followed by the Reverend Bernasko. I went next with my armed Kru-men in bright caps; behind me was Mr. Cruickshank. Between the

ceremonial trees and the palace the distance is about a quarter
of an hour in hammocks ; the different interruptions multiplied
it by three ; at every 100 yards a three-pounder ship's swivel
fired a blank shot and was carried on the shoulder of a porter
to the next station. The direction was north, with a little
westing. A broad, well-worn and carefully cleaned road, hard
with water-rolled pebbles, wound through grass plots, scatterings
of wild cotton heaps, and tufts of cotton between fields of maize
and ' thur ' and under the noble trees detaching the divers
homesteads. An abundance of fetish was also present . . ."

Moving in this manner slowly forward, the procession was
greeted by thunderous cheers from an assembled multitude and
by a carefully arranged song, the refrain of which was :

> Burton, he hath seen all the world with its Kings and Caboceers :
> He now cometh to Dahomé and he shall see everything here.

From this moment the Mission seemed to enter a phan-
tasmagoria ; a blending of comic opera and bloody nightmare.
Entering through the gates of the palace, round which clustered
a crowd of white umbrellas (the sign of a chief) each with its
crude heraldic device, they removed their swords and, passing
up an aisle of crouching Amazons, were halted at a circle of
white sand where they were told to make their obeisances.
Burton and Cruickshank removed their caps and bowed cere-
moniously to a figure hidden in the shadow at the far end, while
the remainder of the natives grovelled in the sand, burying their
faces and pouring handfuls of it over their heads. Then slowly,
while everyone bent double and that curious tinkling bell broke
out, they were led forward to the throne.

At this moment the monster himself emerged into the sunlight and disclosed himself as an athletic man of middle age,
with a strong and ruthless, but not brutal, face, red-rimmed
eyes, powerful limbs enclosed in silver bracelets, and strong
hands with enormous talons growing out inches from the fingers,
which held a body cloth of white calico fringed with green silk
over a pair of purple flowered silk drawers. He was smoking a
long, silver-worked pipe and greeted the Englishmen with a
pleasant smile. Behind him squatted a throng of wives and
slave girls who peered curiously at the visitors. Running his
eye quickly over them, Burton noted that " not a pretty face
appeared ; most had sooty skins, and the few browns showed
negro features. They atoned for this homeliness by an extreme

devotion to their lord and master. It is no wonder that the
King of Dahomé's soul lodges well. If perspiration appears
upon the royal brow, it is instantly removed with the softest
cloth by the gentlest hands ; if the royal dress be disarranged
it is at once adjusted ; if the royal lips move, a plated spittoon
held by one of the wives is moved within convenient distance ;
the king sneezes, all present touch the ground with their
foreheads ; if he drinks, every lip utters an exclamation of
blessing. . . ."

After a few moments of mutual bowing, finger-clicking, and
hand-wagging, the Mission was provided with stools in front of
the throne, a battered table with worn gilt legs that had once
graced some European card-room appeared, and rum, water,
and gin were served. All helped themselves, and another strange
custom made itself known. " After bowing and touching glasses,
the king suddenly wheeled round, whilst two wives stretched
a white calico cloth by way of a screen before him, and another
pair opened small and gaudy parasols, so as completely to
conceal his figure from our gaze. There was a prodigious
outburst of noise. Guns were fired, Amazons tinkled bells, and
sprang watchmen's rattles, ministers bent to the ground clapping
their palms and commoners bawled ' Po-o-o,' cowering to avoid
the dread sight, turning their backs if sitting, and if standing
they danced like bears, or they paddled their hands like the
forefeet of a swimming dog. We were not expected to move." [1]

The toasts were followed by a number of gun salutes ; the
first for the king, a second of eleven guns for Cruickshank, and
a third of nine guns for Burton. The latter at once complained
through his gibbering interpreter, and the king, with grave
excuses, at once ordered two more to be fired. After this for a
time the Mission withdrew.

At the next audience, however, a conversation took place.
This was carried out by the king speaking to his Grand Vizier,
the Vizier to the interpreter, and so to Burton, and vice versa.
Among the first was a demand to know whether the presents
of a horse and carriage and a white woman, as commanded
through Burton's naval predecessor, had been brought. There
was a little awkwardness here, only to be tided over by tact.
Commander Wilmot, leader of the expedition of the previous
year, had brought with him as gift a large coloured picture of
Queen Victoria in full coronation regalia. Gelele had received

[1] For fear of making witchcraft.

this with intense interest, examined its possibilities with a critical eye, and then demanded of Wilmot that the next Mission should bring him a white woman. Wilmot had quibbled uncomfortably and not been definite about this; but, hoping to extricate himself, he had definitely promised the coach and horses. Unfortunately, when reminded of this promise, the Foreign Office, who had not the danger of facing the king in his own country, had jibbed. "With respect to these," they had written to Burton, "you will explain to the king, that in the first place it would be a difficult matter to get English horses out to the Coast, and even supposing they arrived safely at their destination, it would be very doubtful, from the nature of the country and climate, whether they would long survive their arrival." [1]

It was well enough at Whitehall to speak of doubts and difficulties and try to palm off matters with a crimson tent. Burton did his best, but for some time a cloud lingered on the Royal brow; and perhaps there was a touch of conscious humour about the list of presents the king was later to send to the Great White Queen in return. Meanwhile the crate was unpacked and the gifts brought forth and displayed. They were received diffidently, which was not surprising considering that the tent turned out to be useless, the coat of mail too small, and the pipe and belts inferior to those already possessed. The only acceptable object was the silver gilt waiters which were received with some interest and gratification.

There were now more drinks, more healths, shouts, discharges of guns, grovellings, and ceremonious dances, and then the king directed that the Mission should precede him to Abomey, whither he would go when justice was concluded for the wholesale adulteries of his army. Accordingly, the Mission set off the same day and, after a few hours' march through palm groves, arrived at the gates of the straggling capital of this decaying African empire. Greeted by headmen, they marched along broken roads lined with curious gazers, through the city whose red clay houses seemed to lean crazily in all directions. Passing the king's main palace, the walls of which could be seen crumbling, and where there was a room reputed to be completely paved by the skulls of the king's fallen enemies, Burton remarked it as being singularly uninspiring, reminiscent mostly of "an assemblage of farmyards with long thatched barns." They skirted

[1] Foreign Office, 20th August 1863.

this and, after crossing a market-place, reached their own lodging, which turned out to be a barn also with a small hall and sleeping platform, and a small, dark room in the back wall through which Burton at once knocked a hole and provided with a makeshift shutter. In this tiny study, where he worked for a full two months in indescribable heat, he took out his notes and began the long report which would have to be sent to the Foreign Office while he waited for the arrival of the king.

§

Burton had timed his visit to coincide with the king's Annual Customs, a protest against which was to be part of the Mission. The word indicated a certain period of the year set aside for the paying of annual charges or tribute to the king, and the accompanying festivities were marked by appalling human slaughter. In Dahomé the primitive belief that the dead departed to a spot similar to earth was revived, and the theory that a dead king should be accompanied to the Shades by most of his court, all his wives, and a considerable bodyguard was practised. Gelele's father, King Gezo, like an ancient Chaldean, had been followed to the tomb by the massacre of some 500 men, women, and children, who were to make life comfortable for him in the beyond. But even dead he was not out of touch. Like a dutiful son, Gelele kept him *au courant* with Dahoman affairs by a constant flow of messengers, slaughtered slaves, whose spirits bore the messages to him as soon as possible. Any change in policy, any illness, an amusing story, a new drum, or a grandchild was blandly whispered in the ear of some shivering slave who was then decapitated and sent upon his errand. Sometimes the king would dispatch a messneger, omit an item, remember it, and send another on his heels to remedy the defect. To compute the yearly sacrifices and executions was difficult, but Burton, after careful inquiries, estimated that at least 600 or 700 must die ; the major part of them at the dreaded Customs which were soon to commence.

Early on 28th December a discharge of musketry was heard from the palace and messengers appeared requesting the attendance of the Mission, as the king was back and the ceremonies were about to begin. Entering hammocks, Burton and his companions were carried swiftly towards the palace.

Passing through the market-place, they saw an ominous sight. A large victim shed, an open structure not unlike an

English village church and tower, its roof covered by a tattered blood-red cloth, was already full. Some twenty wretches could could be seen crouched on stools, their limbs lashed to a long connecting pole. They were clothed in a macabre uniform, somewhat reminiscent of the Inquisition *san benito* (possibly derived from Portuguese sources), long white pointed caps, spiralled with blue ribbon and calico shifts, bound with red, with a crimson patch over the heart. But they were not, the passer-by noticed, uncomfortable. " The confinement was not cruel ; each victim had an attendant squatting behind him to keep off the flies ; all were fed four times a day, and were loosed at night for sleep . . . It is the king's object to keep them in the best of humours . . . These men will allow themselves to be led to slaughter like lambs. It is, I imagine, the uncertainty of their fate that produces this extraordinary nonchalance. They marked time to music, and chattered together, especially remarking us . . ."

Arriving in the palace yard, which was filled with Amazons, chiefs, and commoners and disclosed in one corner another thronged victim shed, the party halted to await the king, who presently appeared heralded by a cannon-shot and loud applause.

After greetings and compliments, the Europeans sat down, the battered card-table was whisked in front of them and the ceremonies began with a long day of dancing, speeches, and songs. On the second day, the king himself danced a *pas seul* amid tumultuous excitement. The third day was a day of giving, in which the king scattered handfuls of cowrie money in the palace yard, even flinging some into the laps of those in the victim shed. Then, with a loud tinkling of bells and a discharge of muskets, the king, according to Dahoman custom, indicated that, on his guest's intercession, some of the victims would be spared. Taking his cue, Burton rose and pleaded for them, urging that mercy was the great prerogative of kings. Upon this, by the king's instructions, nearly half the victims were untied and brought before him on all fours to receive his clemency. Followed a dance of women ; and then a warlike speech from the king rousing the populace to wrath against neighbouring Abeokuta, in which he declared that his honour could only be redeemed by the country's complete destruction. (This was another point on which the Mission wished to question him.) The ceremonies again concluded with the customary drinking of toasts.

That night was known as Zan Nyanyana, or the Night of Evil. Accompanied by a procession, which, according to instructions, the Europeans refused to join, the king proceeded to the victim sheds to wield the first axe or club and superintend the rest of the slaughter. So far as could be discovered, most of the victims were dispatched by strangling or clubbing and, it was believed, without unnecessary cruelty.

All night the Europeans sat sleepless while outside the continual thumping of the death drum and the echo of musket shots announced the slaughter of the victims. Hot and restless in his little room, Burton, who was appalled but would not allow himself to be carried away by emotion, listened to the drumming and tried to argue the question logically on paper.

" The king takes no pleasure in the tortures and death, or in the sight of blood," he wrote. " Human sacrifice in Dahomé is founded upon a purely religious basis, which not only strengthens but perpetuates the custom. It is a touching instance of the king's filial piety, deplorably mistaken, but perfectly sincere . . . The slain men are mostly criminals and war captives. We can hardly find fault with putting criminals to death when in the Year of Grace 1864 we hung four murderers upon the same gibbet before 100,000 gaping souls at Liverpool . . . and with respect to slaying captives, it must be remembered that this severity depends upon the nature of African wars ; with these people *lex talionis* is the highest experience of law, and after defeat quarter is only given to those who are reserved for slavery or for sacrifice . . ."

But even he quailed when informed by Bernasko that for every man executed in public outside the palace, a woman is slaughtered secretly by Amazons inside.

The next morning, on passing to the palace for the continuation of the ceremonies, Burton found the victim sheds empty. Their inhabitants were not far distant. Several corpses attired in their grotesque shirts and caps were seated tied in pairs to stools at the top of a framework scaffold. Others, stripped naked, were dangling by their heels, legs tied apart, and *genitalia* excised out of respect to the court wives. There was very little blood below, testifying that clubbing or suffocation had been the method of killing. Near the palace gate a dozen decapitated heads were arranged in a neat pattern on the ground. Burton computed that the first Night of Evil had accounted for some fifty victims.

More pageant continued through this day. The Amazons gave a march past and were reviewed by the king. . They revealed themselves in action as quite well-organized troops, consisting of musket women, razor women (armed with giant three-foot decapitation razors), and knife women. These, in close order, discharging their pieces and shouting, circled several times round the yard accompanied by a band of braying horns, whistles, and drums. They were followed by a long procession of the king's possessions terminating in a review of his various equipages, a series of antediluvian barouches, an old English Sedan chair, a brougham with embossed panels, and two American trotting wagons with leathern hoods. Next came a group of hunchbacks drumming on instruments manu-factured from human skulls ; and finally a long procession of all the court officials, who marched and counter-marched until nightfall when the Europeans were dismissed and could return wearily past the already stinking corpses to their cramped lodgings.

A few days of rest were now allowed, and on 4th January the Customs began again with new vigour. More victims were slain, bodies lashed in every imaginable attitude hung from trees, half-hidden by turkey buzzards ; the king danced for his people ; then called upon his guests to dance, whereupon a welcome touch of comedy appeared in this nightmare with the spectacle of Burton and Cruickshank jigging solemnly to a delighted crowd, while the Rev. Bernasko accompanied them with hymns on the accordion,[1] So entranced was Gelele by this performance that he did Burton the great honour of taking his hand and leading him out to do a *pas de deux*. Gelele did a magnificent decapitation dance and Burton tried to keep up with a rendering of a Hindustani jig. The audience went into the seventh heaven of delight and the festivities again terminated in a great drinking ceremony in which Gelele drank from the skulls of two of his greatest former enemies.

§

Six weary weeks had been spent in Abomey without any royal reference being made to the reason of the Mission's visit.

---

[1] Burton was taken to task for thus performing before a crowd of savages. His retort was that dancing in Dahomé was not a diversion but a really important ritual. It would have been discourteous, if not dangerous, to have refused. He did not also add that it was an experience that he would not have missed.

Burton grew weary and then desperate. Repeated hints for an audience were blandly ignored. Finally Burton complained outright to the Vizier. He promised to see at once about it ; and did nothing. The Englishman then announced that he was leaving at once for Whydah ; even if he had to go alone.

The ruse succeeded. Gelele summoned him to a palaver, presented him with the gifts for Queen Victoria, and inclined a cautious ear.

Burton delivered his message ; a reproof that the slave trade still continued, a plea for the abolition of human sacrifices, and a request to allow an English fort at Whydah.

At first the king showed temper, then recovered himself admirably and made a spirited reply, defending slavery on the grounds that it was his only means of revenue. Sacrifice, he asserted with his tongue in his cheek, was only the execution of criminals. On the subject of a fort, no reply was returned. Finally he walked up to Burton, shook hands with him in the English manner, looked at him and made the best criticism ever passed on the traveller. " Batum (Burton), you are a good man, but too angry." Then he bade him farewell and dismissed the baffled Mission.

On 18th February, the party reached Whydah, and a few days later Burton embarked on a warship for Fernando Po. With him he took the royal presents for England's queen :

> A half-starved page boy.
> A green-and-white counterpane.
> A leather pouch to hold tobacco.
> A loin cloth for travelling

And this was all the Foreign Office ever got out of Gelele. His kingdom was shattered a few years later in a war with Abeokuta, its power declined, and it fell into the hands of the French.

Chapter Nine

IMMEDIATELY on her return from Teneriffe, Isabel began agitating for Richard's removal to a post where she could accompany him. She watched the mission to Dahomé with trepidation, sure that with her away from his side some harm would befall him among the heathen. On his safe return she began a further bombardment of the Foreign Office with those wordy, excitable letters of which there must be many in the archives.

A length they drew the following reply.

> Dear Mrs. Burton,
>
> I know the climate in which your husband is working so zealously and so well is an unhealthy one, but it is not true to say that he is the smallest of consuls in the worst part of the world. Many have inferior salaries, and some are in more unhealthy places.
>
> However, if I find a vacancy of a post with an equal salary and a better position, I will not forget his services. I do not imagine he would wish for a less active post.
>
> He has performed his mission to Dahomey very creditably, to my entire satisfaction.
>
> Russell.

Here was a ray of hope and Isabel redoubled her efforts. Any string that could be pulled, however indirectly, was seized by those energetic hands and brought to bear. She spent her days in a round of visits to influential acquaintances. " I can see Mrs. Burton now," writes a contemporary, " talking, talking, talking . . . It seemed to me that this beautiful woman came and talked for whole days at a time, and it was all about ' Dear Richard and the Government '." [1]

At length, in August 1864 when Richard's time for leave returned, she was rewarded. Lord Russell made a move by promoting him to the Brazilian consulate of Santos with an

[1] *In the 'Sixties and 'Seventies*, Laura Hain Friswell.

equal salary, less onerous work, and a climate which, if low-lying and unhealthy, would at least permit Isabel to accompany him.

Isabel was in transports. She went up to Liverpool to meet him, covered him with kisses, and brought him down to London where, in an excess of joy, she persuaded him to visit a Mortlake cemetery and help her choose their future grave.

Meetings with old friends were few and far between. He had a glimpse of Swinburne, with whom he had regularly corresponded from Fernando Po. But the quarrel with Speke was coming to a head and demanded all his energies. The tragic meeting on the platform at Bath followed, and Burton was accused of spreading the rumour that Speke had shot himself. Sick of the whole business, he took Isabel for a short holiday in Ireland, whence they returned after a few weeks and sailed for Portugal, where it was arranged that Richard should sail direct for Rio de Janeiro, and Isabel should return home, pay, pack the heavier baggage, and follow in due course from Liverpool.

After a pleasant stay at Lisbon, excursions into the country, and visits to local bull-fights, they parted once more for a time. Richard embarked at the Tagus, and Isabel " with a heavy heart watched the vessel slowly steaming away." She herself caught the next boat for England to prepare for a grand departure and her first real essay as a Consul's wife.

§

Santos, in the province of São Paulo, is a low-lying alluvial plain on the coast of Brazil about 230 miles W.S.W. of Rio de Janeiro. Situated only a few feet above sea-level, its harbour and lower streets in 1864, before the advent of proper drainage, were a bed of mud, slime, and garbage, breeding fevers as continuous if not as pernicious as Fernando Po. The Consulate was a large one, but had the advantage of a vice-Consul who, fortunately for his superior, had lived in Brazil all his life. This took the more tedious and routine work of the post off Burton's hands, leaving him time to escape into the mountains for health and study.

Speaking the language, as he spoke all his languages, fluently, and having already a deep knowledge of Portuguese literature, history, and etymology, Burton soon settled down into his new post. By the time Isabel arrived from England he had dis-covered the ideal place for recuperation and for Isabel to set up house. This was in São Paulo, the capital, situated 2000 feet above sea-level and some thirty miles distant from Santos. Here Isabel could live away from the vapours, while he, as his work took him to and fro, could spend periods at both towns, returning to São Paulo whenever a rest was needed.

In the Rua do Carmo an ancient convent was found which would make an excellent house. Burton took it at once and had it put in order. He shipped Isabel and the baggage there immediately they arrived.

She fell in love with it at sight. It consisted of several enormous rooms, looking out on the street in front and at the back commanding a limitless view of the horizon. She began an immediate bustle of activity, hired two servants, rearranged the rooms, and began the long process of unpacking her fifty-nine pieces of baggage. Richard was given a room as a study at the back ; for herself she converted a room into a chapel at the side. In the middle, a vast room, previously the refectory, was turned into a combined dining-room, sitting-room, lounge. Rat holes were covered up, shutters repaired, fans, draped photographs, and religious knick-knacks appeared on the whitewashed walls ; in no time a little corner of mid-Victorian England seemed to sprout amid the arid simplicities of Brazil. When all was finished Richard came up from Santos to see how she was getting on. She greeted him, radiant with happiness and pride. This was their first real home.

They had been married four years, and now for the first time they could really take stock of one another. A long bachelor existence in camp, bivouac, and hotel had made Richard somewhat careless in domestic matters. He was indifferent to physical comfort, cared nothing for his surroundings, and had never known the delights of a real home life. As a Consul with a position and an establishment to keep up all this must be changed, and Isabel was determined to change it. She was nothing if not well domesticated in the extravagant Victorian upper-class manner, and with characteristic energy she began to surround her husband with the proper refinements. She demanded and filled the house with servants, organized the culinary arrangements to perfection, and began to make herself leader of such small social circle as São Paulo could afford. For the first time in his life Richard was petted ; his every whim was granted. While he worked, the household moved on tiptoe ; when he was finished, elaborate meals appeared from nowhere. Watched over assiduously he was as carefully protected from financial worries, unwelcome callers, and all other irritations as he was from draughts and infections.

He was not, of course, easy to live with. Often moody and irritable, impatient of servants, and sometimes grossly rude and indelicate with guests, his sneering, domineering, and boasting manner with strangers was always placing him in situations from which it took all Isabel's tact to extricate him. Worst of all, in spite of the soft, silken strands of domesticity woven gently round him, an incurable restlessness would at intervals seize him, when he would rage at the routine of consular work and long to be off alone into the unknown. At such times he seemed impossible. He could settle at nothing, he would stand for hours peering through a telescope at the great mountain ranges on the horizon, or pace restlessly from room to room poring over maps. It would seem then to poor Isabel as if only the slenderest thread kept him from vanishing for ever from her side.

And yet it was not all his fault. There were moments when the Consulate in the Rua do Carmo became almost impossible ; for, if Richard's vices were difficult to live with, Isabel's virtues were often as insufferable. For Isabel took her virtues very seriously, and she had all the lack of humour and sense of proportion of the religious bigot. As we have seen, she took her virtues so seriously that before marriage she had made a list of them ; and once the household had shaken down into its stride she had full leisure to practise them in earnest.

In the virtuous life she had planned for herself, one of the main ordinances, it will be remembered, was that of " doing a great deal of good "—alas, one of humanity's most dangerous resolutions ! Charity to the poor and the inculcation of Catholic religious principles in heretics, these were her aims, and she set about them energetically. In her chapel—" The only really pretty and refined part of my house . . . I painted my chapel myself, white, with a blue border and a blue domed ceiling and a gilt border. I have painted inscriptions on the walls in blue. I have always a lamp burning, and the altar is a mass of flowers . . ." [1]—she decided to hold services with the poor. Below stairs she threw open a large cellar in which vagrants and needy travellers were invited to spend the night, being sped on their way in the morning after breakfast and prayers. No one was

[1] Letter to her mother.

to be turned away from the door. In theory the idea was delightful, and Isabel must have pictured many charming scenes in which the Consul's lovely wife moved gracefully among her dear, doddering poor. But unfortunately her knowledge of human nature was not equal to the demands made upon it. The dear doddering poor who were to receive sustenance and religious succour soon revealed themselves as a series of voracious rascals who made the Consulate a home from home, stole from and insulted their benefactress, and had often to be hurled neck and crop from the place by the Consul himself. There were times when the house was chaos, and Richard, roused from his studies, would emerge distracted upon the most unseemly tableaux.

"On 5th May my landlord's child was christened in my chapel. They asked me to lend it to them for the occasion, so I decorated the chapel and made it very pretty. I thought they would christen the child, take a glass of wine and a bit of cake, and depart within an hour. To my discomfort they brought a lot of friends, children, and niggers, and they stopped six hours, during which I had to entertain them (in Portuguese). They ran all over my house, pulled about everything, ate and drank everything, spat on my clean floors, made me hold the child to be christened . . . I had a very pleasant day ! . . ."

This sort of thing became a common occurrence, and the resulting confusion had almost invariably to be settled by Richard. Sometimes it became dangerous, as happened once when Richard was away, when a drunken sailor broke into the house, threatened the terrorized Isabel with a knife, and would not depart until heavily bribed with silver.

It was difficult to know how to keep her out of mischief; but to occupy her excitable temperament Richard set her lessons to do. He tried to teach her Portuguese, gave her his MSS. to look over and edit, and encouraged her to keep a journal.

In return she began gently, oh so gently, to try to woo him to the Catholic church. From nowhere, it seemed, a rain of suggestive hints descended upon him. He would find religious books with marked passages lying open on his desk ; and in the pockets of his clothing religious trinkets began to discover themselves, so that a handkerchief pulled suddenly from a pocket would send an unsuspected crucifix or medallion tinkling to the floor ; lumps under his pillow would resolve themselves on investigation into sacred images placed there in the firm conviction that their beneficent influences would affect him during sleep ; while constantly and ardently prayers and intercessions for his wayward spirit would rise from the little blue chapel in the Rua do Carmo.

His patience with all this was wonderful. Impatient to a degree with others, with her he seemed to be kindness itself. Indeed, with his cynical, outspoken nature, it must always be one of the finer points in his character that he bore with her so gently. With what an air of resignation would he not listen to her continuous stories of religious phenomena, of souls saved, divine messages, and amazing revelations. " He often looked, oh ! so sad and weary when hearing for the twentieth time how a leaden image had tumbled out of her pocket during a long ride, and then miraculously returned to its despairing owner," writes a relative who knew them both.[1] Sometimes he did lose control and blaze at her : but never for long. The sight of that pale, patient, dramatic face under its aureole of dark-gold hair kneeling below the trumpery altar praying *for him*, disarmed all criticism. She meant so well ; she loved him so dearly.

Yet, apart from these little domestic troubles, for three years life passed uneventfully enough at São Paulo. We find that Richard during this time slips into the background, hidden by consular and literary work : when we hear of him, it is through her. Apart from this, Isabel's letters home are the only records of this three years' retirement ; from them only do we get a glimpse of the first Burton ménage.

15th Dec. 1865.

" I do hate Santos. The climate is beastly, the people fluffy. The stinks, the vermin, the food, the niggers are all of a piece. There are no walks, and if you go one way, you sink knee deep in mangrove swamps ; another you are covered with sandflies ; and a third is crawling up a steep mountain by a mule-path to get a glimpse of the sea beyond the lagoons which surround Santos. . . .

" They think me a wonderful person here (at São Paulo) for being so independent, as all the ladies are namby-pamby. To go up and down by myself between Santos and São Paulo is quite a masculine feat. I am the only woman who ever crossed the Sierra outside the diligence, and the only lady or woman who ever walked across the viaduct which is now a couple of

[1] *Life of Captain Burton*, Georgiana Stisted.

planks wide across the valley, with one hundred and eighty feet to fall if you slip or get giddy. . . . São Paulo itself is a pretty, white straggling town on a hill and running down into a high tableland, which is well wooded and watered, and mountains all round in the distance. No cockroaches, fleas, bugs, and sandflies, but only mosquitos and jiggers. Of course it is dull for those who have time to be dull, and very expensive. For those who are launched in Brazilian society, it is a fast and immoral place, without any *chic* or style. It is full of students, and no one is religious or honest in money matters ; and I should never be surprised if fire were rained down upon it, as in a city of the Old Testament, for want of a just Brazilian. *En revanche* it is very healthy, and only one month's journey to England. . . ."

São Paulo, 9th March 1866.

" I got the same crying fit about you, dear mother, last week, as I did at Lisbon, starting up in the night and screaming out that you were dead ; I find I do it whenever I am over-fatigued and weak. The chance of losing you is what weighs most on my mind, and it is therefore my nightmare when I am not strong ; not but what when awake I am perfectly confident that we shall meet again before another year is out. . . ."

Petropolis, above Rio, 22nd June 1866.

" We went the other day to be presented to the Emperor [1] and Empress. I was in grand toilet and Richard in uniform. The Emperor is a fine man, about 6 ft. 2 in., with chestnut hair, blue eyes, and broad shoulders, and has manly manners. He was very cordial to us, and after a short audience we were passed on to the Empress's reception-room where, after the usual kissing of hands, we sat down and conversed for about twenty minutes.

" The second time the Emperor kept Richard two hours and a half talking on important affairs and asking his opinion of the resources of the country . . . we are now in a position to go whenever we like to the palace *sans ceremonie*. None of the other English here have the privilege. . . . The Emperor has taken a great fancy to Richard, and has put him in communication with him, and all the ministers of state here make a great fuss of him [Richard]. . . ."

[1] Presumably this was the Emperor Don Pedro II.

Rio de Janeiro, June 1866.

" I have been again to the Palace, and to-morrow am going to see the Empress in the evening . . . Richard has given two lectures before a room full of people. The Emperor and Empress were present ; we had to receive them, and to entertain them after in the room prepared for them. I have seen them three times since I wrote, and they always make us sit down and talk to us for some time. I told the Empress all about your paralysis, and how anxious I was about you; and she is so sympathetic and kind, and always asks what news I have of you. She appears to take an interest in me, and asks me every sort of question. Most of my time in Rio has been occupied in going to dinners. . . ."

Rio de Janeiro, 8th July 1866.

" I am still covered with boils, and I cannot sit or stand, walk or lie down, without a moan, and I am irritated and depressed beyond words. I do not know if my blood be too poor or too hot, and there is nobody here to ask. I have a few days well and then I burst out in crops of boils ; and if an animal sting me, the place festers directly. I am very thin and my nose like a cutwater ; and people who saw me on my arrival from England say I look very delicate ; but I feel very well when I have no boils. . . ."

Rio de Janeiro, 23rd July 1866.

" I am still here. Richard left me a fortnight ago . . . Richard is gone to look after the sea-serpent (but I do not tell this as it might get him into a row with the F.O.). I forgot to tell you there is said to be a sea-serpent here one hundred and sixty feet long . . ."

São Paulo, 2nd September 1866.

" To-morrow a little Englishman and woman are to be married. Richard has to marry them. It seems so strange. Fancy him doing parson ! We shall muster about eighty people, Brazilian and English. People marry at five in the evening, and dance after and sleep in the house. Richard says, ' I won't say, " Let us pray." ' He is going to begin with, ' Do any of you know any reason why this man and woman should not be married ? Have any of you got anything to say ? ' Then, shaking his finger at them in a threatening way, he is going to plunge into it. I know I shall burst out laughing."

São Paulo, 15th September 1866.

" I do not think the climate disagrees with me. Of course one does not feel buoyant in great heat ; but it is mere money affairs and local miseries that worry me, and you know we all have them in every latitude. I should not feel justified, I think, in coming home for anything but *serious* illness. I have just domesticated and tamed Richard a little ; and it would not do to give him an excuse for becoming a wandering vagabond again. He requires a comfortable and respectable home, and a tight hand upon his purse-strings ; and I feel that I have a mission which amply fills my hands. Nobody knows all the difficulties in a colonial or tropical home till she has tried them —the difficulty of giving and taking, of being charitable and sweet-tempered, and yet being mistress with proper dignity, as here we are all on a par. I often think a *parvenue*, or half-bred woman, would burst if she had to do as I do. . . . We are leading a very regular life ; up at 5 a.m. and out for a walk ; I then go to Mass, market, and home ; Richard gives me a fencing lesson and Indian Clubs ; then cold bath and dress ; breakfast at 11 a.m., and then look after my house ; practise singing, Portuguese, help Richard with literature, dine at six o'clock, and to bed at nine or ten.

" I am at present engaged with the F.O. Reports ; I have to copy (1) thirty-two pages on Cotton Report ; (2) one hundred and twenty-five pages Geographical Report ; (3) eighty pages General Trade Report. This for Lord Stanley, so I do it cheerfully. . . ."

Rio de Janeiro, 8th December 1866.

" We are nearly all down with cholera. I have had a mild attack. Our *Chargé d'affaires* has nearly died of it, and also our Secretary of Legation. . . . Here people cannot drink or be indolent with impunity. If I did not fence, do gymnastics, ride and bathe in the sea, eat and drink but little, attend to my internal arrangements, and occupy myself from early till late to keep my mind free from the depression that comes upon us all in these latitudes, I could not live for six months. . . .

" When I got the cholera, it was three in the morning. I thought I was dying, so I got up, went to my desk and settled all my worldly affairs, carried my last instructions to Kier [the maid] in her bed, put on my clothes, and went out to confession and communion. . . ."

The Barra, 13th April 1867.

" I write to you from a fresh place. In São Paulo they have been making a new road, and have enclosed a piece of marsh with water five feet deep. The new road prevents this discharging itself into the river beneath, and the enclosed water is stagnant and putrid, and causes malaria in my house. Richard has just returned—knocked up by six weeks in the wilds— and he broke out with fever. I felt affected and the whole house squeamish. I rushed off with Richard to the sea-border, about fifty miles from São Paulo. It would be intensely pleasant if Richard would get better.

" You know I have often told you that people here think me shockingly independent because I ride with Chico [a negro servant] behind me. So what do you think I did the other day ? They have, at last, something to talk about now. I rode out about a league and a half, where I met four fine geese. I must tell you I have never seen a goose ; they do not eat them here, but only use them as an ornamental bird. Well, Chico and I caught them, and slung one at each side of my saddle, and one at each side of his, and rode with them cackling and squawking all the way through the town ; and whenever I met any woman I thought would be ashamed of me, I stopped and was ever so civil to her. When I got up to our house, Richard, hearing the noise, ran out on the balcony ; and seeing what was the matter, he laughed and shook his fist, and said, ' Oh you delightful blackguard—how like you ! ' "

In contrast to Isabel's light-hearted record of these days we have one other picture ; sombre, unsympathetic and perhaps overdrawn, but still of interest. Wilfrid Scawen Blunt, then a newly appointed attaché at the British Legation in Buenos Aires, remembered in after years his impressions of the Burtons.[1] Isabel, " a sociable and very talkative woman, clever but at the same time foolish, overflowing with stories of which her husband was always the hero. Her devotion to him was very real . . ." Burton, he recalls, " seldom went to bed sober. His dress and appearance were those suggesting a released convict . . . He wore, habitually, a rusty black coat with a crumpled black silk stock, his throat destitute of collar, a costume which his muscular frame and immense chest made singularly and incongruously hideous, above it a countenance

[1] *My Diaries*, 1888–1914, Wilfrid Scawen Blunt.

the most sinister I have seen, dark, cruel, treacherous, with eyes
like a wild beast's. He reminded me by turns of a black leopard,
caged, but unforgiving, and again, with that close-cut poll and
iron frame of that wonderful creation of Balzac's, the ex-
gallerien, Vautrin, hiding his grim identity under an Abbe's
cassock."   Blunt spent several evenings with the older man,
" talking of all things in heaven and earth, or rather listening
while he talked, till he grew dangerous in his cups, and, revolver
in hand, would stagger home to bed."

One is tempted to wonder how often the bored Burton gave
way to his fatal habit of *schadenfreude* with a no doubt somewhat
tiresome young attaché ?

§

In June 1867 a three months' leave [1] was granted Burton,
and taking Isabel, as companion for part of the way, he began
a tour of the neighbouring province of Minas Geraes. From
the Emperor he had received a *portaria*, or special licence,
for the journey, and his plan was to visit the famous gold
mines worked by English companies in the mining district
of Minas Geraes, and from there take boat and proceed down
the São Francisco river as far as Paulo Affonso. Isabel was
to accompany him as far as the mines, after which she
was to return home via Rio, leaving him to continue on
alone.

Travelling on horseback and foot via Petropolis and Juiz de
Fora they reached the mines on 23rd July, and made a brief
stay there, during which they undertook the perilous descent
of the notorious Morro Velho mine, where a British company,
exploiting native labour, had sunk a shaft three-quarters of a
mile deep, at the bottom of which squads of miners worked in
conditions of appalling hardship for a bare subsistence. None
of this side of the case touched the travellers. Isabel, who wrote
a graphic description of her descent in an iron pot hung by a
chain, had eyes only for the terrors of the depths ; Richard was
interested in the amount of gold dug.

From here Richard proceeded on towards the São Francisco,
while Isabel returned home. At Sabara, on the banks of the
Rio das Velhas, he purchased a species of Brazilian houseboat,
or *ajojo*, constructed of a roofed platform attached to several
lashed canoes, and for two months swept down the fascinating

---

[1] He had already drifted into the bad habit of taking leave on his own.

rivers, accompanied by a servant or two, a bull mastiff, some Latin Classics, and his beloved Camoens. At times they glided slowly in smooth waters through all the emerald splendour of tropical Brazilian scenery ; then, gathering speed, they would whirl through narrow gorges, dash down rapids, where, piloted by a native, the flimsy craft grazed the fangs of rocks by what seemed a miracle ; and so down towards the terrific and impassable falls of Paulo Affonso. Halts were made on the way to examine gold and diamond diggings and make notes on the country for emigrant purposes. At the falls they disembarked and Burton returned to Santos via Bahia and Rio, after a four months' vacation.

Although his health throughout the trip had been good, the strain of a river journey, which had often necessitated his travelling for hours up to the waist in water, caused a recurrence of old troubles. Fever, which had lain dormant in him for some while, broke out almost immediately on his return. It was the first real indication that the iron constitution, after nearly fifty years of abuse, was beginning to break down permanently. A bad attack of fever gradually developed into a sort of pleurisy which grew so agonizing that every deep breath sent him into a paroxysm of screaming. A Brazilian doctor brought hastily by Isabel cupped the raving man, applied twelve leeches, lanced his body in thirty-eight places, and put a vast blister on his right side ; while Isabel, on the other side of the sick bed, tried her own remedies by dropping holy water on his head, waving charms above him, and decorating his body with a variety of religious symbols.

His recovery was necessarily slow, and with it brought a severe nervous prostration. He grew depressed and irritable. He was, he felt, sick of Brazil, and wearied of consular work and all to do with it. Brazil had given him his illness, it might kill him ; it was also out of the world and held, he was now convinced, no prospects of advancement sufficient to excite a man of his ambition. It was a *cul de sac* from which he must escape as soon as possible.

Once his mind was made up, he acted quickly. As soon as he was firmly on his feet, he applied for sick leave, packed Isabel off home to England, sold up the house and fittings at São Paulo, and began to breathe again like a man. When the requested permission for leave arrived, with an added commission to examine the situation between Brazil and Paraguay, then at war, he gladly seized the opportunity for a pleasant journey on a congenial task.

In August 1868 he left Rio for Monte Video ; whence, after a stay, he proceeded to Buenos Aires, then a small town reeking of rotting flesh and bones from the quantities of its unhygienically slaughtered cattle. Hastily he continued to Paysandu, where he embarked on the Paraná river and steamed slowly down to the battlefields of the Brazilian-Paraguayan armies, past river mines, booms, and naval vessels moored to banks covered with dead Paraguayan soldiers.

His orders were to examine the battlefields and send reports to the Government about the true situation. Like most South American campaigns, the war was a mixture of incompetence, bravery, and cruelty. Gallant Paraguay, flogged on by her lunatic dictator, Francisco Solano Lopez, was being slowly beaten back inch by inch by the opposing forces of Brazil and Uruguay, and the sad story of dogged heroism, attacked at home as well as in the field, was slowly drawing to its close. Even while Burton was in the vicinity, Lopez fled from his capital to the interior, where, deserted by his French mistress, he met a fitting end at the hands of the soldiery. Burton visited the captured capital—of which almost his most vivid memory was (to Isabel's horror [1]) that of a Roman Catholic priest trying to seduce a peasant girl ; thence he continued across the Pampas and over the Andes to Peru.

He was now feeling better. The cares of consular life were behind him, Isabel was five thousand miles away and he was as free as air. South America began to have charms again and he might have prolonged his stay indefinitely ; when out of the blue came a message that roused him like a clarion call.

While seated in a café at Lima, he heard by chance that he had been appointed to the Consulate of Damascus.

He left at once for home.

---

[1] His book on Brazil, which he considerately gave her to " edit," contained several references to Roman Catholic priesthood which offended her. She wrote a preface in which she said, " I protest vehemently against his religious and moral sentiments. I point the finger of indignation particularly at what misrepresents our Holy Roman Catholic Church and at what upholds that unnatural and repulsive law, Polygamy, which the author preaches. . . ." Having a good eye for publicity, Burton let it stand, and had it printed at the beginning of his book. It is probably the most extraordinary preface a woman ever wrote for her husband.

Chapter Ten

THE coveted Damascus appointment, at £1000 a year, had been obtained almost entirely through the energies of Isabel and the influence of her uncle, Lord Gerard of Garswood. But even while Burton was hurrying home, after telegraphing his acceptance, a sudden change of government nearly lost it for him. To warn him of the danger and urgency of his immediate return, Isabel dispatched a letter to him, sending copies of it to Rio, Buenos Aires, and Valparaiso.

London, 7th Jan. 1869.

My Darling,

If you get this, come home at once by shortest way. Telegraph from Lisbon and Southampton, and I will meet you later and have all snug.

Strictly private. The new Government have tried to upset some of the appointments made by the last. There is no little jealousy about yours. Others wanted it, even at £700 a year, and were refused. Lord Stanley thinks, and so do I, that you may as well be on the ground as soon as possible.

Your faithful and attached

Wife.

A few weeks later Burton landed at Southampton and went with some trepidation to the Foreign Office where he was interviewed by Lord Clarendon. He was informed that the objections to his appointment were very serious. Reports had been spread about : (1) that he professed atheism and hated the Christian Church ; (2) that his Pilgrimage to Mecca had made his name anathema among orthodox Moslems ; and (3) he was violently anti-Semitic. In a community in the Holy Land composed of fanatic Christians, orthodox Moslems, and powerful Jews, a British representative of such temper was, Lord Clarendon pointed out, scarcely likely to be successful. Missionaries might refuse to co-operate with him ; indeed they had already complained about his possible appointment; the Moslems would almost certainly distrust him, and he could look for little assistance from Jewish interests. Unless he could convince the Foreign Office of the untruth of these assertions and present them with a written guarantee of good behaviour, it was impossible to see how the appointment could go forward.

Burton replied with characteristic vigour. He scented the usual enemies behind the objections and did not hesitate to attack them. The charges were grossly exaggerated, he explained, and he could well guess whence they had come. They were easily refuted. Far from being mistrusted by Moslems, he was invariably treated as *persona grata* by them, as anyone who had taken the trouble to read the accounts of his journeys to Harar or Tanganyika would agree; his dislike of the Jewish race was a most untrue and unfounded statement based on his strictures of one or two prominent members of the race; as for his private atheism and the trouble it might stir up among the missionaries, surely, he argued, a man's private beliefs need not of necessity impinge upon his public life. If these were the only objections to the appointment of an experienced Orientalist and soldier to a diplomatic post in the Near East, surely they were scarcely worthy of consideration.

But Lord Clarendon knew this was only half the story. Like many other men he admired Burton with reservations; thinking him a useful man but a dangerous and not always reliable one. The Damascus post required one virtue above all others. The virtue was tact; and Richard Burton, Lord Clarendon could not but feel, was not singularly noted for it. Clarendon hesitated, then decided to take the risk and sign the appointment; but he plainly warned Burton that any positive evidence of public feeling against him which might affect his position as Consul would result in his recall. On the other hand, good service had its ample rewards in candidature for those coveted posts of Morocco and Constantinople. Before Burton left he extracted from him a written guarantee to " act with unusual prudence, and under all circumstances to hold myself, and myself only, answerable for the consequences."

With the commission signed, Burton relaxed and gave himself up for a few weeks to society. But to enjoy it was never in his nature. " I have done the London season for the very last time, and shall never return except in autumn or winter. It has been a life of bed at 8 a.m., no breakfast, lunch at 2 p.m., dine at 7.30 p.m. and then soirée. Not so tiring when one's broken to it, but deadly monotonous. . . ." [1]

He visited his parents-in-law, stayed for a few days at Fryston, and once more looked up Swinburne with whom, during his absence in Brazil, he had been in constant correspondence.

Then he took Isabel on a short holiday to Boulogne.

How little, they found, had Boulogne changed since those days, nearly twenty years ago, when they had first met there. How much had they themselves changed! Arm in arm, the young soldier now a greying middle-aged man, the blue-eyed beauty, a stoutish but still good-looking woman, they wandered over the old haunts together, retracing the memories of 1853. How long ago it seemed. Here was the wall where Richard on that sunny, never-to-be-forgotten day had chalked his impudent message to her. There was the ballroom where, trembling with maiden love and jealousy, she had felt his strong sword arm about her in their first dance. Here, too, was Constantin's, where he had fenced his sensational bouts, and the little room overlooking the harbour and the open sea where he had worked through the long hot nights planning the Pilgrimage to Mecca; and there (and once again she visited it with offerings and grateful prayers) the chapel where Isabel with tears of happy anguish had so passionately prayed for love and a great future. Had all she had prayed for come to pass? In her great love, it still seemed so. Her Richard was famous; he had worked for her and give her his love. And now he was taking her, for the first time, to that mysterious, romantic East for which she had dreamed so long, and for which, among these same scenes, she had pined so madly sixteen years ago.

A few weeks later Richard sent her back to England; where she was to complete the paying, packing, and following and meet her husband at a point farther south, while he proceeded leisurely to Damascus via Auvergne and the waters of Vichy.

Scarcely had Isabel gone, than hurrying from Etretat the figure of Swinburne tripped on the scene, to be greeted by Burton with unaffected delight. Already they had arranged to spend a few weeks' holiday together to renew and strengthen the old ties of friendship formed three years earlier, and now they started off on a trip that was to be remembered by both for the rest of their lives.

[1] Letter to Albert Tootal.

What a fortunate combination of place and circumstance was that short holiday in the hills and valleys of Auvergne. To both it came like release from a period of sterility. To Burton after three years of boredom and loneliness in far-off Santos, to Swinburne after one of those black fits when his genius seemed to have deserted him and he could produce nothing but *trivia*. And what a contrast they must have made as they wandered south through that French summer, through Clermont, Polignac, and the vineyards of Puy de Dome. In this strangest of literary friendships we have scant enough information of their doings ; but imagination can well fill in the gaps. They studied botany, they visited ruins, they sat in inns and drank the *vin du pays* ; they visited public libraries, pored over rare manuscripts, and delightedly translated to one another the more salacious passages. They played innumerable practical jokes, tried to outdo one another in being " shocking." What unforgettable days ! Burton's wisdom and knowledge of the strange places of the earth and that " wild Walpurgis Night of Swinburne's talk," intoxicating and heady as champagne, mischievous, profound, and never wearying. One voice alone comes to us out of this period that both were to treasure as a rare and beautiful memory for the rest of their lives. It is Swinburne's. " I feel now," he wrote to a friend simply, " what it is to have an elder brother."

At Vichy they descended upon Lord Leighton and Adelaide Kemble to form a happy quartette. Painter and traveller told stories, Swinburne went through those magnificent frenzies of recitation, and Adelaide, stirred and enchanted, caught some of the lost youth back into her lovely voice :

A woman's voice, divine as a bird's by dawn
  Kindled and stirred to sunward, arose and held
Our souls that heard, from earth as from sleep,
  And filled with light as stars and as stars compelled
  To move by might of music, elate while quelled,
Subdue by rapture, lit as a mountain lawn
  By morning whence all heaven in the sunrise is welled.

And her the shadow of death as a robe clasped round.
  Then : and as morning's music she passed away.
And he then with us, warrior and wanderer crowned
  With fame that shone from eastern on western day
  More strong, more kind, than praise or than grief might say,
Has passed now forth of shadow by sunlight bound,
  Of night shot through with light that is frail as May.

May dies, and light grows darkness, and life grows death ;
  Hope fades and shrinks and falls a changing leaf ;
Remembrance, touched and kindled by love's live breath,
  Shines, and subdues the shadow of time called grief,
  The shade whose length of life is as life's date brief,
With joy that woods on the sunlight past, and saith
  That thought and love hold sorrow and change in fief.[1]

Thus did Swinburne, twenty-five years later, remember the magic of those summer evenings.

But in England Isabel was fretting nervously. She disliked any affection of Richard's which did not concern herself. She feared for his influence on Swinburne and Swinburne's influence on him.[2] "Tamed and domesticated," though Richard was, he must not be let out on too long a chain. So abruptly she arrived at Vichy to look into matters, and the party broke up. Swinburne went to Paris, and Richard and Isabel continued to Turin, where once more they separated ; Isabel to return and finish the business she should not have left, Richard to take the road to Damascus.

§

In 1869 the hand of progress had not yet touched the ancient city of Damascus. She was still much as Kinglake had written of her thirty years before : " This ' Holy ' Damascus, this ' earthly paradise ' of the Prophet, so fair to the eyes that he dared not trust himself to tarry in her blissful shades—she is a city of hidden palaces, of copses, and gardens and fountains, and bubbling streams . . . no mere city, but rather a province, wide and rich that bounded the torrid waste. . . ."

With some such rhapsodic emotion in his heart, Burton must have ridden down into this his new domain. Joy and high hope at that moment surely were his. He was back in his beloved East, among the peoples he knew so well ; his future seemed assured ; both position and power were warm in his hands and the days ahead were lit by the anticipation of pleasant and profitable work. As he rode into the " Street called Straight," brushed shoulders with the desert men, the porters, and the merchants, listened with reawakened memory to the crying of the Muezzin from the minarets [3] and let his tongue

---

[1] " An Evening at Vichy." A. C. Swinburne, 1896.

[2] There is no doubt that Burton taught Swinburne the habit of brandy drinking that later made such a havoc of the poet's health.

[3] The loveliest singing from the mosques of the East is that from the cities of Damascus and Hama.

turn back to the dialects he knew so well, the intervening years
of service in distant and alien lands must have seemed like a
nightmare from which he was just awakening.

§

He found the task which awaited him one that would tax
his capacity to the utmost.[1] In those days the Near East Consulate of Damascus was second only to that at Beyrout which
housed a Consul-General. From Damascus extended a pro-
tectorate over the wide district contained in the provinces of
Aleppo, Baghdad, and Nablus.[2] Capital of Syria and headquarters of the Turkish Government, and a Moslem religious
centre, it was composed of a clashing, restless population of
Moslems, Jews, and Christians.[3] Besides keeping on good terms
with this difficult admixture, the Consul had to avoid any
offence to the Turkish Government and its Wali or governor,
which, in a system composed of bribery, torture, and corruption
was none too easy ; he had also to deal diplomatically yet
firmly with the Druze Arabs of the desert who perpetually
menaced the safety of British travellers.

He entered upon the task with alacrity, and it seemed at
first as if all would go well. He calmed the missionaries, and was
greeted with pleasure by the Moslems. Isabel, too, who arrived
three months later to find him living at an inn, was full of hope.
Was she not going to that place so beloved of Tancred, so often
dreamed about and yearned for ; that perpetual and glorified
fancy dress ball, the romantic East ? And was her own role to
be, well, if perhaps not quite that of a sultana, something not
far short of it ? A role where, in her own words, she could
follow in the footsteps " of Lady Mary Wortley Montagu, Lady
Hester Stanhope, the Princess de la Tour d'Auvergne, that trio
of famous European women who lived of their own choice a
thoroughly Eastern life, and of whom I looked to make fourth."

Bringing the heavier baggage, an English maid, and a St.
Bernard dog, Isabel arrived at Damascus in January 1870.
She was disappointed with this her first glimpse of the East.

---

[1] The facts in the following chapter are drawn mainly from a confidential
report, " The Case of Captain Burton," in the Foreign Office files.
[2] Syria was divided at this time into three *vilayets*. Damascus (which included Homs and Hama), Aleppo, and Jezireh.
[3] The Christians alone must have comprised a difficult problem. During
the author's own political service in Hama there were at least six Christian sects
in the city all mutually and some bitterly opposed to each other, and the Moslems.

" Where are the beautiful gardens of Damascus ? " she asked the *kavass* as she was driven into the narrow streets of the city, and the indicative sweep of his hand had disclosed nothing but " ugly shrubberies, wood clumps, and orchards . . ."

But disappointment was soon forgotten in the excitements of house-hunting and marketing. Ever solicitous of Richard's health, she decided that the city itself, with its narrow, winding streets littered with refuse, its leaning houses and city gates that shut at sunset, was no place for him, and she ransacked the suburbs until she found a suitable house in the district of Salihiyyeh, situated on a sloping hill-side between a mosque and a *hammam*, backed by the sweeping heights of Jabal Kasyum and fronting on to a fragrant orchard of apricots. Here, at a quarter of an hour's riding distance from the Consulate, Isabel settled down to make a home. The house,[1] like most Moslem residences, was large, airy, and cool. Richard's study bedroom was almost level with the tower of the adjoining mosque and from his window he could watch the Muezzin. In Isabel's room at the back was the inevitable chapel. Between these two rooms the house furnishings manifested to the visitor a struggle between Islam and the Church of Rome. Richard decorated the walls with scimitars, crescents, Koranic extracts, praying-mats, and Eastern draperies : Isabel with crucifixes, bleeding hearts, fluttering cherubs, and holy inscriptions. From Richard's bedroom was often to be heard his harsh voice joining in the Call to Prayer from the neighbouring mosque : from Isabel's would come the low earnest sounds of Confession and Prayer. Below stairs the entrance disclosed a courtyard painted in red, white, and blue stripes, with a large recessed room cooled by a splashing fountain, strewn with cushions and carpets, and decorated with potted plants, where receptions were held and deputations met. Beyond it, across the road, was a large garden, the stables, and a loggia in which to sit in the fresh evenings.

In spring and winter the house was delightful, but summer brought the reflected heat from the bowl of surrounding hills, turning Salihiyyeh into a furnace. So, hunting farther afield, Isabel discovered an old limestone barn at Bludan in the Anti-Libanus, eight hours' ride from Damascus and far from its

---

[1] A substantial part of the house still stood in 1947, readily recognisable from Lord Leighton's water-colour. The mosque beside it is practically unchanged. The Consulate has completely disappeared.

torrid heats.   Here, during the summer, they established themselves, riding every so often into the city; and between here
and Salihiyyeh they lived comfortably during the next eighteen
months.   Here Richard, with the copious notes garnered
through twenty-five years of study, began work in his leisure
on the opening chapters of the great book whose inception had
arisen when, as a young Ensign, he had first in the Indian
bazaars and in the arms of his native mistresses listened to the
stories from that greatest book in Eastern literature, the *Arabian
Nights.*   For twenty-five years, in India, in Arabia, Somaliland,
and Africa, he had been gathering notes on the subject.   At
last the work of writing could begin.   Usually he wrote his
books at great speed, working from notes and scarcely ever
revising; but with this, the longest and most intricate of his
labours, he began slowly, with long pauses.   Some hours he would
spend in the Arabic library of Ommayad, the pride of Damascus,
among the rare Persian and Arabian manuscripts; again he
would slip into native dress and visit the *bazaars* to verify some
detail which could be obtained in no other way.   In the intervals
of work he would explore the surrounding country, sometimes
with Isabel, more often alone, visiting the ruins of Baalbek and
the inscriptions at Palmyra, negotiating with the Druze Arabs,
or collecting rare tiles for Lord Leighton's projected Arab room
in Kensington.

Of this period Isabel writes : [1] " Our lives were so wild,
romantic, and solemn, that I could not even bear to sing ; to
dance would have been a profanation. . . . Our days here were
the perfection of living. . . . We rose at dawn—my husband
walked to the Consulate every day at twelve,[2] and remained
there until four or five. We ate twice, at eleven a.m. and at
dusk.   At eleven a.m. anybody who liked of our friends or
acquaintances dropped in and joined us, or sat and talked to
us while we ate.   Immediately after the latter meal, my husband
read himself to sleep.   My work consisted of looking after my
house, servants, stables, and animals ; of doing a little gardening,
of helping my husband, reading, writing, and studying ; trying
to pick up a little Arabic, receiving visits and returning them,
seeing and learning Damascus thoroughly, looking after the

---

[1] *The Inner Life of Syria.*
[2] Burton's hours of work were, for an official in the Middle East, most unusual,
and must have been in summer a sore trial to his Arab visitors, most of whom
would wisely retire to sleep during the hottest hours of the day.

poor and sick of my village and its environs." Besides these
duties, Isabel also collected about her a menagerie of pets
and, to the disgusted amazement of her servants, daily fed on
expensive meat a cohort of the pariah dogs which clear the
refuse from Eastern cities.

But power soon went to her unsteady head like wine. When
she went about the city she rode like an Empress escorted by
four armed *kavasses* who cleared a path before her. Brilliantly
dressed, elaborately coiffured, bowing right and left and twirling
a riding-whip in her gloved hands she felt the cynosure of all
eyes. It was a role which suited her down to the ground. She
was the Consul's wife, an aristocrat and a beauty, and everyone,
willing or unwilling, had to recognize it. To those who bowed
before her in requisite humility she was all gracious smiles and
condescension ; to those who did not, the ever ready riding-
switch was firmly gripped and authoritatively shaken. Then
there were the times when she returned home, dropped the role
of Consul's wife, and became a second Lady Hester Stanhope.
Inserting her stoutish figure into what she fondly imagined was
Eastern disguise, silk bloomers, a yashmak, and a blouse, she
would visit the *bazaars* with a female interpreter and wander
among the Arabs supremely confident that she was helping
Richard and that no one could possibly pierce her disguise.
" Richard was my guide in all things ; and since he adapted
himself to the native life, I endeavoured to adapt myself to it
also, not only because it was my duty, but because I loved it."
Sometimes she entered the *harims*, to whose inmates she must
have seemed like a visitor from Mars. Here she would dramati-
cally throw off her disguise and appear as an Englishwoman.
" I found them very pleasant ; only at first the women used to
ask me such a lot of inconvenient questions that I became quite
confused. They were always puzzled because I had no children.
. . . I asked them how they could bear to live together and pet
each other's children. I told them that in England, if a woman
thought her husband had another wife or mistress, she would
be ready to kill her and strangle the children if they were not
her own. They all laughed heartily at me and seemed to think
it a great joke. . . ."

This was all harmless enough and possibly aroused little
but amusement and compassion among the Arabs ; but there
were other activities of hers which were less kindly received.
Every so often she would attire herself in large yellow button

boots and gaiters, cram her thick hair under a scarlet *tarbush* with a feather, buckle pistol, cartridges, and dagger about her ample waist and, with a Badu veil flowing in the wind, canter about the desert in her third role of " doing a great deal of good." Visiting poor families, she would dispense medicines and advice to the sick, an amiable and praiseworthy labour if not accompanied, where possible, with gifts of little Catholic emblems, murmured prayers, and misguided attempts to rouse the Moslems to a feeling for the True Church. The Sheikhs grumbled, one insulted her and got the riding-whip across his face for his pains ; but acquaintances who came to Burton with warnings that his wife was meddling with fire were greeted with amused indifference. " It pleases her," he would say carelessly, " and it does me no harm."

§

Yet, foolish and laughable though Isabel's behaviour was, it aroused little apparent interest in the city itself. For Damascus society in 1870 was already studded with eccentrics, and contained two characters at least beside whom Isabel and her idiosyncrasies paled into insignificance. From a tower on Mount Olivet, where she fervently awaited the coming of the Messiah, the Marquise de la Tour d'Auvergne, hung with innumerable bangles, would often appear in the Syrian capital ; while through the narrow streets, clad often in the simple smock of a desert woman, stalked the gaunt but still beautiful sixty-four-year old Jane Digby, Lady Ellenborough, whose character and history, if Isabel could have perceived it, far outstripped the romantic heroines of her imagination.

One cannot resist a temptation to pause a moment to consider the relationship between the strange characters of Jane Digby and Richard Burton ; unusual both of them even in the history of British eccentrics in the Middle East. Nor can one but feel that had this aristocratic, independent woman of a score of lovers, wife of an Arab Sheikh, brilliant linguist and musician, been thirty years younger, there might have been much between her and Richard Burton, for they had much in common. Indeed, it is not impossible to imagine that she would have been that almost unbelievable creature, a suitable woman for him, for at many points their characters touched. Turbulent spirits both, despisers of convention, great lovers and passionately drawn to the East. Together

they might have written a bright page in the annals of travel
literature.

Yet even now, they came together like kindred spirits in
their inclinations. Her knowledge of general Arab life almost
equalled his own, her acquaintance with the female side far
exceeded it, and many were the evenings they spent together
in the leafy loggia at Salihiyyeh talking under the stars, while
now in English, now in Arabic, he would question her on female
Arab customs, on the sex intimacies of the *harim*, and her own
experiences there. How much of the knowledge of Moslem
female sex psychology which was to be embodied later in the
famous Terminal Essay to the Arabian Nights came from the
lips of Jane Digby, one can only guess, but knowing the strict
secrecy surrounding the *harim*, the utter impossibility of the
male stranger's entrance to it, and remembering the minuteness
of Burton's descriptions, we must conclude that it was not
insignificant.

For Isabel, Jane was an enigma, alarming and yet perforce
acceptable. Isabel had a natural respect for titles and could
forgive any delinquency—even sleeping with a " black skin "
—provided blue blood had inspired it ; and she accepted Jane's
aristocracy with alacrity, while pitying her character. " It was
curious," remarked Isabel naively, " how she had retained the
charming manner, the soft voice, and all the graces of her youth.
You would have known her at once to be an English lady, well
born and bred, and she was delighted to greet in me one of her
own order. . . . I took a great interest in the poor thing. She
was devoted to her Shaykh, whereat I marvelled greatly. . . .
I could understand her running away with Schwarzenburg, but
the contact with that black skin I could not understand. . . .
Poor thing, she was more sinned against than sinning."

With these three and Abd el Kader the famous Algerian
prince in exile, Lord Leighton, Palmer the traveller, and Tyrwhitt Drake of the newly formed Palestine Exploration Fund,
many enjoyable days were spent at Salihiyyeh. Burton struck
up a close friendship with Tyrwhitt Drake and Palmer, both
alas, to die so soon after ; Palmer by Arab knives in the Wady
Sudr, and Tyrwhitt Drake, while still in his twenties, from
tuberculosis. With these two enthusiasts, Burton worked
frequently on the survey work inaugurated by the Palestine
Exploration Fund. In his book, *Unexplored Syria* (1872), we
have a glimpse of those happy labours, mapping the hills and

valléys of Syria, copying inscriptions at Hama [1] and searching among the ruins of Baalbek and Palmyra. Nor were they without adventures. Many times the party were threatened by the fanatic Badu ; and once at Umm Niran they avoided massacre by the merest chance.

But Burton at last was really happy, and for the first time for many years. One picture of him at this time emerges from the past. Drawn by an eye-witness, it gives us what we so rarely get from his works, a glimpse of the inner man.

" My first sight of Captain Burton," writes this informant,[2] " revealed not only the man in his complex character, but supplied the key to the perplexing vicissitudes of his extraordinary career.

" On his arrival in Damascus, Burton called at my house. My study adjoined the drawing-room, into which he was shown by a native servant. I heard him command the Arab to fetch me in harsh, peremptory tones, which were meant to be obeyed. The servant, not thinking that I was in the study, went to seek me elsewhere. I advanced in noiseless Damascus slippers to the drawing-room door, and I came upon a scene never to be forgotten.

" At one side of the room stood my curly-headed, rosy-cheeked little boy of five, on the other stood Burton. The two were staring at each other. Neither was aware of my presence. Burton had twisted his face into the most fiendish-like aspect. His eyes rolled, exposing the whites in an alarming manner. The features were drawn to one side, so as to make the gashes on his jaw and brow appear more ghastly. The two cheeks were blown out, and Burton, raising a pocket handkerchief to his left cheek, struck his right with the flat of his right hand, thus producing an explosion and making the pocket handkerchief fly to the left as if he had shot it through his two cheeks.

" The explosion was followed by a suppressed howl, something between the bark of a hyena and a jackal. All the time Burton glared on the little fellow with the fiery eyes of a basilisk, and the child stood riveted to the floor as if spellbound and fascinated, like a creature about to be devoured. Suddenly

---

[1] Burton's copies of the Hama inscriptions, published in 1872 in his book *Unexplored Syria*, helped materially to arouse interest in the hitherto unknown evidences of the last Hittite empire.

[2] His name is unknown. Isabel calls him Salih and hints that it is a pseudonym.

a very wonderful thing happened. The little boy, with a wild shout of delight, sprang into the monster's arms, and the black beard was instantly mingled with the fair curls, and Burton was planting kisses all over the flaxen pate. The whole pantomime was gone through as quick as lightning, and Burton, disentangling himself, caught sight of my Arab returning without me, and, instead of waiting for an explanation, hurled at him a volley of exasperated epithets, culled from the rich stores of spicy and stinging words which garnish Arabic literature. Burton had revealed himself to me fully before he saw me. The child's clear, keen instinct did not mislead it. The big rough monster had a big child's heart behind the hideous grimaces. The child's unerring instinct was drawn by affinity to the child's heart in the man."

§

But while the Burton menage was basking happily at Salihiyyeh, about the Consulate itself in Damascus storm clouds were gathering.

It was perhaps impossible to suppose that a man of Burton's character could remain long in an official position in an Eastern city without trouble. He had not the patient and elastic character necessary to steer an official through the rocks and currents of Damascene intrigue. He was impetuous, honest, and tactless, and two of these qualities at least are unfortunate in the character of a consular official. Almost from the beginning of his period of service, enemies, both foreign and domestic, began a campaign of opposition and intrigue.

To understand the charges and complaints which resulted in his unhappy dismissal, it would be as well to examine them in turn, having sifted them from the mass of irrelevant detail which surrounds them. They came principally from three sides : the Wali, or Turkish governor ; the Jews ; and from a certain section of the Christian missionary colony.

With Rashid, the Wali, Burton was soon on terms of mutual distrust. Of the state of Damascus under this man's governorship Burton wrote shortly after his arrival that it was such that "no man calling himself a gentleman and an Englishman, and no man with any pride in the good name of his government, could sit down at his ease before he had effected a radical change. . . ." Rashid was a despot, with influence at Constantinople. He ruled by a system of bribery, corruption, and murder, carried out with that smooth precision of the cultured Turk. All who stood in his way were removed.[1] Burton aroused his antagonism by consistently refusing to countenance his exactions, by paying friendly visits to the Druze Arabs, with whom Rashid was on extremely bad terms, thus fostering in the latter's suspicious mind the idea that the Consul was championing the tribes against him, and by at times behaving with a resolute high-handedness which made many wonder if he were not usurping the mantle of Governor for himself.

An intelligent and patient Consul would at first have moved slowly with the tide. For Burton this was impossible. With the influential Jews of Damascus he was no less abrupt. He found that the three principal Jewish British subjects in the city had practised usury on such a scale that they had depopulated several villages in the neighbourhood. It had been their habit with previous Consuls to apply for powers to force their debtors into paying their enormous interest or be flung into gaol. As the majority of these debtors were ignorant peasants living in the extreme of poverty it had hitherto devolved upon the Consul to make himself party to an inhuman yet legal proceeding : sending a gendarme to force the debtor to pay, sell him up, and throw him into chains. " These protégés," wrote Burton with disgust, " have extended what was granted for the preservation of their lives, liberties, and property to transactions which rest entirely for success upon British protection. . . . I have found villages in ruins, homes empty because the masters had been cast into jail, and women in tears at my feet. I found these things done in the name of England . . ."

Previous Consuls had emerged from this difficulty by turning a blind eye to what did not immediately concern them ; one, Burton's predecessor, is alleged to have accepted bribes. When on Burton's arrival a smiling deputation of these three Jews waited upon him with veiled hints of Arab mares and diamond rings in return for his protection, he almost threw them out of the building. " Il me regard," bleated one of them in a long letter of complaint to the Consul-General at Beyrout, " d'un œil agité ; je n'en connais point la raison." He was shown the reason plainly enough. Burton declared forcibly that he would not have the Consulate turned into a debt-collecting agency,

---

[1] According to Burton, the Consuls of Spain, Italy, and Russia had already been mysteriously recalled. They were the only foreign officials who had opposed the Wali.

nor would he play the part of dun to a rabble of miserable peasants.

It was a praiseworthy gesture, but scarcely diplomatic. The Jews were British subjects, and they were in their rights. Complaints flew to London, backed by local Rabbis, and were taken up by Sir Francis Goldsmid and Sir Moses Montefiore, M.P. Far from Damascus and its intrigues, oppression, and corruption ; far too from the heart-moving desolation of those little villages on the slopes of Lebanon, it seemed to Whitehall that Burton's action was tactless and foolish. From Lord Granville came demands for explanation ; from Eldridge, the Consul-General at Beyrout, who had lived nine years in Syria without ever visiting Damascus, came severe reprimands. Burton held to his course inflexibly.

An even more serious clash, however, was with certain of the British missionaries. Long before he appeared in Damascus they had protested against his appointment. On his arrival they watched him with suspicious trepidation, which, however, rapidly gave way to confidence and even friendship. For to do him justice, Burton went out of his way to placate them. He extended his protection to the Syrian schools, he made the desert routes safe for missionary travellers, and he made the Wali punish promptly any native attempts at intimidation or insult to missionaries or converts. Many were the letters which came to him from the grateful missionaries. "We awaited your coming with doubt," wrote one of them, " but now that you are here we realize that there could not be a better man for the post."

So long as the missions confined themselves to their schools and their philanthropic work they found Burton an admirable protector ; but there was a powerful missionary colony centred in the safe city of Beyrout which had further plans. It became their custom to pay visits to Damascus, make a round of the Moslem prisons with lemonade and tracts, and try to convert the prisoners to Christianity. Head of this colony was a Mr. Mentor Mott, whose name, with that of his wife, Augusta Mott, figures largely in the correspondence preceding Burton's recall. Mott was a religious fanatic with powerful influence at home. Living at Beyrout, safe from the dangers of fiery Damascus, he could not be brought to understand the jeopardy into which his misguided zeal put the lives of the Christians in the city. It was only ten years since, goaded to fury by their leaders and assisted by a passive Turkish soldiery, the Moslems in

Damascus had risen and slaughtered the Christians in the city.[1] Fanaticism, fed by Christian and Jewish importunity, had led to this disaster and the memory of it preyed constantly on the Consul's mind. Mott's indiscretions soon turned Burton from a tolerant observer into an angry opponent. He rescued the man's tracts for him from the prisons where the Moslems had gathered to burn them publicly; but when he found Mott himself, standing in the open *bazaar*, distributing more tracts and surrounded by an angry crowd of Moslems, his patience became exhausted.

" Do you want to be killed ? " he cried, ordering the missionary to leave the city instantly.

" I should glory in martyrdom ! " was the ringing reply; and when told that safe in Beyrout he need fear little, but that every Christian in the city might suffer for his idiocy, he flew into a violent rage and wrote home that Captain Burton was trying to hinder the spread of the Christian faith in the East.

More letters flowed to and fro. More complaints reached Whitehall. Demands for explanations from Captain Burton began to arrive by every post. He replied to them characteristically.

" The charge of religious intolerance is to me a novelty, the world has generally given me credit for something too much the reverse."

Eldridge, the pottering Consul-General at Beyrout, eyed him askance. Was there ever such a man for stirring up trouble ? Why could not he let sleeping dogs lie, as did every Consul in the East ? When two missionaries were attacked and robbed by Druze tribesmen, Burton had them arrested and demanded a fine from them. The Druze complained and sent a deputation to Beyrout to appeal to Eldridge. That temporizer, intimidated, remitted the fine and sent Burton orders to release the prisoners. Burton protested, saying that to do so would make a precedent that would render the desert routes impossible to Europeans. Eldridge insisted, and so the malefactors were freed, shortly after, to repeat their crime. Eldridge wrote home complaining that Burton was antagonizing the Druze and making the country dangerous for travellers; and yet another mark was put against the name of the new Consul at Damascus.

With these enemies combined against him, Burton had a hard struggle to hold his own. But he might have done so were it not for one insuperable difficulty : Isabel.

[1] In July 1860 the Damascus Moslems rose and massacred 3000 adult males among the Christian population.

Isabel gave Burton's critics the handle they really needed. Her well meant but often outrageous behaviour antagonized all who came in contact with her and alarmed even those Moslems who loved her husband. That ever-ready riding-whip, of which Lord Redesdale tells a story,[1] was but the least of her indiscretions. Behind Richard's back she had begun, not only to try to coax, threaten, or buy the Moslem poor into Catholicism, but, driven by repeated failure to desperate devices, she was visiting dying Moslem children and baptizing them over the heads of their bewildered and helpless mothers.

The Turkish Wali complained to Constantinople. Surely a Consul with such a bigoted Roman Catholic wife was a menace to the city? More dispatches went to London. It was represented to Lord Granville that Burton's life was in danger from fanatical Moslems. Still the Foreign Office hesitated to move until they had more positive evidence of this last and most dangerous assertion. This came at last in 1871, and from a different quarter.

In the spring of that year the Burtons, accompanied by Tyrwhitt Drake, the archæologist, commenced a tour of the Holy Land which was to include Jericho, Jerusalem, Hebron, and Nazareth, and the surrounding country. The account of this journey is to be found in Isabel's biography.

All went well until they reached Nazareth, where they camped on a plain outside the city and close to a Greek Orthodox Church. At dawn, on 5th May, Isabel was aroused by an altercation between her servant and a young Copt negro who had been stopped while trying to enter her tent. A scuffle ensued, the Copt threw some stones, and was then seized by the rest of the servants and beaten. At this moment about 150 Greeks emerged from service at the nearby church, formed themselves into a mob, advanced on the camp, and adopted a threatening attitude. Burton and Drake, aroused by the noise, left their tents to investigate and were greeted by a shower of stones. Though struck repeatedly, they stood their ground, marking out the ringleaders, until a shout from a rich Greek

[1] *Memories of My Life.* Isabel entered a Mosque to show some visitors the sights. A poor Moslem was seated in meditation before the shrine of a Saint. He blocked the party's view of the tomb, and, without waiting for him to finish his devotions, Isabel advanced on him with the riding-whip and drove him away in a scene which made Redesdale leave the Mosque in disgust. " If actuated by no higher motive," the latter writes, " she should have reflected upon the harm which such conduct needs must work upon her husband."

in the rear : " Kill them all ! Kill them all ! I will pay the blood money," occasioned a rush in which the two men had to fight for their lives. At length someone fired an alarm shot and a number of Europeans, roused from a nearby camp, came to the rescue. The Greeks fled, leaving one of Burton's servants lying for dead, the other just conscious, Burton himself with a fractured sword arm, and Drake with severe bruises.

Investigation of this unpleasant episode revealed that it was calculated rather than spontaneous and arose primarily from a case in which Burton had protested against the appropriation by the Greeks of Nazareth of certain property belonging to Jewish British protected subjects. The Wali of Damascus, however, only too glad to strike again at his enemy, exaggerated its implications and sent it to Constantinople with a note stating that in his opinion Burton's further presence in Damascus was not only undesirable but dangerous, and that Greeks and Moslems might rise against him and his wife at any moment. He added to this another complaint, unaware of its implied contradiction of the first, that Burton was influencing the Druze Arabs and banding them against the Turks. From Constantinople the protest was forwarded to Beyrout, where Eldridge added his quota, and then it went to London where it finally tipped the scales. Burton must be recalled. The charges against him were too serious to be ignored.

Had anyone taken the trouble to examine these charges carefully, and particularly in their relation to one another, or even had Eldridge any idea of the shifts and mendacity in Oriental intrigue, it might have been seen upon what a mass of contradiction they had been based. H.B.M's Consul, it was claimed by his detractors :

Hated the Jews : and showed preference to Greeks and Christians.

Was hated by the Greeks because he preferred the Jews.

Was hated by the Moslems because he spread Christianity.

Was disliked by the Missionaries because he prevented the spread of Christianity.

Had offended the Turkish Government because he sided with the Druzes.

Was antagonizing the Druzes by not permitting them their legitimate sport of assault and battery.

But no one did take the trouble. It was sufficient, and perhaps rightly so, that pressure from Jewish, Turkish, and British philanthropic sources demanded Burton's recall; and the incident at Nazareth now gave the wanted opportunity for it. It is clear that the temperament needed to carry on service in such conditions was not Burton's.

§

Two months later the blow fell, engineered with an unhappy callousness, much of which must be laid at Eldridge's door. The Burtons were entertaining a party at their summer residence in Bludan. Picnics, excursions, and shooting-parties had been arranged for the guests, and they were about to leave on one of these, when, without warning, a messenger appeared from Damascus carrying a note. It was from the Vice-Consul at Beyrout and curtly informed Captain Burton that, on orders from his superior, he himself had arrived at Damascus the previous day and taken charge of the Consulate over Burton's head.

Burton and Drake saddled their horses instantly and rode furiously to the city. There Burton was handed a letter by the Vice-Consul from H.M. Secretary for Foreign Affairs.

Sir,
        You are informed by a dispatch written to you on the 19th January 1869 by direction of the late Earl Clarendon that very serious objections had been made to your appointment as Her Majesty's Consul at Damascus, and that though his Lordship was willing to allow you to proceed to that post on receipt of your assurance that the objections were unfounded, you were warned that it would be necessary that you should be recalled if the feeling stated to exist against you on the part of the authorities and people of Damascus should prevent the proper discharge of your official duties.

        I regret to have to inform you that the complaints which I have received from the Turkish Government in regard to your recent conduct and proceedings render it impossible that I should allow you to continue to perform any Consular functions in Syria, and I have accordingly to desire that you will, on receipt of this dispatch, hand over the archives of H.M. Consulate at Damascus to the person whom Mr. Consul-General Eldridge will appoint to carry on the duties of the Consulate until further orders.

You will, therefore, make your preparations for return to this country with as little delay as possible.

I am, sir,

Your most obedient humble servant,

Granville.

There was nothing to be done. Grief-stricken, he wrote a note to Isabel at Bludan.

" Don't be frightened—I am recalled. Pay, pack, and follow at convenience."

From Damascus, scarcely allowing himself time to pack, he hurried to Beyrout. In his journal, written in the swaying carriage that bore him over the Bekaa plain on his last journey across Syria, he wrote :

18th August. Left Damascus for ever ; started at three a.m. in the dark, with a big lantern ; all my men crying ; alone in the coupé of diligence, thanks to the pigs. Excitement of seeing all for the last time. All seemed sorry ; a few groans. The sight of B'ludan mountains in the distance at sunrise, where I have left my wife. *Ever again ?* Felt soft. Dismissal ignominious, at the age of fifty, without a month's notice, or wages, or character.

The Turkish Government has boasted that it would choose its own time, when Moslems may become Christians if they wish. The time has now come.[1]

At Beyrout he was cut by Eldridge, and were it not for the hospitality of the French Consul he might have had nowhere to stay.

Then he took the first boat for home.

[1] Burton's record of his travels in Syria is collected in his *Unexplored Syria,* 2 vols., Tinsley, 1872. This is a description of his life as Consul ; an account of his travels in the Syrian desert and Libanus, the discovery of the famous Hama stones, which started the study of Hittite culture, and a collection of Syrian Arabic proverbs. Part of the book is written by Isabel.

Chapter Eleven

THE news of Burton's summary recall from Damascus and the infamous intrigues that had occasioned it evoked a public revulsion in his favour. Not only did the Press take his part, but from Damascus itself a flow of letters appeared from the pens of missionaries, Moslem dignitaries, and English travellers, deploring an unjust act which could only be remedied by its revocation. In Damascus mosques the Moslems prayed publicly for his return, the poor clamoured that now their protector had gone they were in the hands of their enemies, and prophets even saw the decline of Syria in this ignominious recall of one of the few men of integrity and courage that had ever blessed its capital.[1]

In England, after baffling interviews at the Foreign Office, Burton prepared his case, fully documented and argued with what seemed clear and vigorous logic. Reviewing the case in its entirety it seemed impossible that such a case of flagrant injustice should stand; and for a while the dismissed man half-believed that any post might bring him the order to return and take up his Consulship. He forgot that he was a solitary man fighting a bureaucracy and that his case was hopeless from the first.

He was staying at his sister's in Norwood, bitter and silent and more worn and lined than ever. " Never had we known him so wretched, so unnerved; his hands shook, his temper was strangely irritable, all that appreciation of fun and humour which rendered him such a cheery companion to young and old alike had vanished. He could settle at nothing; he was restless, but would not leave the house; ailing, but would take no advice —it was indeed a melancholy spectacle." [2]

Yet public feeling, in spite of the usual fancy fictions that always gathered around him, was strong in his favour; and, when the news reached England of the recall by the Turkish Government of Burton's chief accuser, the Wali, in chains and

[1] The correspondence of this unhappy period is inserted in detail in vol. I. of Lady Burton's " Life ".
[2] Georgiana Stisted, *Life of Captain Burton.*

ignominy to Constantinople, and his subsequent execution, it was felt that no further proof was needed of the vindication of Burton's honour and the rightness of the policy for which he had been condemned.

Once more he wrote to the Foreign Office, setting out the whole case in detail and in the light of subsequent developments, and pleading whether he might not now return to the position from which he had been so unjustly expelled.

This letter occasioned a tactical governmental shuffle. Aware now that they had made, of necessity, an ungracious gesture and damaged the career of a valuable man ; aware, too, that to admit it would be to lay themselves open to public reprimand, the Foreign Office shifted their ground and endeavoured to extricate themselves in the following letter :

Foreign Office, 25th October 1871.

Sir,

I have received your letter of the 16th October, recapitulating, with reference to the cessation of your functions as Her Majesty's Consul at Damascus, the several employments in H.M.'s Consul Service which you have successfully held.

I do not think it necessary to follow you through that recapitulation, or to enter into any review of your conduct in the post which you last held. I am willing to give you credit for having endeavoured, to the best of your ability and judgment, to carry on the duties which were entrusted ; but having come to the conclusion, on a review of the Consular establishments in Syria, that it was no longer necessary to maintain a full Consul at Damascus, at a cost to the public, including salary and allowance, of £1000 a year, your withdrawal from that residence necessarily followed on the appointment of an officer of lower rank, and at a lower rate of salary to perform the Consular duties in that place. Your obedient, humble servant,

Granville.

Thus, having expelled a man from his position in the most ignominious and unjust manner and thown him penniless upon his own resourses with such a character that further employment would be most difficult, they now turned round and implied that they had done nothing of the sort but merely recalled him for reasons of public economy. That this letter is a poor excuse, and the explanation it offers a mere composition of the moment is amply illustrated by a letter from Burton to a friend dated only two months later which also shows the deep interest the latter still had in unhappy Syria.

Howlett's Hotel, Monday, 4th December.

My dear Rathborne,

If you can get a peep at the last "Tablet" do, and you will find Tyrwhitt Drake's account of the Revival movement in Syria. He says it may amount to 20,000—25,000. Do you advise me to draw Lord Granville's attention to it. Mind, the affair is serious. If anything like a massacre takes place, Russia certainly and France probably will interfere and occupy Syria in force. Prussia and Austria will object and then there is a row. You see they have made Damascus a full Consulate. I am now pushing to get the Consul-General up to Damascus. Ever yours truly,

R. F. Burton.

But he soon wearily gave up his attempts to secure official vindication or redress. Indeed circumstances now forced him to turn his mind in another direction. When Isabel returned from Syria with the heavier baggage and they counted up their resources they found that they were practically penniless. Extravagant spenders both, neither had ever been able to save from their joint incomes. Now they were faced, in middle age, with penury.

At all costs Richard must find some work to do. But to what could he turn his hand ? It was the old story over again : lack of official employment was a death-blow to a man who had never experienced anything else. His constant flow of erudite but specialized and unpalatable books brought him nothing ; he knew nothing of commerce, was over fifty and beginning to ail in health.

For a while it was only the generosity of relations and friends that kept them from literal poverty. Invitations flowed in upon them from all sides and their time was spent in a constant round of long visits to country houses. Neglected by his country, the discoverer of Harar and the Lake Regions of Central Africa, the foremost traveller and Orientalist of the day, wandered proudly but pathetically through some of the blackest months of his career. Of this period Isabel records one touching incident. Once, when journeying down to Garswood to stay with her uncle, their worldly capital had sunk as low as a mere £15. Isabel carried the sovereigns in her purse, and during the train journey the latter fell from her lap and one of the sovereigns rolled out of sight between the floorboards. She groped for it in vain and then sat on the floor and, in a flurry of crumpled crinoline and shawl, burst uncontrollably into tears. In a moment Richard was crouching on the floor beside her, his arm round her waist, her head on his shoulder, and thus on the carriage floor alternately comforting one another and clutching their little purse of sovereigns they concluded the journey to Garswood.

Paradoxical creature that could melt at the sight of his wife in tears and yet face the world with a sardonic grin. That the old mocking spirit was not dead we perceive from a characteristic letter that came from him at this time.

Tuesday, 26th October 1872.

Sir,

Yours of 23rd October received.

Reply

I am, Sir, yours most sincerely,

R. F. Burton.

The Secretary,
Anthropological Institute.

In London, while searching for employment, the Burtons entered a round of society. They attended seances, corresponded with Sir William Crookes on the subject of the New Force, attended lectures and meetings. Richard read several papers on anthropological subjects. He met Swinburne again, and Stanley the traveller. The latter records that he proposed that Burton should write his own reminiscences. "He said he could not do so, because he should have to write of so many people."

" ' Be charitable and write only of their best qualities,' I said.

" ' I don't care a fig for charity ; if I write at all I must write truthfully : all I know,' he replied."

And as he watched the proud, sneering face turn away, Stanley cries, regretfully : " What a grand man ! One of the real great ones of England, he might have been, if he had not been cursed with cynicism."

Early in the following year an offer from an independent commercial gentleman for Burton to visit Iceland in the capacity of mining expert and inspect the sulphur deposits there led to a journey which, though uneventful in itself, did much to restore his health and spirits. He returned from Iceland to write the inevitable book *Ultima Thule* (1875), and to receive from the Foreign Office, almost a year after his dismissal, the offer of the Consulate of Trieste with a salary of £700 and a Vice-Consul.

He hesitated : and then accepted, though he was well aware that Trieste was a Consular backwater, from which there could be little hope of promotion. The devils, he said, had shelved him where they thought he would do the least harm, and he despised them for it. But beggars could not be choosers and, with a sigh of mingled relief and regret, he put his affairs in order, said his farewells, and sailed on 24th October 1872, leaving Isabel behind as usual to " pay, pack, and follow."

§

Approaching Trieste from the sea at any time during the 'seventies or 'eighties, the visitor entered an untidy, malodorous harbour whose quay bore evidences of being subjected for long continuous periods to heavy gales and whose backwaters were filled with rotting debris and the outflow of the town drains. Steep, wooded slopes swept down to the water's edge, their nearer folds dotted with villas, their crests giving on to the wild heights of the Karso, while seaward the far horizon glimmered with the snow-covered summits of the Carnian Alps which seemed to hang poised above the blue Adriatic.

Almost immediately behind the Customs sheds and hotels of the harbour a tall block of white buildings met the eye, and approaching and entering these by one of three doorways the visitor would be confronted by a steep flight of 120 steps which would have to be negotiated before reaching a flat at the top.

An Austrian maid would answer the door and usher the breath-less visitor inside, and presently, clad in a long flowing Indian dressing-gown, with a smoking-cap on her head, cigarette in her hand, and several dogs at her heels, Mrs. Burton would bustle forward with words of effusive greeting.

Richard, of course, would be working. " On a book," Mrs. Burton would mysteriously explain, " which I have promised never to read " ; and one would have to proceed almost on tip-toe through the twenty odd rooms of the Consulate and speak in lowered tones.

It was a bizarre and fascinating place, this cosmopolitan eyrie of a great traveller, high above the Adriatic. From room to room, ushered by the talkative Mrs. Burton, the visitor would pass, confronted almost at every turn by some strange incon-sistency of furnishing which would seem to illuminate the conflicting character of the occupants. Crammed from floor to ceiling with pictures, eastern draperies, pilgrim praying-rugs, vases, brass bowls, and ferns, their corners filled with bundles of swords, guns, fencing gear, chronometers, and theodolites, the walls half-hidden in rough deal shelves housing the 8000 volumes of the Orientalist's unique library, above them madonnas rubbing shoulders with eastern chibouques, tinselled altars cheek by jowl with Somali stabbing-spears, and on the tables regiments of photographs—family portraits, Arab groups, Cardinal Wiseman facing a naked Unyamwezi girl with uplifted arms and pouting breasts, a skull or two, some Damascene tiles all resting on a most virtuous Victorian table cloth, aroused in the spectator's mind the feeling that here was the meeting-place of the bivouac and the salon ; the Crescent and the Cross.

At length, outside a closed door, the visitor would be halted. Mrs. Burton would become all gusty whispers. Richard would be inside, working. One tiny peep. . . .

The door would be opened. A glimpse would be had of a long, bare, marble-floored room quartered by a number of plain square tables each littered with manuscripts, notes, and books. At each table a different work was in progress and the great traveller could move from one to the other as the mood took him. Facing a small window and with his back to the door in a hard wooden chair,[1] Burton himself would be seen at work on his *magnum opus*, the *Thousand and One Nights*. At his elbow would be the photostatic copy of the original *Arabian Night's*

[1] Now, with the tables, in the Central Library at Camberwell.

MSS. from the Bodleian, a pile of manuscript notes on all shades of paper, yellowed and faded by Arabian, Indian, African, and Brazilian suns, the garnered researches of twenty-five years, and in that small, feminine, almost indecipherable handwriting he would be covering page upon page in slow laborious translation, halting to think and to consult his notes, to mutter to himself, in Arabic or in English, to chuckle at some happy phrase or knot his thick brows and groan over a difficult one.

The door would shut again on that unforgettable and somehow pathetic picture of England's neglected traveller working in solitude in his third-rate commercial seaport far from the lands he knew and loved so well, and Mrs. Burton would lead one back to her own sanctum, a small but ornate room filled with devotional books, rosaries, a little altar with a flame burning, a prie-dieu, a table littered with pens and paper, a truckle bed. This room, too, had its interest; for from here it was that Burton's wife maintained her constant war of correspondence with the outer world, grappled with creditors, publishers, and printers, fenced round after round with the Foreign Office, declaimed to or pleaded with the Press for adequate recognition of her husband, and meanwhile kept up her own copious diaries and a constant flow of articles and books.

And here in eager, excitable tones she would ask for the latest news from England, society chatter, the discreet scandals; in return she would be full of the petty gossip of Trieste, of their adventures in the mountains, their work, and Richard's ailing health. She would speak of their visits to the Austrian Court. People called Trieste a backwater, but it could boast as high society as any capital. There were the Monpurgo's of Austrian Lloyds and the Sassoons, the two wealthy and powerful leading families. Richard and she had the entrée to their gatherings and to the Court, because she had taken for herself the title of Countess of the Holy Roman Empire, and her visiting-cards read :

Mrs. Richard Burton
née Countess Isabel Arundell of Wardour.

Superstitious and credulous, she would speak too of the many miracles and strange alterations of the course of nature which surrounded Richard and herself. Only a little while back she had woken one morning to see real tears glistening on the

cheeks of her plaster madonna, and a few days later she had
learned that a very dear friend was dead ; or one of her old
confessors was worrying about her in some distant country
and corresponding with her by means of miraculous stigmata
which he caused to appear from time to time in the palm of
her hand ; or alternately it might be the story of the carriage
accident in which everyone was seriously injured except one
person who was carrying a holy medallion given him by Isabel.
Then there were her experiments with Richard.   Richard
practised mesmerizing her for hours and they had got so that
they could communicate to one another without speaking,
they tried table-turning, though this sometimes landed her in
trouble with her local priest, and they dabbled in that wonderful
new discovery called Animal Magnetism.

With this sort of busy life and their work they were perfectly
happy ; and if Richard could get his proper recognition their
cup would be full.   They still kept to the inflexible routine of
the early days of their marriage.   Rising at four or five in the
dawn they would drink a cup of tea over a spirit stove and then
work solidly till noon.   A bowl of soup and a bath and then
they would visit the local fencing-school where they would
fence or batter one another with broadswords for an hour.
There followed another hard spell of work at the Consulate
until evening, when they would relax, stroll up to Trieste's best
hotel and dine well on a half-crown table d'hote.   A simple but
idyllic life, Mrs. Burton would exclaim, and broken by delightful excursions to Rome, Venice, or nearer still to Opçina in the
mountains, where their tired spirits soon picked up, and Richard
could roam the countryside studying and cataloguing the
antiquities of Istria for the inevitable pamphlet.

But of the other side of the domestic picture the visitor
would be kept mercifully ignorant, and he would leave the little
Consulate perched above the Adriatic feeling that he had been
privileged to peep for a moment upon a scene of perfect domestic
bliss.

For Richard was never more difficult than in those early
years at Trieste.   Injustice rankled in his spirit, poverty irked
him, and, though he sought to bury himself in work, those old
frenzies of restlessness would seize upon him, setting him pacing
from room to room like a caged animal, insolent to all who spoke
to him and exploding now and again into those mad and childish
pranks that were the bane of Isabel's life.

More and more difficult did he become with strangers whose society irritated him ; and there were times when he seemed to take a special delight in breaking up Isabel's one important social event, her Friday afternoon salon for ladies. On one of these afternoons, and she blushed with horror whenever she recalled it, he had thrown the refined gathering of Trieste society ladies into an extreme of agitation by stalking suddenly into the room, glowering round the assembly, laying down what appeared to be a MS. in the middle of the tea-table, and walking out again without a word. A most awkward moment ensued when several of the ladies, twittering with curiosity, bent over the MS. lying among the teacups. It was entitled *A History of Farting*.[1]

It was fortunate that the Foreign Office, as if in some measure to atone for their past neglect, allowed him so much freedom during these days, and that there was a Vice-Consul always at hand to take over the routine work. It was only lack of money that hindered him from travelling on his own again. Money, indeed, was one of the major problems of his life at Trieste, and he thought long and often of ways to supplement his meagre income. He did some journalism and reporting, lectured in various cities on a variety of subjects, and even had a fling at commerce, patenting a tonic water of his own, to be called " Captain Burton's Bitters," with a picture of himself on the bottle. " The taste is not over savoury, but the effect upon the liver is grand, enabling it to digest any amount of liquor. . . ."[2]

This production came to nothing, and a few months later we find him turning to new and more adventurous channels in his search for the elusive something that was to make his fortune.

§

To prospect for gold is an activity that appeals especially to the adventurous. The glamour, hardship, constant excitement and anticipation ; and auriferous dreams have sent many a phlegmatic traveller to the waste places of the earth. Ever since his interest had been aroused by the goldfields of California during his visit to the U.S., Burton had been making a study of the prospector's methods ; in Brazil, at Minas Geraes, a

[1] N. M. Penzer, the Orientalist, relates this story, told him by one of Burton's intimates.
[2] Letter to Grattan Geary, June 1876.

theoretical interest had developed into practical planning, and in 1876, with a secret he had kept locked in his bosom for twenty-five years, he felt ready to embark on his own.

In that year, after a grant of six months' leave from the Foreign Office, he took Isabel to India for a holiday. They sailed by the Suez, Jeddah, Aden, and Bombay, a leisurely journey which enabled Richard to visit old haunts and revive forgotten memories. From Bombay they visited Sind, Goa, and the Deccan, changed out of all belief since the extinction of the East India Company. Isabel kept a voluminous journal of their adventures and wrote a book of her own on their return which is infinitely more readable than anything of Richard's.

On the return home via Egypt occurred the opportunity for which he had long been waiting. The story has all the flavour of the *Arabian Nights*.

There was once a caravan of pilgrims returning home from Mecca which took the dreaded overland route to Suez round the spur of Akabah. Struggling day and night, with the Howeitat Arabs harrying their flanks and driving them down to the sea-beaches of Midian for safety, they halted one night in a wadi by the sea. One of the pilgrims dismounted from his ass and went a little distance from his companions to sit alone beneath a tree. With his tired eyes leaning gratefully on the cool waters of the little torrent he rested his cheek upon his hand and then stared hard at the sand-bottom of the wadi. It was glittering strangely. Scooping a few handfuls of the sand and concealing it in a pouch he returned to his party, and on arrival at Alexandria carried his find to a professional assayer. From one handful of the sand the assayer produced a piece of pure gold the size of a grain of wheat and the overjoyed pilgrim, who had made a rough map of the position of the wadi, felt that his fortune was made. He had communicated with the authorities who had done nothing, and then in the careless Oriental manner he had let the matter slide for four years. Then, on a journey from Alexandria to Cairo, he had made the acquaintance of a Persian doctor who afterwards became a close friend of his in Cairo. To him, under a pledge of great secrecy, the pilgrim told his story and showed his grain of gold. But at that time the doctor was otherwise engaged and he could not help, and so for twenty-five more years the matter had lapsed. The pilgrim was Haji Wali of the Cairo *wakalah*, the doctor was Richard Burton in disguise.

Now Haji Wali's story might have been a mere traveller's tale, but for various reasons Burton was inclined to believe him. The coast of Midian has for long been considered an ancient centre of the gold-mining industry. Both classical and Arabian writers speak of Midian gold, and it was well known in 1876 that that comparatively unmapped area was rich in ruined cities and ancient mines. Indeed, it is not impossible that in Midian was centred those mysterious mines of Ophir of which ancient history is full and no man knows the whereabouts.

On his return from India past the Arabian coast which so continually revived in his mind the memories of his famous exploit, the remembrance of this episode with Haji Wali came back to Burton's mind with renewed force. In his youth he had put aside all thoughts of commerce to follow the yearning of his heart for adventure ; now in his age surely the time was ripe to find the wealth that would give him days of ease.

" Throughout the summer of 1877 I was haunted by memories of mysterious Midian. The Golden Region appeared to me in the glow of primeval prosperity described by the Egyptian hieroglyphs. . . . Again I saw the mining works of the Greek, the Roman, and the Nabathæan . . . the forty cities, mere ghosts and shadows of their former selves described in the pages of the medieval Arab geographers ; and the ruthless ruin under the dominion of the Badawin, gradually crept over the land of Jethro. . . ."

The opportunity to be once more in his beloved desert among the Badu, to explore the ancient mines and cities, and find a fortune for himself was irresistible. He was still strong and able ; why should not an expedition be made to this area, led by himself, to survey the unknown country and prospect for gold and minerals ?

At Cairo, after the inevitable delays, he put himself in touch with the Khedive, Ismail Pasha, to whom he communicated his story. This enlightened Egyptian, perceiving that a survey expedition led by such a veteran traveller, even if it failed to find gold, would be of immense geographical value, gladly gave his consent, and guaranteed to finance and provide Egyptian surveyors and miners for the operations.

The enterprise backed by such powerful help and led by unrivalled experience resulted in three expeditions to the unknown Midian during the years 1877-78, an accomplishment which puts Burton's name on the map of Arabia as an explorer of real value. Geographically his surveys of the southern half of the Midian coastal range, supplementing as they do Moresby's official work in the *Palinurus*, far outclass scientifically that more popular *tour de force*, the pilgrimage to Mecca. With Muwaylah as a base, expeditions were made to the Wadis Aynunah and Ziba, to Makna in the Gulf of Akabah, ancient capital of Midian, and finally, inland from Muwaylah, through the coastal Wadi Surr, the porphyritic precipices of the Umm Jedayl, and the dark throat of Wadi Sadr to the unknown Hisma, haunt of the dangerous Howeitat, and westernmost edge of the great central Arabian plateau of el Nejd.

No gold was found, though this did not shake Burton's conviction that it was there, but a large quantity of minerals was collected and a number of valuable archæological finds including Himyaritic and Safaitic inscriptions and coins.

For Burton these were the happiest days he had known since Damascus. In his records of these expeditions, *Gold Mines of Midian*, 1878, *The Land of Midian*, 1879, there are moments when he seems to recapture again something of the long lost colour and vigour of the *Pilgrimage*. Once more, the Arabian Knight, as his friends called him, was in his beloved desert. " At last ! " we hear him cry as he stands again on the threshold of the desert, " once more it is my fate to escape the prison-life of civilized Europe, and to refresh body and mind by studying Nature in her noblest and most admirable form—the Nude. Again I am to enjoy a glimpse of the ' glorious desert,' to inhale sweet, pure breath of translucent skies that show the red stars burning upon the very edge and verge of the horizon, and to strengthen myself by a short visit to the Wild Man and his old home. . . ."

Alas, it was to be his last visit to his beloved desert ; and with the final parting from it he seems to lapse once more into a sullen resignation. Three years later he made another abortive attempt to wring gold from the earth in an expedition to West Africa with Captain Lovett Cameron, but that, too, failed, and again he returned wearily to his dull consulate in Trieste to bury himself more and more in the labours of his *Arabian Nights*, little aware that here, under his hand, was the very gold mine for which he was so ardently searching.

Chapter Twelve

THE next five years passed slowly and uneventfully for the Burtons. Richard laboured at his *Arabian Nights*, punctuating his work with unofficial holidays in Europe. His vice of departing periodically without leave seemed to become intensified with age; and often landed him in awkward situations; but the Foreign Office were very lenient, rarely complaining at the behaviour of what they now saw to be a sick man. A break occurred in 1882 when he was asked by the Government to proceed to Sinai and search for his old friend, Professor Palmer,[1] who, it was feared rightly, had been murdered by Arabs. Eagerly Burton threw a few things together and sailed for Gaza, but he had no sooner set foot on shore than he was recalled. Sir Charles Warren had already accomplished the sad task.

Back again he faced the Trieste round with resigned fortitude. Self pity was the vice which least afflicted him, yet on the 6th December 1883, the following note printed in his journal in red ink comes like a pathetic *cri de cœur*.

" To-day, eleven years ago, I came here; what a shame ! ! ! "

The year 1885 found the Burtons working hard in London under conditions of great excitement and secrecy. The labour of translating the *Arabian Nights* was complete; the copying was in its final stages, a gratifying number of subscribers had been obtained, and volume one of the proposed set of ten was about to issue from the press.

In the days immediately preceding its publication, many doubts assailed both Burton and his wife. Privately printed though it was and markedly labelled as for the student rather than the general reader, there were fears that this monument of industry and learning would not pass the Censor; fears of Governmental displeasure; fears of the police.

Isabel who had promised not to read it, but nevertheless reveals here and there in her works an unaccountable acquaintance with it, was at times bordering on a state of panic. While

---

[1] E. H. Palmer had been one of those Orientalists who had defended Burton in the British press after his recall from Damascus.

the proofs were passing to and fro, her anxiety reached a peak that made her feel like some heroine in a Hoffman story. She saw mysterious strangers everywhere, spent whole hours at a time peering at Dorset Square, through chinks in the window curtains of their chambers at No. 23, or writing agitated letters like the following to her harassed printers :

Dear Mr. Notcutt,

My landlord tells me he thinks the house is watched and he has seen two or three strange people hovering about and advises me to warn our printers not to send messengers but to send by post as they might ask the messenger or others where he came from, or follow him. . . .

Richard was meanwhile grappling with all the difficulties of book production. He had ignored the blandishments of a publisher with an offer of £500, and was bringing out the work himself through Waterlows, the printers, with the same meticulous care that was later lavished by T. E. Lawrence on his eastern classic, *The Seven Pillars of Wisdom*. To Isabel's constant alarms and excursions he turned a deaf ear, summing up his own attitude to public morality with a terse : " I don't care a button about being prosecuted, and if the matter comes to a fight, I will walk into court with my Bible and my Shakespeare and my Rabelais under my arm, and prove to them that, before they condemn me, they must cut half of them out."

Ten volumes had been planned at £1, 1s. a volume, and the names of a thousand subscribers obtained. But a supplementary five volumes were later added bringing the total of royalties received to sixteen thousand pounds, which, after paying the printer, gave the author a clear £10,000.

The first volume appeared in September of that year and at its publication Burton once more became instantly a celebrity. Except for Galland's garbled French edition, the emasculated version from Lane, and Payne's little-known work, the Western world knew comparatively nothing of the poetry, vigour, and life of this treasure house of Eastern customs. Accustomed to regard the *Arabian Nights* as a nursery book suitable chiefly for children, society suddenly found itself face to face in Burton's meticulously annotated pages with all the passion, lust, and glitter of the true East, the real home of the *ars erotica*, and with the fact that the charming stories lisped at mothers' knee took on, in the original, the most sinister and depraving twists.

Volume one of the *Arabian Nights* was the literary sensation of the moment. For every student who supposedly read it for its Eastern lore, five hundred prurient-minded ran avidly through its pages for its amours. Secretly, the forbidden copies passed from hand to hand in the clubs of London, and here and there crept into secluded drawing-rooms to be as eagerly devoured.

" No. 1 caused big sensation," wrote Burton with delighted astonishment to his bibliographer, W. F. Kirby, " wonderful leader about it in *Standard* (Mrs. Gamp of all people) followed by abuse in *Pall Mall*. I have come upon a young woman friend greedily reading it in open drawing-room, and when I warned another against it, she answered, ' Very well. Billy [her husband] has a copy and I shall read it at once. . . . ! ' "

The literary world greeted it mainly with a steady chorus of praise, which almost extinguished the protests of that section of the British public that Burton called " Mrs. Grundy." In literary circles it was felt that no conjunction of author and subject could have been more perfect. The book held a mirror up to its author ; its author had made the book a brilliant background for an exhibition of unique, passionate, and scrupulous knowledge in Eastern life, literature, and sex customs, and psychology. To-day, the famous Terminal Essay, which ranges the whole field of erotic practice in all countries, pales beside the unsavoury investigations of Freud and Krafft-Ebing, but it preceded them by twenty years, it was more catholic, and it is literature.

The *Arabian Nights* contains the very essence of Richard Burton. In reading it, the student approaches nearer to the wild turbulent spirit of him than any other work excepting the *Pilgrimage*.

" This work," he cries in his foreword to the first volume, " laborious as it may appear, has been to me a labour of love, an unfailing source of solace and satisfaction. During my long years of official banishment to the luxuriant and deadly deserts of West Africa, and to the dull and dreary half-clearings of South America it proved itself a charm, a talisman against *ennui* and despondency. Impossible even to open the pages without a vision starting into view ; without drawing a picture from the pinacothek of the brain ; without reviving a host of dead memories and reminiscences. . . . From my dull and commonplace and ' respectable ' surroundings, the Jinn bore me at once to the land of my predilection, Arabia, a region so familiar to my mind that, even at first sight, it seemed a reminiscence of some bygone metempsychic life in the distant Past. . . ."

That the eroticism was bound to be condemned he foresaw ; and against the charge that he had pursued pornography for its own sake, he brought the perfectly proper explanation that his object was " to assist the student of Moslem life and of Arabs, Egyptian manners, customs, and language in a multitude of matters shunned by books, to form a repertory of Eastern knowledge in its esoteric phase, sexual as well as social. . . ."
" Does England," he wrote elsewhere, " forget she is at present the greatest Mussulman Empire in the world ?   How can she rule her people if she does not know them ? "

Once more the warm sun of public recognition fell full upon the tired traveller, reminding the country that its greatest Orientalist and explorer was pining away neglected in Trieste. The chorus of praise so unsuspected, amazed, overwhelmed him. " I seize the opportunity," he wrote, " of expressing my cordial gratitude and hearty thanks to the Press in general, which has received my Eastern studies and contributions to Oriental knowledge in the friendliest and most sympathetic spirit, appreciating my labours far beyond the modicum of the offerer's expectations, and lending potent and genial aid to place them before the English world in their fairest and most favourable point of view. . . ."

But most valued of all were two verses which appeared in the *Athœneum* for 6th February 1886.

To Richard F. Burton :
  On His Translation of the *Arabian Nights*

> Westward the sun sinks, grave and glad ; but far
> Eastward, with laughter and tempestuous tears,
> Cloud, rain, and splendour as of Orient spears,
> Keen as the sea's thrill toward a kindling star
> The sun-down breaks the barren twilight's bar
> And fires the mist and slays it. Years on years,
> Vanish, but he that hearkens Eastward hears
> Bright music from the world where shadows are.
>
> Where shadows are not shadows. Hand in hand
> A man's word bids them rise and smile and stand
> And triumph. All that glorious Orient glows
> Defiant of the dusk. Our twilight land
> Trembles ; but all the heaven is all one rose,
> Whence laughing love dissolves her frosts and snows.
>
> Algernon Charles Swinburne.

Chapter Thirteen

THE success of the *Arabian Nights* led Burton now to undertake an even more risky and scandalous work. This was the translation of an Arabic MS. entitled *The Scented Garden, Men's Hearts to Gladden, of the Shaykh al Nafzawi*. Its subject matter, Burton described himself in a characteristic letter.[1] " Enclosed will show you what my present work is. More than half already done. It will be a marvellous repertory of Eastern wisdom ; how Eunuchs are made and are married ; what they do in marriage ; female circumcision, the Fellahs copulating with crocodiles, etc. Mrs. Grundy will howl till she almost bursts and will read every word with an intense enjoyment. . . ."

Alas, he was not to complete it. A year earlier in 1884 had come the first signs that the iron constitution, racked by a hundred fevers and the hardships of five continents, was at last beginning to break up. Attacks of gout, beginning first as mere twinges, then developing into bouts of acute pain, accompanied by fainting fits and shortness of breath, showed that angina pectoris, an hereditary disease, was already making serious inroads.

Isabel nursed him assiduously. The stairs leading to the top flat of the Consulate at Trieste were found to be too much for him and they moved accordingly into a larger house in a more accessible position. With the added money from the *Arabian Nights* they were able to expand themselves in comfort. A resident physician, Dr. Grenfell Baker, was engaged, and holidays were taken frequently in Switzerland and Tangier.

Burton still hoped that the longed for promotion to Morocco might come ; and when the position fell vacant, he wrote urgently to the Foreign Office, setting out his qualifications, and long record of service. The position, however, was given to another, and thus the last of his hopes died. As if to soften

---

[1] Trieste, 24th September (no date). To Mr. Smithers, his co-translator of Catullus. A MS. copy of part of this translation used to be in the library of the author's father. It was only found after his death, so its origin is not known. Possibly Burton sent extracts to friends.

this blow, however, there came shortly afterwards a telegram from Lord Salisbury to say that, in recognition of the traveller's many services, the Queen had been pleased to make him a K.C.M.G.

Isabel was in the seventh heaven. She was now able to take her place in society and drop that rather peculiar soi-disant title, " Countess Isabel Arundell of Wardour," which previously had given her a somewhat uncertain entrée. Society saw more of them after this. Lady Walburga Paget records, in *Embassies of Other Days*, meeting them in Rome. Both had taken to painting their faces. Richard might still have been taken for an Arab, " an illusion which was strengthened by his staining his under-lids with kohl. His wife still bore great traces of beauty, though she too shared the Eastern predilection for pigments. . . ."

Books still appeared at regular intervals from his pen, but his hours of work grew less, his fits of restlessness increased and often and again he cried out loud for the open air of the wilderness where a man could breathe.

The Foreign Office were infinitely kind. His retirement and pension were only a few months off yet they allowed him almost perfect freedom to wander where he wished. The years 1889 and 1890 show him constantly on the move. Geneva, Montreux, Venice, Brindisi, Malta, Tunis, Algiers, Davos, and the Riviera, restlessly he turns from one to the other accompanied by a solicitous Isabel and Dr. Grenfell Baker.

§

In September 1890 he returned to Trieste to put in a few months' official work before his retirement the following March. About the 12th of October an attack of gout seized him, but was allayed by the doctor and aroused little alarm. But Burton was uneasy. On the 19th October, clad in a crumpled linen suit and Egyptian fez, he spent the day wandering in his garden, plucking flowers, nursing a little bird he found wounded, and working intermittently at his *Scented Garden*. He sighed often and seemed at moments loth to go indoors. When he did so, it was noticed that he was setting his papers in order with a curious lingering care.

In the evening he seemed more cheerful, ate a light dinner, laughed and joked with his companions, and retired to bed about ten o'clock. Isabel kissed him good-night and retired to her own room for evening prayer. But suddenly the dismal howling of a dog outside roused her, and she ordered a porter to go out and see what had happened to the animal.

The stage was now set for the grim comedy that was to follow. Returning, Isabel went into his room again and found him uneasy. He told her he had a gouty pain in his foot. She gently massaged the foot and he dozed, waking now and again to mutter about his dreams.

At four o'clock he was seen to be in difficulties and the doctor was sent for. Some medicine was given but, as the attack seemed no worse than many that had preceded it, the doctor retired to bed again saying that all was well.

At 6.30 the sick man took a rapid turn for the worse. He began to struggle for breath. Isabel fled for the doctor, and returned to find Richard in the agonizing throes of the complaint crying : " Quick, Puss, chloroform—ether—or I am a dead man ! "

But neither could be given him. Isabel clutched him in her arms and held him while the doctor did his best. There were a few moments of agony ; a few moments of convulsions. Then she felt him grow heavier, heavier, and sink back with the death rattle in his throat. It was the end.

For a moment she was stunned with grief. Then she rallied herself. It must not be the end : not yet. Awful as was this moment to Isabel, still more awful was the thought of her loved one dying unabsolved. " Is he dead ? " she asked the doctor. But she would not believe it. He was not dead. He must not be dead ; he must be saved.

There was little time. Put a battery to the dead heretic heart, keep the limbs warm ! The doctor shrugs his shoulders and steps back. Isabel, her face streaked with paint and tears, a huge yellow wig wobbling on her head, rushes from the room for a priest.

She returns with a Slav peasant father. " Is he alive ? " asks the man. The doctor shrugs again, but Isabel's fervent protestations overcome the questioner. She lifts an eyelid. See there, surely, is the gleam of life. No, he is not dead. " Quick, father, quick, before it is too late."

Into the dead mouth is thrust the holy wafer, and while the battery purrs against the dead heart, the solemn tones of the Extreme Unction, broken by Isabel's weeping, fill the little room. Surely that wild untamable spirit will be saved !

Surely the outcast will be received into the arms of Mother Church !

At length all is over, and Isabel's conscience is assuaged. She falls to prayer and weeping, then, as the first light of a new day breaks over the Adriatic and lights up the cold, still face, sardonic in its aureole of crucifixes and candles, she starts, alone, to close the eyes and bind up the jaw of the one she loved so dearly.

Then, silently, she picks up her diary ; that dear, precious diary in which she had recorded so many of her griefs, her hopes, her fears, and writes :

" He looked in a peaceful sleep, with adorable dignity and repose—a very majesty in his death—every inch a man, a soldier, and a gentleman."

§

Richard was saved. He was not in hell fire. But there was his reputation to think of. Suddenly, while praying in her room in Trieste, his spirit appeared before Isabel, pointed, and said sternly, " Burn my manuscripts." Isabel knew what it meant ; it meant all his translations and questionable writings ; it meant his journal kept daily for nearly forty years of his life ; it meant that vile *Scented Garden* on which he had been working so gleefully.

She hurried to the peasant priest and told him all. " Yes, burn them," was his verdict also ; and returning home Isabel went into his little study and gutted it of manuscripts. Aided by the priest, she built a fire, and one by one the valuable sheets, the records of years of labour vanished in smoke. Isabel's purge was complete. She had set her seal upon his body, and now it was set upon his work.

§

Richard Burton was embalmed, and brought to England where, with all the pomp and ceremony of the Catholic Church, he was buried at Mortlake Catholic cemetery. Above his grave Isabel erected a strange yet fitting monument to his conflicting life, a marble Arab tent, filled with the camel bells whose sound he so dearly loved, topped by a cross and crescent and bearing a crucifix and a tablet engraved with a farewell from his friend Justin Huntly McCarthy.

RICHARD BURTON

Farewell, dear friend, dead hero ! The great life
Is ended, the great perils, the great joys ;
And he to whom adventures were as toys,
Who seemed to bear a charm 'gainst spear
Or bullet, now lies silent from all strife
Out yonder where the Austrian eagles poise
On Istrian hills. But England at the noise
Of that dread fall, weeps with the hero's wife.
Oh, last and noblest of the Errant Knights,
The English soldier and the Arab Sheik !
Oh, singer of the East who loved so well
The deathless wonder of the " Arabian Nights,"
Who touched Camœns' lute and still would seek
Ever new deeds until the end ! Farewell !

Thus, incongruously, does one of England's great travellers,
lover of Islam and the East, hater of the religions and conven-
tions of the West, lie in a Roman Catholic tomb in a London
suburb, neglected in death as in life.

§

For six years Isabel lingered on after him, a sad, eccentric
figure, full of strange fancies and superstitions. Much time she
spent in spiritual communication with Richard, who often
appeared to her, and, partly under his guidance, she commenced
that enormous, formless biography, which with the destruction
of all his personal diaries is almost the only record we have of
the man. Racked with internal pains from the inroads of cancer,
she worked on it for years, living much of her time near Mortlake
where he was buried. Ceaselessly she fought for his name and
to defend herself from the charges of wanton destruction of his
work. She finished it, watched it through the press, and then
wrote in relief :

" He always said ' I am gone—pay, pack, and follow.'
Reader ! I have paid. I have packed. I have suffered. I am
waiting to join his Caravan. I am waiting for a welcome
sound—"

That sound came in September 1896. Crippled by malignant
cancer, she died in rooms in Baker Street, and the brave, erratic,
foolish, and pathetic spirit fled in search of its mate.

Richard Burton

CHIEF WORKS :

Contributions to the *Journal of the Asiatic Society*, 1849, including *A Grammar of the Jataki or Belochki Dialect. Notes on the Pushtu or Afghan Language. Scind, or the Unhappy Valley. Sindh and the Races that Inhabit the Valley of the Indus. Goa and the Blue Mountains*, 1851. *Falconry in the Valley of the Indus*, 1852. *A Complete System of Bayonet Exercise*, 1853. *Personal Narrative of a Pilgrimage to El-Medinah and Meccah*, 1855–56. *First Footsteps in East Africa*, 1856. *The Lake Regions of Equatorial Africa*, 1860. *Notes of the Lunar Mountains, and the Sources of the White Nile*, 1860. *The City of the Saints*, 1861. *Wanderings in West Africa*, 1863. *Abeokuta and the Cameroons*, 1863. *A Mission to Gelele, King of Dahome*, 1864 *The Nile Basin*, 1864. *Wit and Wisdom from West Africa : a Collection of 2859 Proverbs, etc*, 1865. *Explorations of the Highlands of Brazil*, 1869. *Letters from the Battlefields of Paraguay*, 1870. *Vikram and the Vampire : Hindu Tale*, 1870. *Proverba Communia Syria*, 1871. *Unexplored Syria* (in collaboration with C. F. Tywhitt Drake), 1872. *Zanzibar*, 1872. *The Castlellieri of Istria*, 1874. *Ultima Thule, or a Summer in Iceland*, 1875. *Gorilla Land, or the Cataracts of the Congo*, 1875. *A New System of Sword Exercise*, 1875. *Etruscan Bologna*, 1876. *Sind Revisited*, 1877. *The Gold Mines of Midian*, 1878. *The Land of Midian Revisited*, 1879. *Translation of Camoens' " Lusiad," with Life and Commentary*, 1880, 1881. *The Kasidah* (poem), 1880, 1894, 1900. *Lord Beaconsfield, a Sketch*, 1882 (?). *To the Gold Coast for Gold*, 1883. *Book of the Sword* (vol. I), 1884. *The Book of a Thousand Nights and a Night* (10 vols.), 1885–86 ; *Supplemental Nights* (5 vols.), 1887–88. Reissued by his wife for " household reading," 1886–88.

POSTHUMOUS PUBLICATIONS :

Translation of Basile's *Pentamerone*, 1893. Verse rendering of *Catullus*, 1894. *The Jew, the Gipsy, and El Islam*, 1897. *Wanderings in Three Continents*, edited by W. H. Wilkins, 1901.

There were further contributions to the *Journal of the Asiatic Society*, 1871. A translation of Gerber's *Province of Minas Geraes*, 1875, and an edition of *The Captivity of Hans Stade among the Wild Tribes of Eastern Brazil* (Hakluyt Soc.) 1874. Translation of *The Lands of Cazembe. Lacerda's Journey to Cazembe in 1798*, 1873.

Works :

Memorial Edition (vols. I–VII), 1873, 1894.

Life :

A Sketch of the Career of R. F. Burton, by A. B. Richards, A. Wilson, and St. Clair Baddeley, 1886. By his wife Isabel, Lady Burton, 1893 ; Second edition by W. H. Wilkins, 1898. *True Life of Captain Sir R. F. Burton,* by his niece, G. M. Stisted, 1896. F. Hitchman, *R. F. Burton, his Early Private and Public Life, with an Account of his Travels and Explorations,* 1897. T. Wright, 1906. W. P. Dodge, *The Real Sir R. Burton,* 1907. *Richard Burton,* H. J. Schonfield, 1936. *The Arabian Knight,* Seton Dearden, 1936.

Index

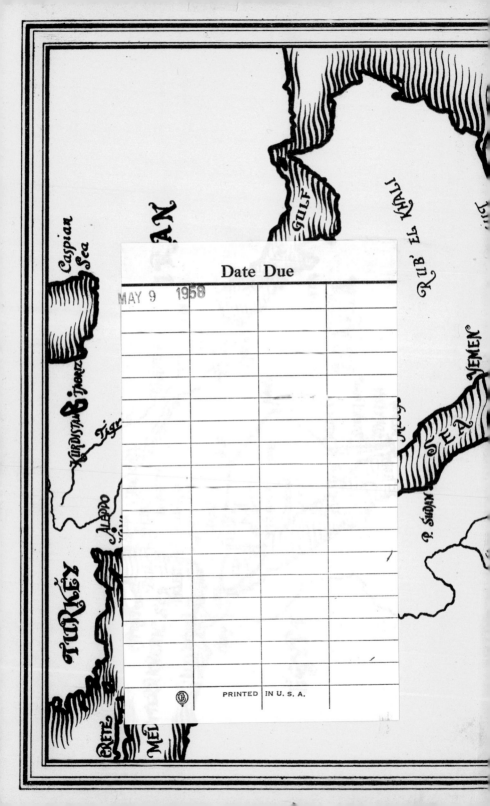

Date Due

MAY 9 1958			
	PRINTED	IN U. S. A.	